Understanding China's Economic Indicators

Understanding China's Economic Indicators

Translating the Data into Investment Opportunities

Tom Orlik

Vice President, Publisher: Tim Moore
Associate Publisher and Director of Marketing: Amy Neidlinger
Executive Editor: Jeanne Glasser
Editorial Assistant: Pamela Boland
Senior Marketing Manager: Julie Phifer
Assistant Marketing Manager: Megan Colvin
Cover Designer: Chuti Prasertsith
Managing Editor: Kristy Hart
Project Editor: Anne Goebel
Copy Editor: Krista Hansing Editorial Services, Inc.
Proofreader: Williams Woods Publishing Services
Indexer: Heather McNeill
Senior Compositor: Gloria Schurick
Graphics: Laura Robbins
Manufacturing Buyer: Dan Uhrig

© 2012 by Thomas Orlik
Publishing as FT Press Science
Upper Saddle River, New Jersey 07458

First Printing July 2011

ISBN-10: 0-13-262019-7
ISBN-13: 978-0-13-262019-2

Pearson Education LTD.
Pearson Education Australia PTY, Limited.
Pearson Education Singapore, Pte. Ltd.
Pearson Education Asia, Ltd.
Pearson Education Canada, Ltd.
Pearson Educación de Mexico, S.A. de C.V.
Pearson Education—Japan
Pearson Education Malaysia, Pte. Ltd.

Library of Congress Cataloging-in-Publication Data:

Orlik, Tom (Thomas Moore), 1978-
  Understanding China's economic indicators : translating the data into investment opportunities / Tom Orlik.
     p. cm.
  ISBN 978-0-13-262019-2 (hardback : alk. paper)
  1. Economic indicators—China. 2. China—Economic conditions—2001- I. Title.
  HC427.95.O844 2012
  339.351—dc22
                                        2011008845

To my wife, Helena, and my parents, Christopher and Judith

CONTENTS

ACKNOWLEDGMENTS

I have received help from numerous individuals and institutions in producing this book. Employees of the National Bureau of Statistics (NBS), China Federation of Logistics and Purchasing, Markit, Market News International, China Economic Monitoring and Analysis Center, Conference Board, Organisation for Economic Cooperation and Development (OECD), Soufun, INTAGE, Customs Bureau, U.S. Bureau of Labor Statistics, and U.S. Treasury all generously shared their time and expertise. I also benefited from conversations with academics and officials at Beijing University, the Chinese Academy of Social Science, and the International Monetary Fund (IMF), as well as numerous other analysts and experts.

I received excellent research assistance from Guo Wei, Jackie Xia, Brandon Li, Lu Ben, Li Bo, Han Ting, and Li Yuxin. Paul Cavey and Bill Adams labored through complete early drafts and provided valuable comments, for which I am very grateful. Logan Wright, David Wilder, Xu Hui, John Canavan, and Fei Yang Adams provided valuable comments on specific sections. My Chinese teacher, Jia Yanfen, suffered with me through reams of official and academic documents on China's economic data. Everyone who writes about China's economic data benefits from the work of Professor Harry Wu and the work of Professor Carsten Holz. I learned a great deal from conversations with both of them and from reading their extensive work and contrasting views on the subject. The structure of the book is indebted to Bernard Baumohl's work on U.S. economic indicators.

The organizations that produce China's economic data are not particularly good at explaining how it is collected or calculated, but some published information does exist. I benefited from material published by the NBS, People's Bank of China, Customs Bureau, and Ministry of Finance. The IMF's General Data Dissemination System has collected and published data on the methodology for some of China's key economic indicators. The OECD's joint program with the NBS has produced some illuminating work on China's economic data, which is available on the OECD's website. Goldman Sachs' Asia Economics Group also did some early work to shed light on key indicators.

I am very grateful to Jeanne Glasser at Pearson, who immediately saw the potential in the book and shepherded it through to publication with consummate professionalism. I am also grateful to Anne Goebel and Krista Hansing at Pearson for their work in preparing the manuscript for publication. Much of the work on the book was done during the time I was working for Stone & McCarthy Research Associates, and I am grateful to Ray Stone and the team for their support and encouragement. I also shared an office with the team at Market News International Beijing Bureau and benefited from the insights of John Carter, Allen Feng, Chen Ying, Connie Young, and Darren Cao into developments in the Chinese economy. Some of the work in preparing the manuscript was completed during my time at *The Wall Street Journal*, and I am grateful to Thorold Barker, Andy Browne, and the team on the "Heard on the Street" column and in the Beijing Bureau for their support and encouragement.

Last but not least, my wife, Helena, cares less than anyone about China's economic data, but has contributed more than anyone to the successful completion of this project. I owe her more than the U.S. owes China.

ABOUT THE AUTHOR

Tom Orlik is a China correspondent for *The Wall Street Journal*, where he writes the "Heard on the Street" column. Prior to joining the *Journal*, he worked for Stone & McCarthy Research Associates as an economist, briefing investors on China's macro-economic data. Before coming to China, Orlik worked for the British Treasury, including work as a speechwriter for the Chief Secretary to the Treasury, advisor to the UK Executive Director of the IMF, and on secondment to the European Commission in Brussels. He has a Master's in Public Policy from the Kennedy School of Government, Harvard, and a Bachelor's in English from University College London. The head of China's National Bureau of Statistics Ma Jiantang made Orlik's 2009 essay on the quality of China's economic statistics recommended reading for all the staff of the statistical system.

CHAPTER 1

Introduction

THE CRUSH

It's a freezing January morning, and a group of 80 or so journalists file past a bored adolescent security guard into the marble lobby of a government building in the center of Beijing. Passing through the lobby, they head up a flight of stairs and show their IDs to another security guard before passing through an airport-style metal detector. They file into a conference room with rows of chairs facing a raised platform, at its center a microphone peeks out through an impressive array of flowers. They huddle in small groups, sipping coffee and talking shop. One member of the Chinese press cleans out his ear with the nail of his pinky finger, cultivated especially long for the purpose. At 9:45 a.m., the door to a side room swings open and a nervous official appears holding a stack of papers. The official is nervous for a reason. Suddenly energized, the journalists surge forward, elbowing each other aside to be the first to see the contents of the papers. The unfortunate bureaucrat is knocked this way and that. The melee continues until her hands are empty. Why all the fuss? Is the Chinese government renouncing its ties with the despotic regime in North Korea? Granting independence to Tibet? Providing the secrets to roasting the perfect Peking duck? No. The 80 men and women are financial journalists. The hapless factotum they have just mobbed is an employee of China's State Council Information Office. The papers they now triumphantly hold in their hands contain the figures for China's gross domestic product (GDP) in the final quarter of 2009.

It is now 9:50 a.m. The journalists have opened their mobile phones and are calling in the numbers to their colleagues in news rooms around the capital. GDP has grown by 10.7% year on year in the final three months of 2009, up from 9.1% in the third quarter. China has emerged first and strongest from the worst economic crisis since World War II. But alongside the news of surging growth comes something more troubling. Inflationary pressure has returned, and sooner than expected, to the Chinese economy. Consumer prices rose 1.9% in the year to December, up from 0.6% in November. Food prices increased even more, up 5.3% compared to a year ago. The journalists have a few short minutes to make sense of it all. What is the news? Will surging growth send the Shanghai Composite Index, the price of a barrel of oil, and the value of the Australian dollar and the Korean won surging upward? Or does the return of inflation signal the end of the good times? The journalists call in their numbers to colleagues at the newsrooms of Dow Jones, Market News International, and Reuters. There's a minute of frantic checking and rechecking of the numbers. "GDP grew 10.7% in the fourth quarter and 8.7% for the year as a whole, right?" A pause. "Right." At 10 a.m., the embargo on broadcasting the news is lifted. In trading rooms in Shanghai, Hong Kong, Tokyo, Taipei, and Singapore, screens light up with the data. In the State Council Information Office, a group of gray-suited officials has filed onto the platform, and the press conference begins. Ma Jiantang, the smiling head of the NBS, starts to read from his prepared statement. "You could say 2009 was a good harvest for the Chinese economy," he says. But financial markets aren't listening to his statement; they're already trading on the data.

In China, the Shanghai Composite Index is flat. At first sight, this is something of a mystery. If growth is on track, it should be good news for equities. Investors should be rushing to buy, not standing by indifferently. But the markets are thinking not just about what the data says about the state of the economy, but also about how the government might react. With growth on track but inflation rearing its ugly head, the markets fear the stimulus party might be drawing to a close. The Shanghai Composite Index fell almost 3% the previous day, on the suggestion that banks would tighten their lending. A higher-than-expected reading for growth and inflation heightens concerns that the end of the stimulus is near. The biggest potential losers from a tighter policy stance—companies in the banking, property, and commodities sectors that benefited from a lending- and investment-driven 2009—start to fall. On the Hang Seng Index, Industrial and Commercial Bank of China, the world's largest bank by deposits, falls 2.9%. In Australia, iron ore miners BHP Billiton and Rio Tinto fall 1.7% and 3.2%. The Aussie loses 1.1% against the greenback. In New York, it is still 9 p.m. on January 20, and the markets are closed. Investors have a night to sleep on the data. When they wake up on January 21, they will find that markets across Asia have fallen. Higher inflation, not faster growth; the end of the stimulus, not the beginning of the recovery—those were the main takeaways from China's economic data. The day after the release of China's GDP data, the Chinese tail wags the U.S. dog and the Dow Jones Industrial Average falls more than 2%.

Back in the State Council Information Office, Ma Jiantang has finished reading from his statement and it is time for questions and answers. The first question comes from a representative of China Central Television: "Has the Chinese economy now overtaken that of Japan to become the second largest in the world?" Mr. Ma smiles while a functionary reads the question again in English for the benefit of the foreign journalists. "As to where China's economy ranks in the world, experts and scholars can do their own research," he says. "But the reality is that China remains a developing country, and on a GDP per capita basis, we are not even in the top 100 countries in the world." The average Chinese person might be pulling in just USD4,000 a year. But 1.3 billion people earning not very much still adds up to a lot. In 2010, China's GDP totaled CNY39.8trln, equivalent to USD5.9trln. In the world GDP rankings, China overtook fourth place Germany to move into bronze medal position in 2007, and in 2010 outstripped Japan to claim the silver. China might not yet be number one—and might not be number one within the next decade. But China moves markets. The mainland's own equity markets are moved more by the story of growth and inflation told by the economic data than they are by the profit and loss of the companies listed on them. Mainland firms make up more than 50% of the Hang Seng Index, and the Hong Kong markets move in tandem with the mainland. Regional markets in Japan, Korea, and Singapore rise and fall with news of the economic fortunes of their big neighbor, and major news can move markets in the United States and Europe. China is the world's biggest consumer of iron ore and copper, and the second largest consumer of oil. Commodity investors pore over China's import, industrial value-added, and fixed-asset investment data for signs of changes in its appetite. The drama of yuan appreciation is the focus of attention for the foreign exchange markets. A capital account that remains closed to speculators limits the scope for betting on the yuan, but the Korean won, Singapore dollar, and Australian dollar are traded as proxies for yuan appreciation and the China growth story. The eyes of the world's financial markets are focused on China, and the lens through which they see it is China's economic data.

HOW RELIABLE ARE CHINA'S ECONOMIC STATISTICS?

With so much attention on developments in the Chinese economy, the reliability of China's economic indicators has been the subject of some controversy. In the popular imagination, the production of China's economic data is regarded as a crude political farce: the controlling hand of the Communist Party intervening arbitrarily to direct the level of key indicators before they are published. In the past, that image was not too far from the reality.

In the Great Leap Forward, Chairman Mao's disastrous attempt to shift a backward agrarian economy to a modern industrial economy in a few short years, the failure of the statistical system contributed to catastrophe on a grand scale. Mao's plan to accelerate the development of the economy required producing an agricultural surplus that could be sold to fund investment in a modern industrial base. Whipped into a patriotic frenzy, and knowing that their future depended on meeting unrealistic targets for the production of grain, local officials engaged in rampant falsification of data. At the height of the insanity, in summer 1958, some provinces were boasting annual output of 10,000 pounds of grain per mu. Those numbers were already crazy. A mu is 1/15 of a hectare, and in the 1950s that area of land could be expected to produce around 1,000 pounds of grain a year. But even these bloated reports were soon surpassed by other provinces claiming output of 20,000 or even 30,000 pounds per mu. The point of the production data was not to reflect reality, but to generate the good news required to support morale among comrades and meet the unrealistic expectations of the higher-ups. But reality is distorted at a cost. The higher the production figures, the greater the tax owed to the central government. In some provinces, the exaggerated claims were so great that the entire harvest had to be handed over as tax, used to fund investments and extravagancies that China could ill afford. In some parts of the country, the only crops left behind were grown by villagers in secret locations, away from the acquisitive eye of the local production teams. But such success stories were few and far between. Tens of millions died in history's greatest man-made famine.

That was 50 years ago. Some things have stayed the same in the last 50 years, but a lot has changed. At its heart, the cause of over-reporting output during the Great Leap Forward was the divided loyalties of local officials, torn between the reality of stubbornly unchanging grain yield and the dream of career progression that depended on meeting unrealistic targets for output. That conflict of interest was slow to be resolved. The biggest reform-era controversy over China's economic data, a GDP growth figure for 1998 that many experts regard as grossly inflated, has been laid at the door of the exaggerated claims made by local officials. But NBS headquarters in Beijing is no longer reliant on the unreliable inputs it receives from local bureaus. Across the key industrial output, fixed asset investment, and retail sales data, the largest enterprises in the country report directly to the NBS in Beijing. Where there is a conflict between local and national data, the NBS typically resolves it in favor of the reliable national figures. The GDP data is a case in point, with the national total announced by the NBS consistently below the sum of the GDP reported by the provinces.

The second problem that bedeviled the grain data during the Great Leap Forward was the belief that boosting morale through exaggerated claims was more important than reporting reality. The audience for China's economic data might have expanded beyond the agricultural workers of the 1950s, but the numbers continue to play a role at home and abroad in buoying confidence in the China growth story. The magic 8% figure for GDP growth, in particular, has an almost talismanic significance. But if the government is ever tempted to play fast and loose with the statistical reality, there are also forces pulling in the other direction. The Information Age has reduced the scope for the use of economic data as an instrument of propaganda. Official data is available instantly around the world over the Internet. A horde of sophisticated and cynical journalists, spreadsheet-wielding economists, and hard-nosed investors are following developments in the Chinese economy. The extent of the 1950s famine was revealed only by demographers poring over the population data decades later. If an inconsistency arises today, a lot of people will know about it very quickly. The fact that the NBS was happy to announce GDP growth of 6.1% year on year in the first quarter of 2009, the lowest level in a decade, suggests that the powers-that-be realize that the benefits of supplying credible official data are greater than the costs of reporting an unwelcome reality.

Measuring a rapidly changing economy remains a challenge. One of the problems of the Great Leap Forward was that China's leaders were blinded by a belief in their own hocus-pocus technology. Mao genuinely believed that revolutionary fervor plus new planting techniques could result in massive increases in grain output. Changes in production techniques made it more difficult to measure output, or at least obscured for a time the fact that output was little changed. The dislocations of reform-era China might be less wrenching than those of the 1950s, but the mainland is still changing fast. The economy is many times larger today than it was in 1978, new sectors are driving increases in output and employment, new products are entering consumers' shopping baskets, and new property is coming online in the housing market—keeping track of developments is an enormous challenge. In some areas, the NBS has made an effort to keep its measuring tools sharp and clean. To keep track of GDP, the NBS has expanded its survey from a primitive 16 sectors to a more respectable 94 and has significantly improved its coverage of the services. But in other areas, surveying tools and techniques have been slow to adapt to a changing reality. Consider China's creaking system for measuring developments in labor markets. In 1978, 100% of the workforce was employed in the state sector, and a survey based on wages in state-owned enterprises worked well enough. In 2010, that number was less than 10%, and a wage data survey that continues to focus on a privileged subset of state-sector workers makes little sense. Survey tools that lag behind the reality of a changing China are a more serious problem for China's economic data than political interference.

A recalcitrant population continues to add to the problems. The NBS is not the State Administration of Taxation or the Public Security Bureau. But a culture of deceit among Chinese people when it comes to dealing with officials of any kind makes it difficult for the NBS to collect solid baseline information. In the Great Leap Forward, peasants growing crops outside the greedy gaze of the local production team distorted the data. Fifty years later, the problem is small businesses that keep three sets of books—one for the taxman, one for investors, and one for themselves—or rich households that refuse to disclose the income they receive from graft. The problem of a sample set that is incapable of telling the truth to anyone in an official badge remains, and that adds to the difficulties the NBS faces.

Finally, the NBS and other arms of the government charged with the production of China's economic data do themselves no favors by treating straightforward information on methodology with a degree of secrecy more suited to guarding the location of nuclear weapon silos. Transparency on the methodology underpinning key data points has improved considerably from the situation a few years ago. In 2010, for example, the results of a new effort to measure wages in the private sector were published alongside details of the survey approach and a discussion of some of its limitations. But crucial details of the methodology on key indicators are still kept hidden. The weights of different components in the consumer price index (CPI), for example, are public information in most countries and enable an easy check on the reliability of the official data. In China, the NBS does not disclose the weights, making it impossible to verify if movements in the index represent changes in prices or changes to the calculation method. Partly as a result, confidence in the CPI data is so low that, in some months, the rumor in the market before the release of the data comes in two parts—one on the real level and one on the level the NBS will announce. The statisticians do not have an enormous fund of good will and faith in the official data to draw on. By withholding key details of how the data is calculated, the NBS and other institutions raise doubts, perhaps unnecessarily, about its reliability.

The reality of China's economic data today is not the crude controlling hand of the Politburo dictating the GDP growth figure. It is an increasingly reliable and comprehensive set of economic indicators that remain compromised in some areas by the difficulty of measuring a rapidly changing economy, imperfect surveying methods, a recalcitrant sample set, and continued political sensitivity surrounding some numbers. The system is not perfect. Some data points are more reliable than others. But neither is it a farce. As shown by the mad scramble for the GDP data in the State Council Information Office and the billions of dollars that are traded instantly on its release, the shortcomings in the data are no impediment to the market reaction.

A MONTH IN CHINA'S ECONOMIC DATA

Most months in the Chinese economic calendar follow the same pattern of data releases, and a glance at the schedule for a typical month provides a way to highlight the more important data points.

1st: The China Federation of Logistics and Purchasing (CFLP) and HSBC Markit Purchasing Managers Indexes give the markets their first glimpse into the state of the manufacturing sector in the month just past. For some investors who do not follow China closely, this is the data point that is watched.

10th: Customs' import, export, and trade surplus data gives a read on the state of foreign demand for China's products and domestic demand for raw materials. Commodities markets keep a close eye on China's imports of iron ore and crude oil. The trade surplus is a monthly flashpoint for pressure on China's exchange rate regime.

10th–15th: People's Bank of China (PBOC) data shows the strength of loans, deposits, and money supply growth. These are data points that can drive the markets in the short term (through a boost to liquidity) and the long term (through the strong relationship between changes in credit and money supply and growth and inflation).

11th: NBS data on industrial value added, fixed asset investment, and retail sales keep the markets up-to-date on the China growth story. The CPI and producer price index (PPI) data reveal whether inflation is set to spoil the party. The 11th-day data dump is the main event in the monthly calendar. In the mass of data, the two points that get the most attention are industrial value added (a proxy for growth of the whole economy) and CPI (the best measure of overall inflation).

18th: NBS house price data provides a flawed but widely watched read on China's bubbly property sector.

The exceptions to the normal monthly pattern are at the beginning of the year and in months when the quarterly GDP data is published. In the beginning of the year, the NBS delays the publication of data on industrial value added, fixed asset investment, and retail sales for the first two months until March, to smooth out the effect of the Chinese New Year. In months when the GDP data is published, the NBS delays the 11th-of-the-month data release to coincide with it. That normally means publication on around January 20 for the fourth quarter GDP data, and April 15, July 15, and October 15 for the first, second, and third quarter data.

WAITING FOR RELEASE OF THE DATA—OR NOT

The regular monthly calendar is a way to keep track of what data is released when. But in China, not everyone is waiting for the official release to see the data. Economic data and information on key policy decisions are often in the market days ahead of the official announcement. If the markets latch on to a credible rumor for an important data point, the reaction can happen ahead of the official release. Important information leaks into the markets in several ways:

- Officials in the know share information with family and friends, enabling them to make a profit before it is made public. In June 2005, weeks before the government announced the end of the yuan's peg to the dollar and a one-off 2% appreciation, insiders were turning up at banks with briefcases full of dollars to change into yuan, planning to make a fast buck when the government removed the peg. In most months in 2010, the CPI data was in the market, correct to one decimal place, days ahead of the data release. Investors with strong links to official sources saw the data first and were able to take a profitable position based on their information advantage.

- Senior officials sometimes abandon protocol and announce the data before the official release date. Premier Wen Jiabao is a repeat offender. In March 2010, he told a group of foreign business leaders that China expected a trade deficit for the month some weeks ahead of the official data from the Customs Bureau. In March 2009, he was so excited by a rebound in industrial value added that he announced it himself before the NBS had a chance.

- Official information can be collected from unofficial sources ahead of the data release. Data on bank lending never used to be particularly important. The banks could be counted on to lend CNY200 billion or so a month, higher in the beginning of the year and lower in the end, but not normally with enough variation to move markets. In 2009, that all went out the window. A surge in bank lending was the major factor contributing to the recovery in the real economy and the rebound in the equity markets. With investors focused on the lending figure, the financial press has started to work contacts with the banks to get an advance estimate. Industrial and Commercial Bank of China, Bank of China, China Construction Bank, and Agricultural Bank of China account for around half of total lending. For a journalist with good contacts, four phone calls can produce a reasonable estimate of lending for the month. That number is normally in the markets ahead of the PBOC data release.

• The monthly data on industrial value added, fixed asset investment, retail sales, CPI and PPI, and the quarterly GDP data is announced to the financial press about 15 minutes ahead of the public announcement. In theory, this allows the data to be released to the markets in an orderly way. Any organizations that take advantage of the 15-minute window to jump the gun and release the data early should be severely punished. In practice, Chinese news organizations, especially state media outlet Xinhua, break the embargo with impunity. Foreign news organizations, which are kept on a tighter leash, are left fuming as their Chinese competitors break the rules to gain a competitive advantage.

It adds up to a messy and confusing picture, with insiders benefiting from advance information and everyone else chasing rumors. For foreign investors, the chance of being out of the loop when decisions or data are leaked is one of the frustrations of working in the Chinese markets.

A YEAR IN CHINA'S ECONOMIC DATA

Chinese holidays (some of them fixed, some of them floating), political set pieces, and changes in the season affect what is happening to the data. Keeping an eye on the calendar makes understanding what is going on easier.

January and February: New Year's Holiday Plays Havoc with Data

Chinese New Year is the main event in the annual calendar, the equivalent of Thanksgiving, Christmas, and New Year's Day in the United States rolled into one, but stretched over an entire week. Airports and railway stations are packed with workers returning home for the most important holiday of the year. Work on construction sites grinds to a halt, factories cease production, and the financial markets are closed. With the New Year falling in January some years and February in others, the calendar plays havoc with the economic data. The NBS attempts to overcome the problem by publishing some of the main data points for January and February together. Data that is published for separate months, including data on trade from the Customs Bureau, needs to be treated with caution because of the seasonal distortion.

The holiday also impacts the financial markets. With households hungry for cash to pay for train tickets and to stuff into red envelopes as gifts for family members, and firms demanding extra funds to pay a New Year's bonus, the banks run short. Short-term interest rates kick up, and the PBOC injects liquidity to make up the shortfall. Throw the chance of very bad weather impacting economic activity into the mix, and data for the first two months of the year needs to be treated with caution.

March and April: Twin Work Meetings Set the Direction of Economic Policy

With the New Year's festivities over, March's main event is the government's twin work meetings. In theory, the National People's Congress (NPC) is China's highest authority. In practice, key decisions are shaped by a smaller group at the October meeting of the Communist Party's Central Committee. That does not mean the NPC is without interest. The premier's work report sets out the government's overall economic policy stance and the priorities for the year, including a target for GDP, CPI, and money supply. The National Development and Reform Commissions (NDRC) expand on that with targets for trade, fixed asset investment, and retail sales. The budget sets priorities for government spending and the target for the fiscal surplus or deficit. The Chinese People's Political Consultative Conference is second fiddle to the NPC, but it takes place in parallel and provides the financial press with a rare opportunity to doorstop decision makers and ask them difficult questions.

In April, following the confusion caused by Chinese New Year, GDP data for the first quarter brings some welcome clarity on the state of the economy. Publication of the GDP data is typically preceded by a meeting of the State Council, chaired by the premier and with all the main economic policy actors in the room. The State Council reviews the economic data ahead of its publication, agrees on the direction of economic policy for the quarter ahead, and sometimes makes decisions on the use of key policy instruments such as the interest rate. In April 2010, the State Council meeting resulted in the announcement of a crackdown on bubble prices in the real estate sector.

May and June: No Rest for the Workers

Until 2007, workers enjoyed a week-long holiday in May. From 2008, that was reduced to a single day, on May 1. The change from a week-long to a single-day holiday affects the seasonal pattern in the historical data, and the 1-day holiday continues to reduce working days in May relative to April and June, which can have an impact on the month-on-month data.

July and August: Political Slumber and Natural Disaster

Beijing summers are hot. The temperature pushes up into the high 80 degrees Fahrenheit. In the Deng Xiaoping and Jiang Zemin era, China's leaders sloped off to Beidaihe, a nearby coastal resort, for a few weeks of swimming and political intrigue. Hu Jintao decided that an annual holiday for the entire leadership did not fit with the image of simple living he wanted to project, so the Beidaihe retreats fell out of favor. But being in Beijing does not appear any more conducive to making difficult decisions. The publication of GDP data for the second quarter in early July is preceded by the normal meeting of the State Council. But in general, the summer months are not heavily populated with major political or economic events.

Natural disasters are not confined to the summer months. Snowstorms in the winter and earthquakes anytime they please have claimed lives and treasure in recent years. But the summer months are particularly prone to natural calamities. Floods can damage infrastructure and put a dent in output for the industrial and agricultural sectors. July 1 also marks the date of the founding of the Chinese Communist Party in 1921, a sensitive anniversary.

September and October: National Day Holiday, Central Committee Meeting

The moon festival in September or October and National Day at the beginning of October introduce further confusion into the economic data. The fall holidays are not as important as the New Year's festivities. There's no exodus of migrant workers from the factory back to the farm, construction continues, and shops stay open. But the two holidays put a significant dent in working days, especially for white-collar workers, and affect the economic data for September and October. The National Day Holiday on October 1 is also the anniversary of the founding of the People's Republic of China in 1949.

In mid-October, a meeting of the Central Committee of the Communist Party brings together China's most senior decision makers. The meeting has assumed a new importance under the leadership of Hu Jintao as a forum in which important economic decisions are made. The October 2010 meeting came ahead of a decision to raise interest rates and anticipated a shift in economic policy out of crisis response and into neutral mode. The Central Committee meeting also sets the tone for the meeting of the NPC in March the next year.

November and December: Central Economic Work Meeting

In the first half of December, the main event is the Central Economic Work Meeting. With the president and premier in attendance, the meeting brings together senior leaders from central departments and provincial governments for 3 days of discussions. The meeting sets the tone for economic policy in the year ahead, identifying the overarching stance for monetary and fiscal policy, and setting out priorities for structural reform.

How This Book Works

This book is organized into chapters that cover different aspects of the economy; for example, the second chapter covers indicators of national output, and the third chapter indicators of investment. Within each chapter, there are sections devoted to individual indicators. The information on each indicator is organized as follows:

Market sensitivity: Is this a high-sensitivity indicator that always gets the attention of the markets (such as GDP or CPI), a medium-sensitivity indicator in which an unusual movement might spark some trading activity (such as fixed asset investment or retail sales), or a low-sensitivity indicator that does more to inform the market's overall assessment than it does to trigger an immediate response (such as nonperforming loans or yuan deposits in the Hong Kong banking system)?

What is it? This is a brief description of the indicator and what it measures, including the units in which it is published. Being clear about the units in which the data is published is especially important in China, because of the considerable variety of approaches and conventions that often differ from those used in the United States. The main points to watch for are these:

- **Currency:** Is the data published in yuan (as with the GDP data) or dollars (as with the trade data)?

- **Units:** Is the data published in individual units (as with the wage data), tens of thousands (as with floor space under construction), millions (as with yuan deposits in the Hong Kong banks), or hundreds of millions (as with fixed asset investment)? Tens of thousands (万, wan) and hundreds of millions (亿, yi) are units peculiar to the Chinese counting system.

- **Period:** Does the data cover the current month (as with retail sales) or the year-to-date (as with fixed asset investment)?

- **Real or nominal:** Does the data account for changes in prices (as with industrial value added) or not (as with wages)?

Chinese news release on the Internet: Where can you find the Chinese data release on the Internet?

English news release on the Internet: Where can you find the English data release on the Internet?

Release time: When can you expect the publication of the data?

Frequency: Is it a daily, weekly, monthly, quarterly, or annual indicator?

Source: Who is producing the data? This could be the NBS, PBOC, CFLP, Hong Kong Monetary Authority, U.S. Bureau of Labor Statistics, or someone else.

Revisions: Is the data subject to revisions (as with the GDP data) or not (as with almost everything else)?

Why is it important? Why do the markets care about this indicator, and what does it say about the Chinese economy?

How is the data calculated? Where does the data come from, and how is it put together? Are there any reasons—political or technical—to doubt the accuracy of the data?

Interpreting the data: What does the data release look like, what are the most important takeaways, and how should they be interpreted? If the data is typically published in a table, you can see a copy of it here, with labels indicating the key points, linked to explanatory notes. For tables that are published on a timely basis in English, the English table is shown. For tables that are not published in English, or published in English only after a long delay, you can see a copy of the Chinese table with the main terms translated into English. For some of the larger tables, some of the less relevant data points are left out. For example, in the table of China's imports by product (Table 5.4 in Chapter 5), the table includes imports of crude oil and iron ore, but not imports of pesticides or other smaller components of China's import bill. Data omitted from the original is indicated by an ellipsis in brackets: [...]

Market impact: What impact does this data release typically have on equity, commodity, and currency markets?

CHAPTER 2

National Output

GROSS DOMESTIC PRODUCT

Market sensitivity: High

What is it? Quarterly and annual report on the size and growth of the Chinese economy, published in nominal level (CNY100mlns) and real growth (YoY % and QoQ %)

Chinese news release on the Internet: www.stats.gov.cn

English news release on the Internet: www.stats.gov.cn/english/

Release time: Quarterly data at 10 a.m. on the 15th day of the first month of the following quarter, annual data at 10 a.m. around January 20 in the following year

Frequency: Quarterly

Source: National Bureau of Statistics (NBS)

Revisions: During the following year, revisions are made to annual and quarterly estimates as more complete information is available. Major revisions to historical data are made as a result of the economic census, which takes place every 5 years.

Why Is It Important?

This is the big one. The GDP data is the most complete indicator of the state of the Chinese economy. It is the government's scorecard on the success or failure of its policies. It is the number that, more than any other, shapes the world's perception of China. Thirty years of growth averaging close to 10% year-on-year (YoY) has transformed China from an inward-looking basket case to a giant of the global economy. A GDP that has outstripped first that of Britain and France, then Germany, and now Japan, to place China at number two in the world rankings, has installed China's leaders at the top table for decisions on everything from climate change in Copenhagen to reform of the international financial system in Washington, D.C. A GDP that has increased in size many times over since 1978 has transformed China's population from Mao suit-clad peasants worried only about where the next meal is coming from to the 1.3 billion customers the world's retailers most want to meet, and has raised China's industry from the smoldering ashes of backyard steel furnaces to the world's largest consumer of iron ore and producer of steel.

In the years before the financial crisis, China enjoyed 10 sequential quarters of unbroken double-digit growth. That growth was unbalanced, with investment and exports the ugly sisters at the ball, and domestic consumption wondering whether a very large pumpkin and two oddly attired field mice were good to eat. But for many investors, the quarterly GDP data was all they needed to know about the China growth story. In the post-crisis world, with diminishing returns to further investment, the U.S. consumer gazing woefully at his recently dismembered credit card, and the Chinese consumer happier to hide cash under the mattress than spend it at the shops, double-digit growth may soon be just a distant memory. The focus of attention now is on how far and how fast China's GDP growth will slow, and what that slowdown means for equity, commodity, and currency markets. The torrid years of double-digit growth are over. But China's GDP data will remain a focus of attention, a gauge of the transition to a sustainable development path.

The 1998 Controversy

Despite being the focus of so much attention—or perhaps because of it—China's GDP data is also the subject of widespread controversy. Two episodes in the turbulent history of China's GDP data illustrate the institutional and technical challenges the NBS faces in making the calculation.

First, in 1998, the Asian Financial Crisis brought the region's economy grinding to a halt. A closed capital account protected China from the speculative attacks that crippled Thailand, Indonesia, and South Korea. But with major trade partners sliding into recession, China was not immune to the effects. Falling growth in energy consumption, airline passenger numbers, and imports all pointed to a sharp slowdown in growth. But if the economy was indeed sliding into recession, it was not evident to the NBS. Official data for the year shows GDP growth of 7.8%, down only slightly from 8.8% in 1997 and within spitting distance of the magic 8% that is believed to be the minimum required to maintain social stability. The 1998 GDP data has generated a storm of controversy. Academic economists have expended much energy in either defending the NBS calculation or, more common, attacking it and offering their own alternative estimates. Professor Thomas Rawski at the University of Pittsburgh has led the charge, concluding that the 1998 GDP data was inconsistent with evidence of slower growth from energy consumption, air travel, and output of key products such as steel and cement, and arguing that growth for the year was probably in a range between –2% and +2%. Professor Harry Wu of Hitotsubashi University in Tokyo and the late Professor Angus Maddison were equally stern, concluding on the basis of their own index of industrial production that China's GDP grew just 0.3% in 1998 (–0.1% in Professor Wu's recent updated results). Their alternative estimates of GDP growth from 1992 and after are shown in Figure 2.1. Professor Carsten Holz of the Hong Kong University of Science and Technology has weighed in forcefully on the other side, concluding that though there are inherent difficulties with calculating the GDP of a large and rapidly developing economy, it is difficult to identify systematic biases in the NBS data or to arrive at compelling alternative estimates.

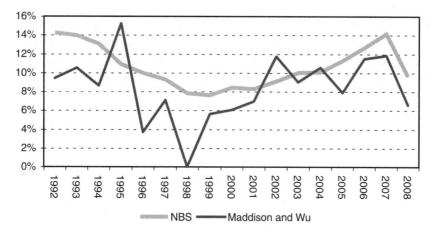

Figure 2.1   *GDP growth: NBS versus Maddison and Wu estimate (YoY %)*
Data Source: NBS, Maddison and Wu

The government has never admitted any problem with the data. Indeed, in a revision to the historical GDP data as a result of the 2004 economic census, the 1998 figure was the only one that was left untouched. But it has come close. The story that has trickled out in speeches and articles in the official press points the finger of blame at an excess of enthusiasm from local officials. Caught between the reality of an economy in crisis and the dream of career progression that depends on delivering growth that hits the 8% mark, officials engaged in rampant falsification of production data. Premier Zhu Rongji spoke of a "wind of embellishment and falsification" that swept through the statistical system. An article in the NBS in-house magazine, *Economics Education,* even developed a game theoretic model to explain how exaggeration by one official could trigger a wave of exaggeration by other officials, a kind of Chinese bureaucratic version of keeping up with the Joneses. In the years that have followed, controls on local statistics offices have been improved, more data is reported directly to the NBS headquarters in Beijing (bypassing the embellishing hand of local leaders), and more surveys and other checks on the accuracy of data collected at a local level are now conducted. These checks and balances have freed the national-level data from the impact of local exaggeration—or "adding water," as it is called in China. But local-level GDP data, especially for more backward provinces, remains deeply unreliable. In the Wikileaks scandal that broke at the end of 2010, it was revealed that even China's premier-in-waiting, Li Keqiang, had little faith in the provincial GDP data. Speaking to the U.S. ambassador in 2007, when he was still party secretary of Liaoning province, Li said that the provincial GDP data was "man-made" and, therefore, unreliable. To keep a handle on the growth rate of the Liaoning economy, he relied on tracking electricity consumption, rail cargo volume, and bank lending.

A Disservice to Services

Lying local officials aren't always the problem with China's official growth data, and the NBS doesn't always err on the upside. As the second episode in the troubled history of China's GDP calculation shows, the sheer size and complexity of the Chinese economy can also defeat the statisticians, and the official numbers can understate the true size of the economy. In 2004, China conducted an Economic Census, including a thoroughgoing attempt to come to grips with one of the most slippery parts of the economy: the services sector. With legions of statisticians on the ground in street-side cafes, foreign-language schools, and IT support centers, the NBS was able to get a more accurate gauge of the total output of this important but overlooked sector of the economy. The result was an upward revision of GDP for 2004 of a whopping CNY2.3 trillion, adding 16.8% to the size of the Chinese economy. How could the regular annual accounting exercise have overlooked such a large chunk of China's output? Part of the reason is that the services sector is made up of many small enterprises and informal operations. Adding up the output of a million local hairdressers, half of them with no accounting ledger and half with a ledger that conceals as much as it reveals, is a bigger challenge than taking stock of the output of the big modern firms that dominate the industrial sector. But that's not the entire story.

The NBS now uses the United Nation's approved System of National Accounts as the basis for calculating GDP. But in the early reform era, the Material Product System, borrowed from the old U.S.S.R., was employed. As might be expected from a scheme devised in Soviet Russia, the Material Product System is rather good at measuring physical outputs (such as the tons of steel and cement valued by central planners) and less good at measuring the intangibles produced by the services sector. Some of the biases in the old system linger in the new, and that's another reason the NBS missed such a large volume of services output. After the embarrassment of the 2004 census, the NBS made a serious attempt to overcome the deficiencies of its coverage of the services sector. New service sector industries, accounting for most of the output that was missed in the years before the census, were brought into the fold of the annual survey. But counting the output of a rapidly evolving services sector remains a challenge for China's statisticians. In 2009, the next round of the Economic Census discovered another CNY1.3 trillion in GDP that had previously been overlooked, adding 4.4% to the estimated size of the Chinese economy. Once again, the lion's share of the addition came from the services sector. A 4.4% addition to GDP in 2009 is considerably smaller than the 16.8% addition in 2004; the NBS is getting better at counting service sector output. But undercounting the services sector remains the most serious methodological problem for China's national accounts.

Political pressure to the right of them, technical weakness to the left of them: China's GDP data is under fire from all sides. Small wonder, then, that at the beginning of 2009, with the government vocally committed to its 8% growth target for the year and the economy hovering on the brink, there was concern that the NBS would come under pressure to cook the books. Much to the surprise of many commentators, the NBS came through the challenge rather well. The official GDP statistics tell a story of the sharpest slowdown in growth in more than a decade in the second half of 2008, with the economy hitting a trough in the first quarter of 2009 and then a rapid rebound starting in the second quarter and continuing over the course of the year. This story is confirmed by the V-shaped path traced out by retail sales, fixed asset investment, and export data. Back in 1998, the mismatch between strong GDP growth and weak growth in air passenger traffic, energy consumption, and output of cement and steel rang alarm bells. In 2009, the air passenger, cement and steel series followed the same pattern as the GDP data. The rebound in electricity output was a little slower, and that rang alarm bells. But the NBS explanation that a slower recovery in some electricity-intensive sectors was the reason for the mismatch appeared credible. If the NBS is fabricating the 2009 GDP data, it is also fabricating all the other data for the year, and that is difficult to believe. The NBS has never fully answered the charge of political interference in the calculation of GDP growth, and, even in the absence of political interference, measuring the size and growth of an economy as large and dynamic as that of China remains a challenge. But in the face of the 2009 economic crisis, where misreporting would have presented an even greater threat to its credibility than the 1998 debacle, the NBS has acquitted itself rather well.

How Is the Data Calculated?

$GDP = Pvt + Invt + G \text{ spending} + Net \text{ exports}$

There are three approaches to calculating GDP: the expenditure approach, the income approach, and the production approach. The expenditure approach is familiar from macroeconomics textbooks; it takes GDP as the sum of household consumption, investment, government spending, and net exports. This is the approach on which the calculation of GDP in the United States is based. The income approach calculates GDP as the sum of payments to the original factors of production: wages paid to workers, profits earned by business, taxes on production, and the consumption of fixed capital. Finally, there is the production approach which calculates GDP as the sum of value added across all sectors of the economy.

In China, the NBS publishes quarterly production-side GDP data. On an annual basis, the production-side data form the basis of the official figures, but expenditure-side data is also published.

Annual Data—Production Side

For the annual production side GDP data, the NBS breaks down the economy into 94 sectors. The approach to data collection and calculation varies across each of them, but the NBS has three general approaches:

1. For 51 sectors, the data is sufficiently complete and robust to allow calculation of output and value added directly. Those 51 sectors include key contributors to GDP, such as industry, agriculture, and finance, and account for 60% of the total.

2. For 32 sectors for which data is available on only a subset of output, value added is calculated for the subset for which data is available and then is extrapolated to the entire sector using the proportion of total value added produced by the subset in the last census year. So if the subset for which data was available accounted for 30% of value added for the sector in the census year, it is assumed to continue to account for 30% in the year for which the calculation is made. The extrapolation approach is used to calculate value added for the retail, construction, and other sectors, which account for a total of 35% of GDP.

3. For 11 sectors for which annual data is inadequate, the NBS estimates output and value added based on data from the census and the growth rate of a reference indicator that should be correlated with the growth of the sector. This approach is clearly less satisfactory than the other two, but because it covers just 5% of GDP, there is limited scope to distort the overall reading.

Breaking down the economy into 94 sectors represents a considerable advance from the situation even a few years ago. Before the 2004 economic census, the NBS relied on a breakdown into just 16 sectors (this is one of the reasons the statisticians missed such a large chunk of services sector output). But 94 sectors is still a long way behind an average of 200 for most developed economies.

Quarterly Data

For the quarterly data, a compressed timetable means that the NBS has to make the calculation based on a coarser sector breakdown and less complete data set. The quarterly data is based on a breakdown of the economy into just 17 sectors and makes greater use of the reference indicator method than is the case with the annual data:

- For 14 of the 17 sectors, the statisticians rely on extrapolations based on indicators that should move in line with growth for each sector. That means looking at value added for the sector in the same period last year and multiplying it by an indicator that should track the growth of the sector over the last year. Among the 14 sectors that are covered in this way are real estate, retail, transport, and finance.

- For the remaining 3 sectors of the economy—industry, construction, and agriculture—the NBS looks at total output for the current period and multiplies it by the ratio of total output to value added for the same period in the previous year.

With a less granular breakdown of sectors and a less comprehensive data set, the margin for error in the quarterly data is wider than for the annual data. The NBS does not always publish revisions for its quarterly data, but when it does, they can be substantial. In 2010, the quarterly growth rates for 2009 were revised from 6.1%, 7.9%, 9.1%, and 10.7% YoY to 6.6%, 8.2%, 9.7%, and 11.4%. This changed the shape of the downturn and recovery, suggesting the downturn was less severe and the recovery more rapid than previously thought.

Expenditure Data

For the expenditure-side calculation, the NBS needs data on household and government consumption, capital accumulation, change in inventories, and net exports:

- **Household consumption:** The basic data comes from the NBS surveys of urban and rural households. Recent independent research by Professor Wang Xiaolu of the China Reform Foundation has called into question the accuracy of the NBS data on income and expenditure for China's richest households. With China's richest households understating their income by a considerable margin, the NBS calculation of GDP on the expenditure side may be an underestimate.
- **Government consumption:** Data on government spending is provided by the Ministry of Finance.
- **Capital accumulation:** Data is based on the NBS's own survey of fixed asset investment (FAI) and data from the Ministry of Land and Resources. The crucial difference is that FAI is a gross figure, whereas capital accumulation is a net figure.
- **Change in inventories:** Calculating change in inventories is notoriously difficult, not just in China, but everywhere in the world. In China, wild swings in inventories in some years suggested that the NBS was using it as a residual to close the gap between the expenditure and production side data. But in recent years, this category has started to behave in a more reasonable manner. Data is collected from NBS surveys of the industrial, retail, and construction sectors.
- **Net exports:** This data is assembled from a combination of Customs and State Administration of Foreign Exchange data.

Getting to Current Prices

This exercise gets the NBS an estimate of GDP at current prices, or nominal GDP. But the real question is how much GDP has grown. To answer that question, the NBS has to strip out the impact of inflation on its estimate and work out GDP at constant prices, otherwise known as real GDP. Different deflators are used to calculate GDP at constant prices for different sectors of the economy. The consumer price index (CPI), producer price index (PPI), retail price index, and an index of the change in price of fixed assets all come into play. It is also possible to calculate a deflator for the economy as a whole, referred to as the GDP deflator. In the United States, the GDP deflator is published and is an important guide to the extent of inflationary pressure. In China, the NBS does not publish a deflator for its GDP series.

First Estimate, First Check, Final Check

For the annual production-side data, the calculation of China's GDP goes through 3 stages. The initial estimate is normally published on January 20 in the following year. This initial estimate gets all the attention, but it is also based on partial information and is subject to large revisions as new information becomes available. With more complete information available, including complete accounting information and the results of sampling surveys for several additional sectors, by the end of the year, the NBS is in a position to make a more complete estimate. A final estimate, based on the complete data set, is produced in the middle of the second year. These revised estimates typically receive little attention, but they can be quite large. GDP growth for 2007 was revised up from 11.4% in the first estimate to 13.0% in the final estimate. Both 2008 and 2009 saw smaller but still substantial increases in the growth rate from the first to the final estimates. The NBS also makes revisions to historical data on the basis of the economic census, which takes place once every 5 years. In the past, these revisions have been quite significant—remember the 16.8% addition to the 2004 GDP after the discovery of previously uncounted output from the services sector. But as the NBS annual data-collection methods improve, the likelihood of massive revisions to historical data on the basis of the census is reduced.

Interpreting the Data

Table 2.1   *Gross Domestic Product (GDP) (First Quarter, 2011)*

	Absolute Value (100 million yuan)	Growth Rate Over the Same Period Last Year (%)	
Gross Domestic Product	96,311	9.7	◀ 1
Primary Industry	5,980	3.5	2 ▶
Secondary Industry	46,788	11.1	
Tertiary Industry	43,543	9.1	

Data source: Adapted from NBS

For all the market attention to the Chinese GDP statistics and all the debate on its accuracy and reliability, the actual quarterly data release is rather a disappointment. Investors familiar with the granular detail of the GDP data released by the United States, European, and many Asian and emerging market economies will immediately be struck by the paucity of information in the Chinese equivalent. The U.S. quarterly GDP data release runs to 13 closely typed pages and breaks contributions to GDP into more than 50 categories. The NBS might be making the annual calculation based on a 94-sector breakdown and the quarterly data based on 17 sectors. But the data release breaks GDP down into only three not particularly useful categories and could fit—without too much difficulty— onto a postage stamp. The main takeaways are:

1. Until 2011, the highlight of the data release was the YoY growth rate, which is published in real terms. Investors have become accustomed to double-digit growth for the Chinese economy. In the future, the markets will have to come to terms with growth lodged firmly in single digits, and even below the 8% figure which has been the government's official target since time immemorial. Why is 8% the magic number for the

Chinese government? One theory is that it is related to paramount leader Deng Xiaoping's pledge to quadruple the size of the economy from 1980 to 2000. Another view is that it is the relationship between growth and employment that is the main motivation. With millions of young people entering the labor markets every year in the 1990s and early 2000s and the former employees of defunct state-owned enterprises also looking for work, the government calculated that only growth above 8% would generate a sufficient number of jobs to ensure social stability. So what happens if growth now dips below the magic 8% level? Probably not much. Deng's target is long since achieved, and changing conditions in China's labor markets mean that lower growth might not be the disaster for employment which everyone expects. The demographic dividend has been used up and the reform of the state sector is ancient history. With fewer young people entering the labor force and more old people leaving it, there is less need to create millions of new jobs every year. A shift in the structure of the Chinese economy would also help out. The current slant toward heavy industry generates a lot of output but not a lot of jobs. If the government achieves its objective of a shift away from low-employment heavy-industry and toward the high-employment services sector as the main driver of growth, that will also ease the transition to the world below 8%.

From the first quarter of 2011, the YoY data has had to share the limelight with a new arrival as the NBS began publishing a seasonally adjusted quarter-on-quarter (QoQ) figure for GDP growth. This is an important step forward for China's GDP data. Other major economies, including the United States, use the QoQ seasonally adjusted annualized rate as the benchmark for measuring the growth of GDP. By adopting the same approach, China has taken a step toward bringing its data into line with international standards. "QoQ seasonally adjusted annualized rate" is a bit of a mouthful, but its meaning is actually quite straightforward. *QoQ* means a comparison of output in the current quarter with output in the previous quarter (as opposed to the same quarter a year ago—which is the comparison made by the YoY data). *Seasonally adjusted* means that the statisticians have adjusted for seasonal factors—like changes in the number of working days—that might affect output. *Annualized* means that the QoQ number is multiplied according to a compound growth formula to give the growth rate for the entire year if the current rate of growth was sustained.

For the first quarter of 2011, the new approach shows China's GDP growing at 2.1% QoQ or 8.7% on an annualized basis, compared to 9.7% using the old YoY calculation. The difference between the results produced by the two approaches is significant—indicating that the current momentum of the economy was slower than the YoY figures suggested. The QoQ approach to measuring growth is more volatile than the YoY approach, showing higher peaks and lower troughs in the growth rate. The NBS avoided controversy by publishing only a data point for growth in the first quarter of 2011. But a historical series would have shown growth slowing extremely sharply in response to the economic crisis in the fourth quarter of 2008. QoQ annualized data

calculated by the People's Bank of China—which publishes its own series in its quarterly report on the macroeconomy—shows growth hitting a trough of 3.7% in the
fourth quarter of 2008, before rebounding strongly to 6.4% in the first quarter of 2009
and 14.9% in the second. The YoY data from the NBS shows the economy hitting a
trough of 6.6% growth in the first quarter of 2009 and recovering only slowly in the
following quarters.

   The different growth rates shown by the YoY and QoQ data have far-reaching
implications for the markets and for policy makers. For the markets, the steady rapid
growth shown by the YoY data has been fundamental to shaping perceptions of the
China investment story. Would the jagged ups and downs traced out by the QoQ
data—suggesting the Chinese economy was veering wildly between overheating and
overcooling—have inspired the same level of confidence? In the future, the introduc-
tion of QoQ data means markets will have to get used to not just a slower rate of
growth, but also a more volatile pattern of growth. For policy makers, the focus of
attention should be the current momentum of the economy, shown by the QoQ data.
The Chinese government kept the economic stimulus in place far into 2010, claiming
that the recovery was not yet stable. The QoQ data, which shows the economy
rebounding sharply from the second quarter of 2009, calls into question the wisdom of
keeping the economic punch bowl spiked with cheap credit for quite so long.

2. The data release also includes the breakdown of the nominal level of GDP, and the real
   YoY growth rates, for the three broad sectors of industry. *Primary industry* refers to
   the agricultural sector. *Secondary industry* includes mining, heavy industry, manufacturing, and utilities. The *tertiary sector* is services. Over the course of the reform era,
   the share of the primary sector has withered, from more than 30% of GDP in 1979 to
   around 10% in 2010. The remainder of output is split between the secondary and tertiary industries, which account for around 48% and 42%, respectively. One of the key
   challenges for the Chinese economy in the years ahead is to shift away from reliance
   on heavy industry as a driver of growth and toward a greater role for the services sector. That should mean faster growth in the tertiary sector.

   The more interesting breakdown is the contribution of consumption, investment,
   and net exports to GDP. The NBS spokesman sometimes throws out an estimate of the
   quarterly expenditure-side breakdown in the press conference which accompanies
   release of the production-side data. But quarterly expenditure-side data remains a work
   in progress, and the definitive statement of the breakdown only appears with the
   annual data. The expenditure-side data is an important input into the debate on the
   imbalanced structure of the Chinese economy. In the period from 2000 to 2009, the
   data shows the share of household consumption in GDP falling from 46% to 35%, and
   the share of capital formation rising from 35% to 47%. For all the official rhetoric on
   the importance of rebalancing the economy toward a greater role for consumption, the
   data shows the structure of the economy moving in the wrong direction.

Market Impact

Equities: The quarterly GDP data is the most complete reflection of the state of the Chinese economy. But what it gains in completeness, it loses in timeliness. Monthly data on trade, investment, retail sales, and industrial value added has already done a lot of the legwork in keeping investors up-to-date on the state of the economy. The GDP number itself is often leaked to the market before publication. A number that is in line with expectations generated by the monthly data and the market rumors often has little impact on the markets.

With GDP a focus for policy makers, investors also have to factor in the likely response of the government. Strong GDP growth is a sign that the economy is in a healthy state, which should be good news for equities. Weak GDP growth should have the reverse effect. But weak growth is also an indicator that the government is about to send out invitations to the stimulus party, and strong data is a warning that the policy punch bowl might be down to its last dregs. The anticipated response from the government, as much as the data itself, can be the decisive factor that moves markets.

Commodities: China is resource poor and on a resource-intensive development path. Put those two facts together, and it's clear why a strong GDP growth figure is bullish for commodity markets. In the future, as China attempts to transition from investment-led to consumption-led growth, that relationship between growth and commodity demand might break down. But the road toward rebalancing is long, and many more barrels of oil and tons of iron ore will be consumed along the way.

Currency: The main concern for the government in how much it allows the yuan to appreciate is the impact on domestic growth and jobs. Strong GDP growth means the government can allow the yuan to appreciate a little faster; weak GDP growth can slow appreciation to a snail's pace. The period of yuan appreciation from 2005 to 2008 coincided with years of double-digit growth. The pause in the yuan's rise against the dollar from August 2008 to June 2010 coincided with the sharpest slowdown in growth in more than a decade. Strong Chinese growth is also positive for the world economy, especially for commodity exporters such as Australia and Asian neighbors such as Korea and Singapore. With China's capital account closed, currency markets respond to the GDP data by taking a position in proxies such as the Australian dollar, the Korean won, and the Singapore dollar.

INDUSTRIAL VALUE ADDED

Market sensitivity: High

What is it? Report on industrial value added output, broken down by ownership type, sector, and product (current month and year-to-date, real, MoM %, and YoY %)

Chinese news release on the Internet: www.stats.gov.cn

English news release on the Internet: www.stats.gov.cn/english/

Release time: 10 a.m. on the 11th day of the following month. March, June, September, and December data is released later, to coincide with the quarterly GDP data.

Frequency: Monthly, data for January and February released together

Source: NBS

Revisions: No

Why Is It Important?

The Chinese economy is an industrial economy. For all the talk of rebalancing from manufacturing toward services as a driver of growth, the share of manufacturing and heavy industry in GDP is higher now that it was a decade ago. Steel mills, cement kilns, aluminum smelters, textile sweat shops, mobile phone factories, and automobile assembly lines remain the main engines of China's development. Industrial value added is equal to almost 50% of GDP, and the industrial and manufacturing sectors employ more than 210 million workers—27% of the workforce. The industrial output data offers a monthly snapshot of the most important sector of the Chinese economy. It is the most valuable and most closely watched, of the monthly indicators of the overall state of the Chinese economy.

How Is the Data Calculated?

Rapid growth in the economy, and continued concern about the quality of data reported by local officials, create problems for the industrial value-added data.

Expanding Sample Size

The rapid growth in China's industrial sector makes it difficult to maintain a consistent approach to measuring value added. In 1994, only 460,000 firms in China were classified as operating at the village level or above. The initial approach to measuring industrial output, which ran from 1994 to 1997, covered all these firms. From 1998, the NBS survey covered all state-owned enterprises and private firms with operating income of more than CNY5 million a year. After 2007, the CNY5 million threshold was extended to cover the state sector as well. That didn't stop the sample from continuing to swell in size, from 160,000 firms in 1998 to 430,000 in 2009. The NBS has now decided that a sample of 430,000 is simply too unwieldy. With a small group of large firms accounting for the majority of value added, and data on a large group of small firms less reliable and more costly to collect, the NBS has decided that, from 2011 on, the threshold for inclusion will be increased to firms with an annual operating income of CNY20 million a year.

For the firms above the threshold, two reporting methods are used. For the biggest 40,000 firms in the country, which together account for more than 60% of total output, the raw data is reported directly to the NBS headquarters. For everybody else, the local statistical bureau is responsible for collecting data, which is then transmitted up the administrative chain. In the past, the main channel for distortions in China's economic data was local officials over-reporting local industrial output. Direct reports by the largest firms in the country cut out the statistical middle man and reduce the scope for local exaggeration distorting the data. But the continued role of local statistical bureaus means there is still a chance the embellishing hand of provincial chiefs is adding a few yuan to local output data.

What Happened to Level Data?

Until the end of 2006, the NBS published the real growth and nominal level of industrial value added. In August 2006, for example, the NBS data release showed that total industrial value added for that month was CNY735.55 billion, up 15.7% from a year earlier. From the end of 2006 on, the NBS published only the real growth rate. The omission of data on the nominal level of value added has raised a number of eyebrows and prompted multiple attempts to find out what is going on. The most compelling explanation is that the NBS headquarters believes the output data it receives from local statistical bureaus is exaggerated and is making a downward adjustment to the growth rate to correct for that exaggeration. To hide its well-intended but difficult-to-justify data tweaking, the NBS stopped publishing the nominal level of value added.

The data for 2006 and 2007, when the NBS stopped publishing the level of output, provides some support for this theory. Enterprises above the CNY5 million threshold for inclusion in the monthly data typically account for around 85% of industrial output. Calculations by Professor Carsten Holz show that in 2006, industrial output for this subset added up to an implausibly high 99.7% of total industrial output. In 2007, it came to an impossibly high 109.3%. Either businesses below the CNY5 million threshold had negative output for the year, or the NBS is massaging the growth rate down.

Getting to Real Value Added

Getting from the raw output data to an estimate of value added means subtracting the value of intermediate inputs from the value of final output. Consider steel as an example. To calculate the value added of a steel producer, the value of iron ore and coking coal (inputs) must be subtracted from the value of steel (output). Making that calculation is time consuming, so for the monthly data, the NBS dispenses with the niceties and multiplies total output for the month by the ratio of total output to value added for the previous year. Given the time constraint, this approach makes sense. But with the ratio of value added to total output changing from year to year, it also introduces a certain margin of error into the calculation.

The final step in the calculation is to get from the nominal rate of growth to the real rate of growth. The NBS uses the producer price index as a deflator.

Interpreting the Data

Table 2.2 *Industrial Value Added—July 2010*

Indicators	July Absolute Magnitude	July Increased YoY (%)	Jan-July Absolute Magnitude	Jan-July Increased YoY (%)
1 ▶ **Value-Added of Industry Above Designated Size**	...	13.4	...	17.0
2 ▶ Value-Added of the Main Industrial Sectors				
Manufacture of Textile	...	11.1	...	11.6
Manufacture of Chemical Raw Material and Chemical Products	...	13.7	...	17.6
Manufacture of Nonmetal Mineral Products	...	18.5	...	20.7
Manufacture of General Purpose Machinery	...	21.0	...	21.5
Manufacture of Transport Equipment	...	15.9	...	27.1
Manufacture of Electrical Machinery & Equipment	...	18.9	...	18.5
Manufacture of Telecommunications Equipment, Computers and Other Electronic Equipment	...	13.8	...	19.3
Production and Supply of Electric Power and Heat Power	...	10.4	...	13.8
Smelting and Pressing of Ferrous Metals	...	6.0	...	15.8
3 ▶ Output of Major Products				
Crude Oil (10,000 tons)	1722	6.4	11570	5.3
4 ▶ Generating Capacity (100 million kWh)	3776	11.5	23478	17.9
Pig Iron (10,000 tons)	4758	-1.9	35197	14.4
Crude Steel (10,000 tons)	5174	2.2	37548	18.2
Steel (10,000 tons)	6767	9.7	46587	23.1
Cement (100 million tons)	16492	16.6	100904	17.4
Automobile (10,000 sets) o/w:	134.2	17.1	1045	42.3
Autocars (10,000 sets)	67.7	9.7	527.8	40.1

Source: Adapted from NBS

1. The focus for market attention is the year-on-year growth in industrial value added for the current month. Industrial value added is not the same as GDP, but it is the monthly indicator that provides the most comprehensive assessment of the state of the economy and is viewed by the markets as a proxy for overall growth. Another reason this number receives a lot of interest is that industry is the most sensitive of the three sectors of the economy to changes in the demand or policy environment. The agricultural sector is blown hither and thither by floods and droughts. Output for large chunks of the service sector is impervious to the economic cycle. But changes in foreign demand, interest rates, or the exchange rate can have a marked impact on the

industrial sector. Factories can slow production to zero or accelerate from 50% to 100% capacity utilization in the space of a few weeks in response to the changing environment. That makes changes in industrial value added a more sensitive indicator of the state of the economy than, for example, retail sales. At the beginning of 2011, the NBS began publishing a number for seasonally adjusted month-on-month (MoM) growth in industrial value added, alongside the existing YoY measure. The MoM growth rate provides better information about the current momentum of the economy.

2. The NBS also provides a breakdown of output growth for each of the most important sectors of industry:

   - The textile sector was ground zero for China's explosion onto the global scene. The share of the Pearl River sweat shops in China's total industrial output has fallen back from 5.9% in 2001 to 4.2% in 2009, and low-cost competition from South Asian countries threatens to push it down further. But China's textile mills are still a bigger source of employment than the computer and mobile phone sectors combined. A slowdown in growth in textile production might not immediately catch the attention of the markets. But if slower growth threatens bankruptcies and unemployment, it might well catch the attention of policy makers.

   - Design of the technology that goes into mobile phones and computers might remain outside the grasp of Chinese manufacturers, but putting together pieces made elsewhere is no problem. China is the world's largest manufacturer of mobile phones and computers, with Taiwanese firms such as Foxconn at the fore. Production of telecommunication, computers, and electronic equipment accounts for 8% of industrial output, one of the largest and fastest-growing sectors.

   - Nothing says a country has arrived on the world scene like its own brand of automobiles. A decade ago, Chery, BYD, and Geely were just a glint in an entrepreneur's eye. Now they are jostling for a share of not just the Chinese market, but also global markets. Toyota, Honda, and Volkswagen are among the foreign brands that have located major production facilities in China. Transport equipment accounts for about 7% of China's total industrial output.

3. In addition to the industry breakdown, the NBS provides data on the volume of output for 8 categories of product. Output of steel and cement are a particular focus for investor attention:

   - Steel production capacity above 700 million tons a year in 2010 and more under construction makes China the largest producer in the world. But with domestic demand running at less than 600 million tons a year, there is substantial excess capacity in the sector. Increasing steel output in China might be good news for iron ore miners in Australia and Brazil, but it is often bad news for foreign steel producers, with the risk that China's overproduction will spill over onto global markers and depress prices.

   - With construction and the real estate sector a mainstay of final demand in the Chinese economy, markets pay close attention to movements in the production of cement as a leading indicator of the construction cycle. In the run up to the 2008 financial crisis, growth in output of both cement and steel fell earlier and more sharply than growth in industrial value added as a whole.

An oddity of the unit output data for specific products is that it typically grows at a slower rate than industrial value added as a whole. In Table 2.2, only cement and automobile production is growing at a faster rate, and major categories of products such as steel and oil are growing considerably more slowly. Some analysts have cited this as evidence that China is exaggerating growth in industrial value added. In fact, the explanation is more innocent. First, the raw output data does not take account of changes in quality. If China's automobile manufacturers are making more stylish cars, allowing Beijing residents to enjoy the capital's famous traffic jams in greater comfort, that would show up in the value added data but not in the unit output data. Second, the product data covers older varieties of product where growth in output is likely to be lower than the average. The growth in China's industrial value added is in leading-edge machinery and electronic products, where factories are ramping up to full capacity, not pig iron and cement, where the government is clamping down on old and high-pollution plants.

4. Electricity production has a special place in the world of China's economic indicators. Ever since Professor Thomas Rawksi blew the whistle on China's 1998 GDP statistics, citing the mismatch between falling electricity output and stable GDP growth, markets have kept a close eye on the electricity output data. Even Vice Premier Li Keqiang has said that the electricity data is a better guide to growth than GDP, at least at a provincial level. Government statisticians might lie, the reasoning goes, but volts do not. Any divergence between growth in electricity output and growth in overall industrial value added is seized upon as evidence of new statistical fraud by the NBS, and the electricity output data is frequently in the markets ahead of the publication of overall value added data.

But as Figure 2.2 shows, the relationship between industrial value added and electricity output is not always so straightforward.

- In 2009, electricity output growth stayed in negative territory for some months after industrial value added rebounded. Some commentators cried foul. But as the NBS was at pains to point out, the discrepancy was not because the electricity output data was correct and the value added data was fabricated, but rather because certain energy-intensive sectors (notably metals processing) were lagging behind the recovery in the industrial sector as a whole.

- Factories with their own off-grid generators complicate the picture. When China's power grid reaches full capacity, China's factories flick a switch and their own generators swing into life. That output is not captured in the NBS data.

- China's households can also throw a wrench in the works. About 11% of China's electricity demand comes from the household sector. An unusually hot August can mean hundreds of millions of households keeping the air-conditioning on for longer, generating a surge in electricity output that has little to do with changes in industrial value added.

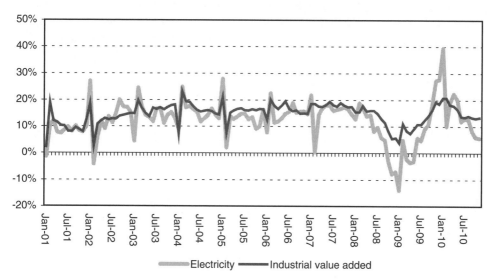

Figure 2.2 *Industrial value added versus electricity output (YoY%)*
    Source: NBS

Market Impact

Equities: The key question for equity markets is whether the shift in industrial value added is expected. PMI data from the China Federation of Logistics and Purchasing and HSBC Markit does a decent job of anticipating moves in industrial output. If the NBS data is in line with expectations generated by the PMIs, the markets might have already priced in the change. If the data is a surprise on either the up or the down side, that can result in a sharp reaction from equity investors.

Commodities: Seventy percent of China's energy demand comes from the industrial sector. China's steel furnaces are a bottomless pit into which Australia and Brazil pour their iron ore. Every piece of electrical equipment and car that is made requires copper wire. It is easy to see why strong growth in industrial value added is bullish for commodities markets. But with China a leading producer of steel and aluminum, strong growth in domestic production for some categories of product can also depress global prices, as overcapacity spills out on world markets.

Currencies: For China's policy makers, strong growth in industrial value added is an indication that growth and employment are on track, and that means more scope for yuan appreciation. Strong growth in industrial output can also be good news for proxies for yuan appreciation, and the China growth story in the Australian dollar, Singapore dollar, and Korean won. But with the PMI data already signaling the direction of travel, a surprise in the industrial value added data is needed to move the currency markets.

FISCAL REVENUE AND EXPENDITURE

Market sensitivity: Low
What is it? Monthly record of the government's incomings and outgoings, published in nominal level (CNY100 million) and growth (YoY %)
Chinese news release on the Internet: www.mof.gov.cn/
English news release on the Internet: n/a
Release time: Around the 12th day of the following month
Frequency: Monthly, with data for January and February sometimes released together
Source: Ministry of Finance
Revisions: No

Why Is It Important?

The memory might have been washed away by the CNY9.5 trillion in new loans issued by China's banks in 2009, but the government's first response to the financial crisis was through fiscal policy. It was the promise of CNY4 trillion in new investment at the end of 2008 that pulled the Chinese economy back from the brink. The day following the announcement of the stimulus package on November 9, the Shanghai Composite Index rose 7.2%, the Hang Seng rose 3.5%, and copper futures on the London Metal Exchange kicked up 3.1%. The CNY4 trillion push was a one-off, and the impact of fiscal data is not normally so marked. But the monthly release from the Ministry of Finance does provide an insight into the impact of the government sector on the real economy and the financial sector, and offers another way of thinking about the pace of growth. Over a longer time frame, fiscal data is an important part of understanding the government's structural reform agenda, and the deficit or surplus adds to or subtracts from China's national debt.

How Is the Data Calculated?

The framework for China's fiscal accounts is based on the International Monetary Fund's Government Finance Statistics Manual. But adoption of an international framework is no guarantee that the fiscal data is free from problems. In the 1990s, a drive by the central government to increase its own sources of revenue at the expense of local exchequers led to rapid growth in off-balance sheet revenue raising and spending by provincial capitals. In 2009, an explosion in borrowing by investment vehicles backed by guarantees from local government further muddied the fiscal waters. With an unknown but substantial amount of local revenue raising and spending going on outside the watchful gaze of the Ministry of Finance, the fiscal data does not present a complete picture of government activity.

Interpreting the Data

Deficit or Surplus?

The monthly fiscal data provides a means of tracking the net impact of government activity on the economy. If expenditure exceeds revenue, the government is running a deficit for the month and giving an additional impetus to growth. If revenue exceeds expenditure, the government is running a surplus—with the effect of reigning in growth. At the end of 2008, in the face of the financial crisis, the government promised an "active" fiscal policy to support the economy through the difficult times ahead. In 2009, the Ministry of Finance's budget targeted a deficit equal to 3% of GDP. In 2010, with the worst of the crisis over, the deficit target was shifted down to a smaller but still significant 2.8% of GDP. But as Figure 2.3 shows, the government as a whole ran a surplus in almost every month of both years. The only time a significant deficit appeared was in the final month of the year, when spending departments realized they hadn't used part of their budget and emptied their accounts in a hurry, hoping to avoid having the funds disappear back into the coffers of the Ministry of Finance. In the period from January to November 2009, the government ran a budget surplus of CNY715 billion. Only in December did the public sector get stimulus minded and run a deficit of CNY1.45 trillion.

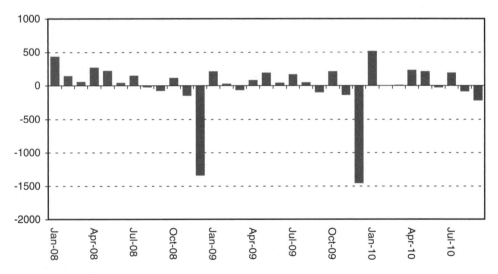

Figure 2.3 *Monthly fiscal balance (CNY, billions)*
Source: Ministry of Finance, author's calculations

The end of year spending splurge is huge. From 2008 to 2010, the December government deficit averaged more than CNY1 trillion. That level of government spending concentrated in a single month also has a marked impact on the financial system. Until they are ready to spend them, government departments hold their funds on deposit at the Central Bank. At the end of the year, the spending splurge means they empty their deposits. All that cash ends up as new deposits at the commercial banks. With CNY1 trillion in extra deposits on their hands, the temptation for the commercial banks is to lend it out—making loans is how the commercial banks make a profit. To prevent an end-year lending surge, the Central Bank often anticipates the government's move to empty its deposits and raises the commercial banks' reserve requirement ratio in tandem—forcing the banks to put their extra cash on reserve rather than lending it out.

In the longer term perspective, the deficit or surplus also adds to or subtracts from China's national debt. The figures for China's public debt are the subject of some controversy. If the Ministry of Finance is to be believed, at the end of 2010 central government debt added up to an insignificant CNY6.8 trillion or 17% of GDP. But that number considerably understates the total extent of the government's liabilities. A proper understanding of China's public debt has to consider a number of additional points:

- Local government debt was significant going into the financial crisis. Jia Kang, the head of a research institute under the Ministry of Finance, put the total at CNY4 trillion in 2008. Throw in the CNY7.7 trillion that the China Banking Regulatory Commission says local governments borrowed indirectly in 2009 and 2010, and total local government debt at the end of 2010 is around CNY11.7 trillion, or 29% of 2010 GDP.

- Bonds issued by the China Development Bank and other policy banks owned by the government are equal to CNY5.2 trillion, or 13% of GDP.

- Debt issued by the Ministry of Finance to pay for the recapitalization of the banking system at the end of the 1990s, and undigested obligations in the asset management companies that took on the banks' bad debt are equal to CNY3.0 trillion—8% of GDP.

- In early 2011, the Ministry of Railways owned up to total debt of CNY1.8 trillion (5% of GDP), mainly accumulated over the course of financing investment in China's high speed rail network.

Throw in an estimate of bad loans in the banking system as a result of the 2009–2010 lending splurge and China's debt-to-GDP ratio at the end of 2010 is probably closer to 75% of GDP than the official 17% figure.

This 75% is not a crazy number—it is lower than the total for the United States (92%) and Japan (220%). In the context of a rapidly growing economy, a low cost of borrowing for the government, and with almost all of the debt denominated in yuan, most analysts believe there is no immediate cause for concern. But total debt is far higher than the official figures suggest, and that is a constraint on the government's freedom of policy maneuver. When inflation rises, for example, the Central Bank's willingness to raise interest rates is reduced by the cost it imposes on government borrowers. Most of the cost of funding improvement in healthcare and education falls on local governments. With the cost of servicing debt high and resources limited, local government's ability to finance promised improvements in public services is also limited.

Revenue as a Way to Track Growth

Change in government revenue provides another way to track growth in the economy. If growth is solid, the government should be enjoying higher receipts from value added tax, corporate tax, and income tax. If growth is falling away, tax receipts should also be down. As Figure 2.4 shows, the relationship does hold in broad terms, but the fiscal story and the growth story do not entirely coincide, for various reasons:

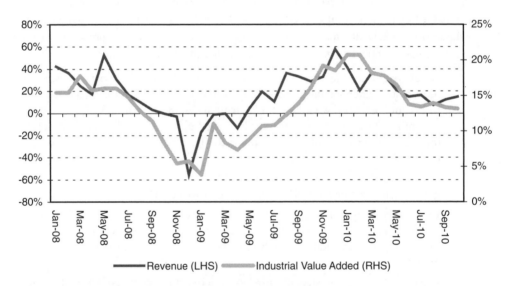

Figure 2.4   *Government revenue growth versus industrial value added growth (YoY%)*
Source: Ministry of Finance, NBS, author's calculations

• The government uses fiscal policy to balance out the fluctuations in growth. In the bad times, the government taxes less and spends more, to give the economy a boost. In the good times, the government taxes more and spends less, to prevent rapid growth from tipping over into overheating. In the fourth quarter of 2008, with the economy teetering on the brink of crisis, the increase in spending by the government was the largest in 20 years. In 2009, to support the infant recovery, the government cut taxes to the tune of CNY500 billion, the equivalent of 10% of total revenue in the previous year. A fiscal policy that leans against the prevailing economic winds also affects the relationship between revenue and growth.

- Changes in the efficiency of tax collection affect revenue growth independent of the economic cycle. In the second half of 2009, the Ministry of Finance launched a major initiative to raise tax collectors out of their collective stupor. The result was revenue growth that rebounded even faster than the economy itself.

- GDP and industrial value added data, the two main measures of growth, are published in real terms that account for movements in prices. The fiscal data is published in nominal terms. In the first half of 2009, growth in revenue was in negative territory. But because the CPI showed that prices were also falling, the real situation was not as bad as the nominal data suggested.

Spending Priorities

How the government spends its money says a lot about its priorities. Beijing is committed to raising the share of household consumption in GDP. Achieving that objective means addressing the weak provision of health, education, and welfare services that force households into a high level of precautionary saving. The government has made ambitious commitments to free universal education and basic healthcare, and if these are to be delivered, they will require a step change in spending. The monthly data does not give a particularly good sense of the trend, but on an annual basis, the data provides an opportunity to see if the government is putting its money where its mouth is. The record since 2005, when the government made improving the quality of health and education a priority, shows the level of spending increasing rapidly; but spending as a percentage of GDP still low compared to other emerging market economies. Public spending on education of around 3.1% of GDP, and public spending on health of just 1.2% of GDP in 2010, put China near the bottom of the middle-income country class.

Market Impact

On occasion, changes in fiscal policy can have a marked impact on the markets. The announcement of a CNY4 trillion stimulus at the end of 2008 was a major boost for the Shanghai Composite and for commodity markets. But that was a one-off event, and the regular monthly fiscal data does not normally attract much attention from investors.

FREIGHT AND PASSENGER TRAFFIC

Market sensitivity: Low
What is it? Report on transportation of goods (100 million tons and 100 million ton kilometers) and passengers (100 million passengers, 100 million passenger kilometers) by road, rail, air, and water
Chinese news release on the Internet: www.stats.gov.cn
English news release on the Internet: www.stats.gov.cn/english
Release time: Normally with a delay of at least 1 month
Frequency: Monthly
Source: NBS
Revisions: No

Why Is It important?

On a trip to Hong Kong at the beginning of 2009, the express train from the airport passed by the port on the way toward Central Station. Hong Kong's port is one of the busiest in the world, a staging post for China's exports before they continue their onward journey. Twenty-foot equivalent units, the brightly colored building blocks of globalization, are normally piled toward the sky. But on that day, there were none. The empty port spoke more vividly than any trade statistic ever could of the sorry state of the world economy and the dire straits in which the Chinese export sector found itself. Transport data, statistics on the brute tons of freight hauled and the raw number of passengers carried, provides another way of thinking about the state of the real economy. The logic is easy to understand. If demand is strong, inputs need to be shipped to the factory and outputs need to be shipped to the port. If the economy is flourishing, consultants should be on the plane to meet clients and households should be buying plane tickets for weekend breaks. If growth is headed south, the number of goods and people in motion should be reduced.

In China, where doubts about the reliability of the official growth data persist, a glance at the transport data has additional appeal. Transport data, similar to the GDP data, comes from the National Bureau of Statistics and might be tarred with the same brush. But GDP data is hot, the focus of international attention and the subject of political pressure. The stakes on the transport data are a lot lower—perhaps it is more trustworthy? That logic has certainly appealed to some well-respected commentators on the Chinese economy. For University of Pittsburgh economist Professor Thomas Rawski, very low growth in air passenger numbers back in 1998 was the smoking gun that convicted the politicians of murdering the GDP data. Even Vice Premier Li Keqiang has remarked that railway freight is a better guide to the strength of growth than GDP, at least at a provincial level. As Figure 2.5 shows, growth in railway freight does follow roughly the same pattern as growth in industrial value added, albeit with considerably more volatility. More than a decade on from the 1998 controversy, doubts about the reliability of the official growth data are less prominent than they were. Transport data also has its own problems and peculiarities. But tons hauled and passengers carried remain powerfully evocative. The transport data still provides a window into the state of the real economy and a cross-check against the official growth statistics.

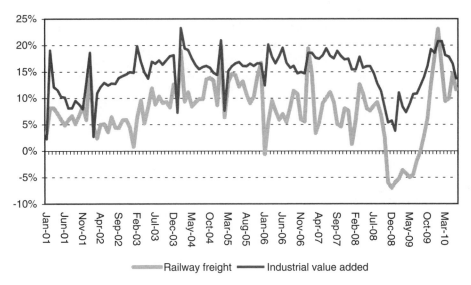

Figure 2.5 *Railway freight versus industrial value added (YoY %)*
Source: NBS

How Is the Data Calculated?

The NBS relies on inputs from a variety of sources for its transport data. The Ministry of Railways, Ministry of Transport, and Civil Aviation Administration of China are all in on the act. Collecting information on freight and passenger volumes on rail and air is straightforward. The railway and airline companies, which are few in number and in many cases state owned, submit the complete information on a monthly basis. Water transport is also straightforward. The ports keep complete records of the tonnage that comes in and goes out, and these records form the basis of the NBS data.

Where things get a bit trickier is on the roads. Motorways are okay. They have toll gates, and the toll operators can keep a record of the number of trucks and passenger cars that pass through. What is impossible to keep track of is the large volumes of freight and the passenger journeys made on local roads. The inadequacy of the data collection in this area was underlined in 2009, when the volume of highway freight mysteriously doubled from 118 billion kilometer (km) tons in March 2009 to 263 billion km tons in April 2009. The NBS offered no explanation, but it can only be assumed that a more comprehensive survey revealed many more journeys than were previously known. The numbers for highway freight and passengers need to be treated with some caution. With highway freight and passengers making up a substantial part of the total, so does the aggregate data.

Interpreting the Data

Table 2.3   *Total Volume of Transportation—May 2010*

Indicators	Unit	May	Growth Rate over Same Month Previous Year (%)	Jan-May	Growth Rate over Same Month Previous Year (%)
Total Volume of Freight	100 million tons	26.55	16.3	123.63	16.2
Railways	100 million tons	3.10	12.8	14.98	15.3
Highways	100 million tons	20.32	17.0	94.25	16.3
Water Carriage	100 million tons	3.13	15.7	14.37	16.5
Civil Aviation	10,000 tons	46.73	36.0	220.45	40.8
1 ▶ Total Turnover Volume of Freight Transport	100 million ton-km	11310.21	16.3	53268.61	16.3
2 ▶ Railways	100 million ton-km	2373.63	15.0	11383.35	14.6
Highways	100 million ton-km	3489.43	18.1	16462.89	18.2
3 ▶ Water Carriage	100 million ton-km	5431.74	15.6	25353.60	15.8
Civil Aviation	100 million ton-km	15.41	62.2	68.77	61.4
Total Volume of Passenger Transport	100 million persons	26.63	8.0	133.39	7.0
Railways	100 million persons	1.38	6.9	6.83	6.7
Highways	100 million persons	24.84	8.1	124.67	7.0
Water Carriage	100 million persons	0.20	-2.1	0.85	-3.8
Civil Aviation	100 million persons	0.22	18.2	1.04	16.5
4 ▶ Total Passenger Kilometers	100 million persons-km	2207.28	9.1	11451.15	10.5
Railways	100 million persons-km	679.83	8.1	3698.65	8.0
Highways	100 million persons-km	1200.98	6.5	6140.60	9.7
Water Carriage	100 million persons-km	6.08	-2.8	25.63	-6.5
Civil Aviation	100 million persons-km	320.39	22.8	1586.27	20.3
Total Volume of Freight Throughput in Major Coastal Port above Designated Size	100 million tons	4.67	11.8	22.04	19.1

Source: Adapted from NBS

1. Total volume of freight says how much tonnage was hauled. Total turnover volume is the more interesting statistic because it says not just how much, but also how far. In Table 2.3, the data for May 2010 shows total turnover of freight growing 16.3% YoY, a number that was consistent with the 16.5% growth in industrial value added in the same month.

2. China's railway system is one of the most crowded in the world. In February 2008, under the combined weight of bad weather, winter demand for coal (which is transported by rail), and peak passenger demand at Chinese New Year, the system broke down. Several cities experienced brownouts because supplies of coal could not reach power plants in time. Premier Wen Jiabao made a public appearance at a railway station in Hunan province to calm a fractious crowd of travelers. That breakdown in the rail system was one of the reasons the government made it a focus for investment in 2009 and 2010—adding substantially to capacity. The wider point is that supply constraints in the transport infrastructure introduce a bias into the transport data. Even if demand for railway freight is strong, it cannot grow faster than the capacity of the railway system to haul it. This is one reason transport data needs to be treated with caution as a proxy for growth.

3. The vast majority of water-bound freight is accounted for by imports and exports, handled through the giant coastal ports like Shanghai and Ningbo in the Yangtze River Delta, Guangzhou and Shenzhen in the Pearl River delta, and Dalian in the North Eastern Bohai rim. The data on water-bound freight reflects the health of the export sector.

4. Passenger transport data needs to be interpreted with some caution, for two reasons. First, strong seasonal variations distort the figures. Anyone who has lived in China knows that the week-long New Year holiday is not a good time to travel. Railway stations and airports are jammed with travelers returning home for the most important holiday of the year. The roads out of Beijing and Shanghai come to a standstill. A surge in travelers at this time of year is normal seasonal variation, not evidence of a booming economy. With the New Year's holiday falling in January some years and February in others, interpreting the year-on-year change in passenger numbers at the beginning of the year is also fraught with difficulty. Second, developments in passenger transport are not always reflective of developments in the real economy. The government's belated response to the outbreak of SARS in 2003 saw passenger volumes collapse. Air travel in May 2003 was down 77% YoY. But the fall in passenger transport overstated the impact of disease on the economy as a whole.

Market Impact

Transportation data, with all its limitations, is a decent measure of the overall level of economic activity and provides a common-sense cross-check against the more politically sensitive GDP numbers. But the data arrives too late (some weeks behind the main macroeconomic indicators for the month) to spark a reaction from the markets.

CHINA FEDERATION OF LOGISTICS AND PURCHASING'S PURCHASING MANAGERS INDEX

Market sensitivity: High
What is it? Monthly index of business conditions. Results between 0 and 100, with 50 the line that separates improving from deteriorating conditions
Chinese news release on the Internet: www.chinawuliu.com.cn/
English news release on the Internet: www.chinawuliu.com.cn/en/news/
Release time: 9:00 a.m. on the 1st working day of the following month
Frequency: Monthly
Source: China Federation of Logistics and Purchasing (CFLP) and NBS
Revisions: No

Why Is It Important?

The financial markets are enraptured with China's Purchasing Managers Indexes (PMIs), for good reason:

- The PMI data covers the most important section of the economy, with manufacturing accounting for almost 50% of GDP.
- The data provides direct access to the views of business managers, unfiltered by the embellishing hands of local government officials.
- The data is available early, on the first business day of the month—and does a decent job of anticipating movements in the industrial value added data that comes out almost two weeks later.
- It is a month-on-month (MoM) indicator, providing insight into the current momentum of growth.
- It is based on an internationally recognized and comparable methodology, and its older brother in the United States is well regarded as a guide to the state of the economy.

Three contenders compete for the heavyweight PMI crown. The reigning champion is the China Federation of Logistics and Purchasing (CFLP) PMI, which weighs in with the largest sample and the most comprehensive publicly available data set. The main challenger is the HSBC Markit PMI, which suffers from a smaller sample set but boasts complete independence from the controlling hand of the government. The plucky outsider, hoping to land a few quick jabs by publishing results early and covering a different set of questions, is the Market News International (MNI) survey.

How Is the Data Calculated?

The CFLP survey began life in 2005. It covers a panel of 820 businesses in China, designed to ensure representative coverage by sector, ownership type, and region. The CFLP does not disclose the exact composition of the sample, but it does reveal that the sample mirrors the contributions of different sectors, ownership types, and regions to industrial output. In practice, that means the sample is divided into 20 sectors, with ferrous metals, general equipment, and chemicals having the largest shares. Firms from the prosperous East Coast make up about 40% to 50% of the sample, with firms from the Central and Western provinces making up the balance. It is widely believed that the CFLP sample set is slanted toward state-owned enterprises. In fact, the team that led the survey insists that, regarding ownership structure, the sample closely mirrors that of the industrial sector as a whole.

The methodology is based on that of the U.S. Institute of Supply Management (ISM). The survey is conducted midmonth, with responses collected over the Internet. Respondents are asked to comment on 11 different areas:

- Production
- New orders
- New export orders
- Backlog of orders
- Stock of raw materials
- Purchasing of inputs
- Imports
- Input prices
- Inventories
- Employment
- Supplier delivery times

For each of these areas, respondents are asked whether the situation in the current month is better than, the same as, or worse than the previous month. The score for each question is the sum of the percentage that answered "better" + 50% of the percentage that answered "same." So if 20% of respondents said they had received more export orders this month than last, and 60% reported the same level of export orders, the score for the export orders subindex would be 50: 20 + (60 * 0.5) = 50.

The way the index is constructed means that a score of 50 indicates no change over the situation last month, a score above 50 means growth or improvement, and a score below 50 means contraction or deterioration. In the previous example, a score of 50 for the new export orders subindex means there has been no change in export orders from last month to this month.

To get from the subindexes to the overall score for the PMI, CFLP takes a weighted average of the five most important subindexes:

PMI = (New orders * 0.3) + (Production * 0.25) + (Employment * 0.2) + (Supplier delivery times * 0.15) + (Stock of raw materials * 0.1)

These components and weights are almost identical to those used in the ISM survey in the United States and the HSBC Markit survey in China.

The CFLP PMI is seasonally adjusted. But a pronounced pattern of rises and falls in the index around major holidays suggests that it is not seasonally adjusted enough. On average between 2005 and 2010, the CFLP PMI rose more than 3 points compared to the previous month in March, gave back those gains with a 3-point fall in May, rose more than 2 points in September, and fell back 2 points in October. These regular rises and falls suggest that the results are affected by the timing of Chinese New Year, which falls in January or February, and the national holiday, which falls in October. Till the CFLP adopts a better approach to seasonal adjustment, movements in the index at these times of year should be interpreted with caution.

Interpreting the Data

The headline reading on the CFLP PMI grabs the attention of the markets. A reading above 50 points to improving conditions in the manufacturing sector—normally including higher levels of new orders and output. A reading below 50 points to deteriorating conditions, with orders and output falling away. But expansion is the natural state of the Chinese economy. Over the 5 years from 2005 to 2010, the PMI managed an average score of over 53 and dipped below 50 in only 7 of the 60 months. So the key question is not whether the PMI is above 50, which it almost always is, but how far above 50 it is and whether it is higher or lower than in the previous month.

The financial crisis tested the mettle of China's three business sentiment surveys, and as Figure 2.6 shows all three put in a decent performance. With the Chinese economy sailing into the stormy waters of the crisis, all three indicators showed growth slowing from the start of 2008. The CFLP index pointed to negative growth from the beginning of the third quarter—among the first data points to identify the rocks ahead. Coming out of the crisis, all three surveys signaled a rebound, but subtly different results reflected differences in the sample sets. The government's CNY4 trillion stimulus and a surge in bank lending that kick-started the recovery was channeled mainly through the state sector. The MNI index gives the largest weight to state-owned firms, so it showed the most striking rebound. The state sector share in the CFLP sample is in line with its share in the economy as a whole, so it also showed a strong rebound. The HSBC sample is weighted toward small private businesses that were slower to feel the benefits, so it rebounded relatively weakly (a different approach to seasonal adjustment may also have played a part).

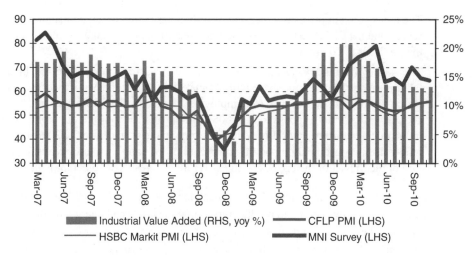

Figure 2.6   *Industrial production versus PMIs: PMI readings above 50 indicate expansion.*
Source: NBS, CFLP, HSBC Markit, MNI

The CFLP subindexes provide a more detailed insight into the state of the manufacturing sector:

- The index of production is the best guide to the current state of manufacturing output. The CFLP team that put the survey together say that the index of new orders is the best guide to the immediate future. In practice, the two indexes move closely together.

- The index for new export orders provides insights into the state of the export sector. With export orders typically placed 2 to 3 months ahead of shipment, movement in the PMI export orders index is not normally immediately reflected in the Customs data.

- The index of imports is a useful measure of the strength of domestic and foreign demand. China's imports fall into two main categories: imports of raw materials for the domestic industrial sector and imports of inputs into the export processing trade. So a strong reading for the imports index points to robust demand at home and abroad. A fall points to the reverse. In the second half of 2008, the fall in the PMI import index gave a clear signal of the coming collapse in exports and industrial value added.

- The supplier delivery times index is volatile, but it is also a useful gauge of spare capacity in the economy. The idea is that if the economy is overheating, supply bottlenecks increase and delivery times lengthen. If there is spare capacity, that should be reflected in shorter delivery times. One point to note is that the delivery times index is reported in opposite terms to the other components of the PMI. A reading over 50 means delivery times are shortening (pointing to spare capacity in a cooling economy) and a reading below 50 means they are lengthening (pointing to overheating).

- The index of input prices is a measure of inflationary pressure in the manufacturing sector, and the CFLP series has a solid track record of anticipating movements in the producer price index.

- The employment index is a much more sensitive measure of movements in China's labor markets than the famously awful official data. Where the Ministry of Human Resources and Social Security's unemployment data and the NBS wage data showed virtually no response to the 2008 crisis, the CFLP measure of employment in the manufacturing sector dropped like a stone in the final quarter of 2008 and rebounded just as quickly in the first quarter of 2009, painting a more realistic picture of the impact of the crisis, and the government's response, on employment.

The CFLP PMI also includes a detailed breakdown of the headline PMI and some of the main subindexes by sector and product type—raw materials and energy, producer goods, intermediate goods, and consumer goods. A slowdown in new orders for the textile sector might drag down the headline reading for the new orders subindex, but the ferrous metals smelting sector might gain a growing number of new orders. The sector breakdown allows for a more differentiated understanding of what is going on in the manufacturing sector.

Market Impact

Equities: The PMI data is the first meaningful data point the markets receive on the state of the economy in the month just past. It also has a good record of anticipating the change in the official industrial value added series. That makes it a focus of attention for equity markets. A strong reading can send the Hang Seng and the Shanghai Composite Index higher; a weak reading can push them lower.

Commodities: China's industrial sector is one of the world's largest consumers of energy and the world's largest consumer of metals. High readings on the PMI are a sign that growth is on track, and that is generally good news for commodities demand.

Currencies: Currency markets also pay attention to the PMI data as an early indicator of the overall state of the Chinese economy. A high reading can be good news for other regional currencies, which are traded as proxies for yuan appreciation and the Chinese growth story.

The markets are not the only group keeping an eye on the CFLP PMI. Policy makers are also paying attention, with the CFLP briefing the National Development and Reform Commission, Ministry of Finance, and other key institutions on the results of the survey at a monthly meeting.

HSBC MARKIT PURCHASING MANAGERS INDEX

Market sensitivity: High

What is it? Monthly index of business conditions. Results are between 0 and 100, with 50 the line that separates improving from deteriorating conditions.

Chinese news release on the Internet: n/a

English news release on the Internet: www.markiteconomics.com/

Release time: 10:30 a.m. on the 1st day of the following month. From 2011, a flash reading, based on 85% to 90% of the total PMI survey results for the month has been published a week earlier.

Frequency: Monthly

Source: HSBC and Markit Economics (formerly CLSA and Markit Economics)

Revisions: No

Why Is It Important?

The HSBC Markit PMI is the challenger for the heavyweight survey crown. Weighing in with a sample of just 430 companies, it is already conceding some advantage to the CFLP survey's muscle-bound 820. It also loses points from the judges for not publishing full details of the results to nonsubscribers and having no breakdown of results by sector. But it gains points for a superior approach to seasonal adjustment of its results, and, for those who continue to suspect political interference in China's data, for its complete independence from the controlling hand of the government.

How Is the Data Calculated?

The survey covers a panel of around 430 businesses in China. Sectors and regions are weighted according to their contribution to GDP, with the weighting revisited every year to account for changes in the structure of the manufacturing sector. As Table 2.4 shows, in the current sample, the largest sector weights go to the extraction and energy sector (18%), chemicals and plastics (12%), food and drink (11%), and basic metals (11%).

In terms of size, small businesses with 1–499 employees make up the largest share of the sample (40%), medium-size businesses with 500–2,499 employees (31%) are next up, and large businesses with more than 2,500 employees (29%) are the smallest part of the sample. That weighting gives small, private firms a larger share in the HSBC survey than in the CFLP survey.

Table 2.4   *HSBC Markit PMI Sample by Size and Sector*

Description	1–499	500–2,499	2,500	Total
Food and drink	20	16	12	48
Textiles and clothing	15	18	6	39
Electrical	14	14	17	45
Chemicals and plastics	24	17	11	52
Transport	8	16	9	33
Timber and paper	15	1	3	19
Basic metals	22	11	15	48
Mechanical engineering	16	11	8	35
Extraction and energy	20	20	38	78
Other	15	10	5	30
Total	**169**	**134**	**124**	**427**

Data Source: Adapted from HSBC Markit

The range of questions covered by the HSBC Markit survey is almost entirely identical to that of the CFLP survey. The one significant difference is that the HSBC Markit survey adds a question on output prices (not covered by the CFLP survey) and has no question on imports (covered by the CFLP survey). The approach to calculating the value of the subindexes and the PMI itself is also identical to the approach the CFLP uses.

The HSBC Markit PMI has a more sophisticated approach to seasonal adjustment than the CFLP PMI. That means it provides a better read on the state of the manufacturing sector around the major holidays in January, February, and October.

Interpreting the Data

The main takeaway from the data is the headline reading for the PMI. A reading above 50 indicates that conditions in the manufacturing sector have improved relative to the previous month; a reading below 50 means they have deteriorated. The HSBC Markit team says that, as a rule of thumb, a reading between 50 and 55 points to a moderate improvement in operating conditions, and a reading between 55 and 60 points to strong improvement. The same is true below the 50 line, with readings between 45 and 50 suggesting a moderate deterioration, and lower readings pointing to a more marked decline.

Compared to the headline reading for the PMI, the subindexes receive relatively little attention, particularly because HSBC Markit does not release full details of the levels to nonsubscribers. The main focus of attention for the markets is the subindexes of production, new orders, and new export orders. Indexes of input and output prices provide an insight into upstream inflationary pressure, and the difference between them shows whether firms are being squeezed between higher input and lower output costs or firms are benefiting from higher margins. The employment index is a more sensitive measure of changes in the labor market than the official unemployment and wage data.

Market Impact

Equities: The equity markets focus on the PMI data as the first meaningful reading on the state of the Chinese economy in the last month.

Commodities: China's industrial sector is the main contributor to China's demand for energy and the most important driver of global demand for metals. The PMI data is the first chance commodities investors have to get a sense of the state of Chinese demand.

Currencies: Strong PMI data is good news for the proxies for the Chinese growth story in the Australian dollar, Singapore dollar, and Korean won.

MARKET NEWS INTERNATIONAL CHINA BUSINESS SURVEY

Market sensitivity: Low

What is it? Monthly index of business views on current operating conditions and the outlook for the immediate future. Results are between 0 and 100, with 50 the line that separates improving from deteriorating conditions.

Chinese news release on the Internet: n/a

English news release on the Internet: www.marketnews.com

Release time: 9:35 a.m. on the final Friday of the month

Frequency: Monthly

Source: Market News International (MNI)

Revisions: No

Why Is It Important?

The outside bet for the business sentiment survey crown is the Market News International Survey. Weighing in with a sample size of just 180, it packs less punch than either the CFLP or the HSBC Markit surveys. Till the start of 2011, with the results published at the end of the month covered in the survey, a few days before the results of the other surveys were available, the Market News product could land a few jabs before the heavyweights had limbered up. But with HSBC now publishing a "flash" based on results from 85% to 90% of its sample several days before the MNI results are available, that first mover advantage has been taken away.

How Is the Data Calculated?

The MNI survey dates back to 2005, with a methodology modeled on Japan's Tankan and the U.S. Institute of Supply Management's surveys. In the middle of every month, the survey team contacts the board secretaries and investor relations directors of around 180 companies and conducts short telephone interviews covering their views on the current state and future expectations for operating conditions. The sample consists of Chinese firms listed on either the mainland or Hong Kong markets. In practice, with state-sector firms disproportionately represented among listed companies, the MNI survey is more tilted toward firms with government ties than either the CFLP or the HSBC Markit surveys. For this reason, the MNI team believes its survey is more sensitive to changes in government policy than competitors' surveys.

Seventy-five percent of participants are involved in the manufacturing sector; the remaining 25% are involved in services. The inclusion of service-sector firms is another point of difference from the CFLP and HSBC approach, which treats manufacturing and service-sector firms separately. The sample is refreshed every month, with an entirely new set of firms from China's listed universe asked for their views.

Questions cover a slightly different set of subjects from the CFLP and HSBC surveys. Respondents are asked for their views on the current conditions and expectations for conditions three months down the line in these areas:

- Overall business conditions
- Productive capacity
- Production
- Interest rates
- New orders
- Impact of the exchange rate on business
- Employment numbers
- Financial position
- Inventory
- Order backlog
- Input prices
- Availability of credit

As in the CFLP and HSBC approach, the score for each index is 100% of the percentage of respondents that gave a positive answer, plus 50% of the percentage of respondents that gave a neutral answer.

Where the MNI survey differs is in how the headline figure for business conditions is derived. In the CFLP and HSBC surveys, the headline reading for the PMI is the weighted average of the indexes for new orders, production, employment, supplier delivery times, and stock of raw materials. The MNI survey dispenses with these niceties and simply asks respondents for their assessment of current business conditions. That difference in methodology, combined with a sample populated with an entirely new set of companies every month, accounts for the more erratic movement of the MNI index compared to the CFLP or HSBC PMIs.

Interpreting the Data

Table 2.5 *MNI China Business Sentiment Survey—Current Conditions*

Current Conditions	Sep-10	Aug-10	Jul-10	Sep-09
1 ▶ Overall Business Condition	69.54	62.16	64.94	60.47
Productive Capacity	53.79	57.85	70.63	55.21
2 ▶ Interest Rates You Pay	52.36	52.05	49.44	55.88
New Orders	66.36	61.16	67.68	60.00
Need to Hire More Employees	58.68	58.74	57.19	55.45
Financial Positions	53.66	55.12	65.67	60.80
Order Backlog	56.67	49.44	51.54	50.00
Input Prices	67.04	64.48	57.39	54.00
Production	67.48	60.33	63.95	60.80
3 ▶ Effect of Yuan Exchange Rate	44.66	44.31	43.40	43.06
Prices Received For Your Products	62.50	53.47	49.35	51.04
Inventories	44.94	50.00	34.56	44.00
Availability of Credit	51.30	49.61	57.47	55.41

Source: Adapted from MNI

1. The most important data point is the index of overall business conditions. A reading above 50 means that participants in the survey generally view conditions as improving from the previous month. A reading below 50 means conditions are getting worse. The financial crisis provided the first serious test of the survey's capacity to anticipate movements in industrial output, and it put in a decent performance. The index of overall business conditions began to turn down in July 2008, hit a trough in December 2008, and rebounded sharply in February 2009, anticipating the rebound in the NBS index of growth in industrial value added. A rebound that was stronger than that of either the CFLP or the HSBC index probably reflects a bias toward the state sector—which benefited disproportionately from the government's stimulus measures—in the sample.

2. One of the unique features of the MNI survey is the index on interest rates. Businesses are asked if the interest rates they pay are higher, lower, or the same as last month's. In China, the Central Bank sets benchmark lending rates. But commercial banks have the freedom to lend at a discount of 10% to the benchmark rate or as high above it as they can find customers willing to pay. The banks raise and lower the rates they charge around the benchmark rate in accordance with the creditworthiness of the borrower, the availability of credit, and the circumstances of the economy. The index of interest rates paid provides insight into the rates firms are actually facing in the market. At the beginning of 2010, the Central Bank continued to insist that monetary policy was unchanged. The benchmark lending rate was still 9 months away from a move. But in reality, tighter credit conditions meant businesses were already paying higher rates on their loans. The MNI data told that story, with the index of interest rates paid moving from 47.58 in November 2009 to a high of 76.06 in March 2010.

3. The index measuring the impact of the yuan exchange rate provides a snapshot into the views of business on China's most controversial economic policy. The main consideration for the Chinese government in determining the exchange rate remains the impact on domestic businesses. No matter how much pressure there is from Washington, D.C., Beijing will not allow appreciation at the expense of bankruptcies in the export sector and unemployment up and down the East Coast. The export data tells part of the story of the impact of the exchange rate, but not the entire story. Exports could continue to grow even as exporters were pushed to the point of bankruptcy by tighter margins. To get a read on what is happening at the firm level, China's decision makers are looking at the results of surveys a lot like the MNI survey. If businesses are complaining loudly about the impact of the exchange rate, that is an important factor in the government's decision making on the pace of appreciation. A fall in the MNI index of the impact of the exchange rate to 32.64 in June 2008, down from 70.28 the previous year, showed that the appreciation shoe was starting to pinch. As Figure 2.7 shows, the low reading in the MNI survey anticipated the government's decision to put appreciation of the yuan on hold for the course of the financial crisis.

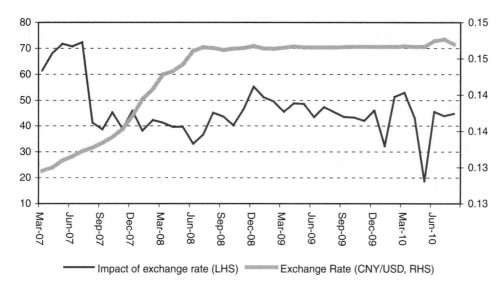

Figure 2.7   *MNI survey on impact of exchange rate versus exchange rate*
Source: MNI, China Foreign Exchange Trading Center

Table 2.6   *MNI China Business Sentiment Survey—3-Month Outlook*

		Sep-10	**Aug-10**	**Jul-10**	**Sep-09**
1 ▶	Overall Business Conditions	63.58	67.23	68.18	61.15
	Productive Capacity	61.36	65.70	70.63	54.17
	Interest Rates You Pay	55.19	51.64	50.00	52.94
	New Orders	64.49	65.63	68.29	58.24
	Need to Hire More Employees	54.79	60.14	52.61	53.18
	Financial Position	53.25	57.48	67.00	59.66
	Order Backlog	58.89	51.11	54.62	46.67
	Input Prices	62.59	56.90	53.98	51.33
	Production	62.60	65.29	69.19	60.23
	Effect of Yuan Exchange Rate	46.12	45.93	45.75	44.44
	Prices Received For Your Products	58.57	55.56	45.42	52.60
	Inventories	48.88	47.40	37.50	47.33
	Availability of Credit	52.61	50.39	54.60	50.68

Source: Adapted from MNI

1. Part of the added value of the MNI survey is the forward-looking aspect, with participants asked to comment on their expectations for the situation 3 months down the line. Business behavior is shaped not just by current conditions, but also by expectations about the future. If new orders are down but businesses expect them to pick up 3 months from now, that is reason for optimism. If new orders are down and businesses expect them to stay down, that is not good news. At the end of 2008, business

views on the current situation were dire, with the index of overall business conditions dipping to 35.2. But expectations of the future never dropped below the 50 mark that separates optimism from pessimism, as China's state owned enterprises correctly anticipated that the government's stimulus would turn things around.

Market Impact

With the headline result on overall business conditions volatile, and the detailed results of the survey restricted to MNI clients and Bloomberg subscribers who pay for access to the data, the MNI survey is not currently a market mover.

NATIONAL BUREAU OF STATISTICS LEADING ECONOMIC INDICATOR

Market sensitivity: Low
What is it? Composite indicator of the position of the Chinese economy in the economic cycle
Chinese news release on the Internet: www.stats.gov.cn
English news release on the Internet: www.stats.gov.cn/english
Release time: Around 6 weeks after the month covered by the data release
Frequency: Monthly
Source: NBS
Revisions: No

Why Is It Important?

Where is China in the economic cycle? Sailing into a boom or plunging into a bust? In a sea of economic data, it can be difficult for investors and policy makers to get their bearings. The macroeconomic climate index, compiled by the China Economic Monitoring and Analysis Center (CEMAC) at the National Bureau of Statistics, is intended to cut through the uncertainty. The statisticians at CEMAC have pored over the complete set of China's economic data and tried to work out which indicators normally move ahead of the economic cycle, which move in line with the cycle, and which lag behind. They bundle the results into a leading index, coincident index, and lagging index.

How Is the Data Calculated?

The leading index shown in Table 2.7 attempts to anticipate turning points in the economy and consists of indicators that typically move ahead of the growth cycle. Some of the components of the index are themselves composite indicators calculated by CEMAC.

Table 2.7 *Leading Indicator Components and Weights*

Indicator	Weight
6 Composite Leading Indicators o/w:	**78.67%** o/w:
1. Index of Hang Seng–listed mainland firms	–10.00%
2. Product sales ratio	–19.17%
3. Money supply (M2)	–20.00%
4. New investment projects	–20.00%
5. Freight o/w:	–17.50% o/w:
Total freight	–50.00%
Port throughput	–50.00%
6. Real estate development o/w:	–13.33% o/w:
Floor space under development	–50.00%
Commercial floor space under development	–50.00%
Consumer expectations	**9.33%**
Slope of Treasury yield curve	**12.00%**

Source: Adapted from China Economic Monitoring and Analysis Center (CEMAC)
Key: o/w = of which

The coincident index shown in Table 2.8 consists of indicators that typically move in line with the economic cycle. The income index and the demand index components of the coincident index reflect the income approach and expenditure approach to the calculation of GDP.

Table 2.8   *Coincident Indicator Components and Weights*

Indicator	Weight
Industrial output	14.75%
Employment	12.50%
Income index o/w:	32.00% o/w:
Government tax revenue	−26.67%
Industrial profits	−33.33%
Household disposable income	−40.00%
Demand index o/w:	40.75% o/w:
Fixed asset investment	−33.33%
Retail sales	−40.00%
Imports and exports	−26.67%

Source: Adapted from CEMAC

The lagging index shown in Table 2.9 consists of indicators that typically move behind the economic cycle.

Table 2.9   *Lagging Indicator Components and Weights*

Indicator	Weight
Government spending	13.60%
Commercial loans	21.80%
Household deposits	13.40%
Consumer Price Index	21.00%
Business inventories	30.20%

Source: Adapted from CEMAC

In addition to its system of leading, coincident, and lagging indicators, CEMAC publishes an early warning index. This index attempts to capture in a single number whether the economy is too hot, too cold, or just right. The index is a composite of 10 different indicators, shown in Table 2.10. For each of these indicators, CEMAC has reviewed the historical data and attempted to define what range of readings is consistent with economic stability, what range indicates overheating, and what range points to too much slack in the economy. For industrial output, for example, year-on-year growth of between 10% and 16% is deemed to be consistent with economic stability. Growth above 16% indicates that the economy is moving toward overheating, and above 18% suggests overheating. In the other direction, a reading below 10% suggests the economy is cooling down, and anything below 8% suggests that the economic temperature is excessively chilly.

Table 2.10 *Early Warning Index—Components and Weights*

	Over-heated	Slanted toward overheating	Stable	Slanted toward overcooling	Over-cooled	Weight
Industrial output	>18	18–16	16–10	10–8	<8	1.2
Retail sales	>28	28–18	18–9	9–7	<7	1.2
Fixed asset investment	>45	45–30	30–15	15–11	<11	1
Foreign trade	>34	34–26	26–10	10–3	<3	0.8
Fiscal revenue	>28	28–24	24–11	11–4	<4	0.8
Industrial profit	>223	223–47	47–2	2– –12	<-12	1
Urban household disposable income	>17	17–13	13–8	8–4	<4	1.2
Total loans	>24	24–22	22–13	13–10	<10	0.8
Money supply M2	>30	30–23	23–14.9	14.9–14.1	<14.1	0.8
Consumer Price Index (CPI)	>118	118–108	108 - 100	100–99	<99	1.2
Warning index	>136	136–116	116–83	83–63	<63	1.0

Source: Adapted from CEMAC

The components are given weights between 0.8 and 1.2, depending on how important CEMAC believes they are. Industrial output is an important reflection of the state of the economy and is weighted at 1.2. Fiscal revenue is less important and is weighted at 0.8. By summing the weighted monthly readings for each of these indicators, CEMAC arrives at the score for the index.

Interpreting the Data

Table 2.11 *Macroeconomic Climate Index—June 2010*

	3	2	1	
Date	Monitoring Signals	Coincident Index (Year 1996=100)	Leading Index (Year 1996=100)	Lagging Index (Year 1996=100)
2009.09	103.3	98.2	105.0	90.8
2009.10	110.7	99.5	105.7	92.0
2009.11	117.3	100.4	105.4	93.2
2009.12	116.7	102.1	105.4	93.8
2010.01	114.0	103.1	104.7	95.0
2010.02	104.7	103.9	104.7	95.8
2010.03	106.0	104.1	105.0	96.3
2010.04	107.3	104.0	104.4	96.3
2010.05	114.0	103.7	103.4	97.3
2010.06	106.7	103.0	102.8	97.4

Source: Adapted from NBS

1. As Figure 2.8 shows, the leading index does a decent job of forecasting turning points in the economic cycle. Going into the financial crisis, it peaked in February 2008, 4 months ahead of the coincident index, and hit a trough in November 2008, 3 months ahead of the coincident index. With the effects of the stimulus starting to wear off in October 2009, the leading index peaked again, pointing to another slowdown in growth. Sure enough, in March 2010, the coincident index peaked and growth started to moderate. According to CEMAC, in the last decade, the leading index has led the coincident index by an average of 4 months.

2. The coincident index is meant to provide information on how the economy is doing right now, especially to identify turning points in the economic cycle. In the financial crisis, the coincident index points to June 2008 as the peak of the cycle and February 2009 as the trough.

3. The early warning index provides an alternative window into the current state of the Chinese economy. According to CEMAC, a number between 83.33 and 116.66 is consistent with stable growth. Anything outside that range on the upside suggests overheating; anything outside on the downside suggests too much slack. The early warning index is a fun idea, and the pronounced ups and downs of the index give a strong sense of the position of the economy in the cycle. But attempting to capture the complexity of the Chinese economy in a single indicator appears like an over simplification, and with all the component parts available before the index is published, it's not a focus for market attention.

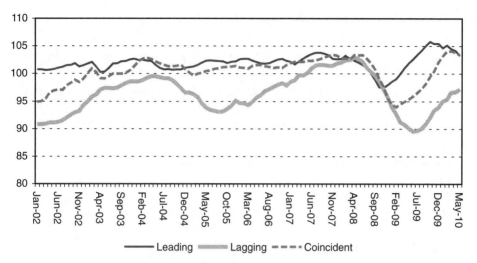

Figure 2.8 *Leading, coincident, and lagging indicators*
Source: China Economic Monitoring and Analysis Center

Market Impact

For much of the last decade, the Chinese economy has traveled in only one direction: up. Small wonder, then, that an indicator that promises to predict turning points in growth has received little attention. But as the sharp slowdown in 2008 demonstrates, China is not immune to the vicissitude of the economic cycle. The NBS leading index did a decent job of anticipating both the downturn and the rebound. As the Chinese economy enters the uncharted waters of slower growth, the leading index could receive increased attention as a guide to the outlook.

One group that is already paying attention is China's policy markers. CEMAC hosts a seminar every month at which it presents the latest reading to staff at the People's Bank of China (PBOC), National Development and Reform Commission, and other stars in China's economic policy constellation.

CONFERENCE BOARD LEADING ECONOMIC INDICATOR

Market sensitivity: Medium

What is it? Monthly indicator of the future growth path of the Chinese economy, indexed to 100 in 2004

Chinese news release on the Internet: www.conference-board.org/data/bcicountry. cfm?cid=11

English news release on the Internet: www.conference-board.org/data/bcicountry. cfm?cid=11

Release time: Around 6 weeks after the end of the month

Frequency: Monthly

Source: The Conference Board

Revisions: Yes, frequent minor revisions as new data becomes available

Why Is It Important?

There's no shortage of economists with crystal balls of some kind, promising a glimpse into the misty future of the Chinese economy. The Conference Board, a venerable U.S. research institution that produces leading economic indicators (LEI) for the United States, Europe, and Japan, has more claim to expertise in the art of prophecy than most. The Conference Board's China LEI is a recent addition to the forecasting family, making its first appearance in May 2010. Similar to the NBS leading index, it is a composite indicator, made up of data series that tend to move ahead of the economic cycle. If everything is working as it should, the Conference Board's LEI should peak 6 to 8 months ahead of a downturn in growth, and trough several months ahead of a recovery—providing the markets with a heads-up on the road ahead.

How Is the Data Calculated?

The first question for any LEI is, leading what? Like the NBS, the Conference Board has eschewed the use of growth in industrial value added or GDP as a measure of the current state of the economy and designed its own coincident economic indicator (CEI). The Conference Board CEI brings together a set of five monthly indicators that typically move up when the economy is shifting up a gear, and move down when growth is falling away. Specifically, the CEI brings together industrial value added, retail sales of consumer goods, manufacturing employment, electricity production, and the volume of passenger traffic. The data for these series is seasonally adjusted and, in the case of retail sales, deflated. Each of the components is equally weighted but adjusted for volatility, so components that tend to have larger fluctuations do not dominate the index and components that have smaller fluctuations are not lost in the noise.

With the movements in growth traced out by the CEI as a basis, the Conference Board has scoured the universe of Chinese economic data for indicators that tend to move ahead of the coincident series. That search has yielded six indicators that the Conference Board thinks do the job:

- **Consumer Expectations Index:** Since 1990 the NBS has conducted a monthly survey and asked consumers about their satisfaction with current conditions and their expectations about the future. In theory, the consumer confidence index should anticipate the ups and downs of household consumption.

- **China Federation of Logistics and Purchasing (CFLP) PMI Export Orders Subindex:** Every month, the CFLP asks about 820 businesses a range of questions on current operating conditions. One of those questions is whether export orders are up or down from the previous month. With orders placed 2 or 3 months ahead of shipment, the index should predict changes in export growth.

- **CFLP PMI Supplier Deliveries Subindex:** The CFLP also asks businesses about the length of supplier delivery times. As suppliers run close to full capacity in booms, delivery times lengthen. If demand slows, suppliers have more spare capacity and delivery times speed up. That means the index should measure changes in capacity utilization.

- **Total Loans Issued by Financial Institutions:** This is a monthly data series published by the PBOC that keeps track of total loans issued by China's banks. With banks the main source of credit in the Chinese economy and loan growth a key instrument of government policy, the loan data has a solid track record in anticipating peaks and troughs in economic activity.

- **5,000 Industrial Enterprises Diffusion Index: Raw Materials:** The PBOC conducts a quarterly survey of senior managers of 5,000 companies, gathering their views on business conditions. Among other things, respondents are asked to comment on whether they think supplies of raw materials will be adequate, moderate, or inadequate in the current and subsequent quarters. The answers to that question capture the outlook for the cement, steel, and other raw material sectors that are key beneficiaries of China's investment-driven growth. Because the survey is conducted on a quarterly basis, the Conference Board estimates the value of this component for months when no survey has taken place.

- **Total Floor Space Started:** This is a monthly NBS data series that measures the total floor space of newly started buildings. The idea is that changes in this indicator should move ahead of changes in real estate investment, which accounts for around 20% of all investment activity in China and is the largest single source of demand for raw materials. In 2008, the sharp decline in floor space started led the slowdown in the wider economy.

As with the CEI, the six components of the index are given equal weights, adjusted for volatility. This means components that typically exhibit large movements do not dominate at the expense of more stable components.

The choice of components for the LEI might have been the best on offer when the Conference Board crunched the numbers back in 2009. But they are not perfect. Consumer confidence has a weak track record of predicting movements in retail sales, supplier lead times is extremely volatile, and the PBOC diffusion index is available only once every three months. Aware of these weaknesses, the Conference Board has said that its current choice of indicators is provisional and subject to revision as new and better data series become available.

Table 2.12 *Summary Table of Composite Economic Indexes*

		2010			6-month
		Apr	May	Jun	Dec to Jun
1 ▶	**Leading Economic index (LEI)**	144.6	145.9 r	147.0 p	
	Percentage Change	0.0	0.9 r	0.8 p	3.7
2 ▶	Diffusion	16.7	83.3	50.0	66.7
	Coincident Economic index (CEI)	183.0	184.6	186.4 p	
	Percent Change	1.4	0.9	1.0 p	7.6
	Diffusion	100.0	80.0	80.0	100.0

Source: Adapted from the Conference Board
Key: p = preliminary; r = revised

Interpreting the Data

1. The takeaway for the markets is the latest reading on the LEI. This is the Conference Board's estimate of the outlook for growth in the months ahead. An acceleration in growth in the LEI suggests that growth is set to accelerate a few months down the line. A deceleration suggests slower growth. A historical data series stretching back to 1986 has done a decent job at predicting changes in the business cycle and fluctuations in growth. But that is no surprise. The Conference Board's LEI was designed based on this historical data. The series since the launch of the LEI in May 2010 is too short to make any judgment on the indicator's forecasting skills. For what it's worth, in Table 2.12, the data for June 2010 shows the LEI at 147.0, up 0.8% from May. That 0.8% compared with a 0.9% increase in May, suggesting that the outlook for growth was stable. In this instance, the Conference Board's indicator did a better job of forecasting the outlook than many professional economists, whose predictions of a sharp

slowdown in growth were proved wrong by a steady performance by the Chinese economy in the second half of 2010.

2. A composite index such as the LEI can be moved by many components together or by an extreme move in one or two of the components. The diffusion index measures the proportion of the components of the LEI that are on the move. The higher the reading for the diffusion index, the more broad-based the rise in the components. In general, a shift in the LEI brought about by a broad constituency of components should get more attention than a shift brought about by an extreme move in one or two components.

Market Impact

The Conference Board LEI has had a rough start to life. The result for April 2010, the first month the indicator was published, had to be corrected downward after a calculation error was discovered. That correction coincided with a crash in the mainland's equity markets, with the Shanghai Composite Index down 3.1% on the same day. In fact, with global markets also sharply down and Chinese investors largely unaware of the existence of the Conference Board and its new indicator, the downward correction and the collapse in the markets was probably a coincidence. But it was not an auspicious start, and the discovery of a further calculation error the following month compounded the infant indicator's woes and earned it a savaging from the financial press. But it is in its early days, and if the LEI can establish a solid forecasting record, it will start to get attention for the right reasons.

ORGANIZATION FOR ECONOMIC COOPERATION AND DEVELOPMENT COMPOSITE LEADING INDICATOR

Market sensitivity: Low

What is it? A composite indicator providing a broad picture of the outlook for the Chinese economy, focusing on turning points in growth

Chinese news release on the Internet: n/a

English news release on the Internet: http://stats.oecd.org/index.aspx

Release time: Around the 10th to 15th of the following month

Frequency: Monthly

Source: Organization for Economic Cooperation and Development (OECD)

Revisions: Yes, frequent minor revisions as new data becomes available. The entire series is revised every 5 years as part of a regular review.

Why Is It Important?

Plenty of economists are peddling a model for predicting the future of the Chinese economy. The NBS has a leading economic indicator. The Conference Board has one, too. Rounding out the set of economic soothsayers is the Organization for Economic Cooperation and Development (OECD) and its Composite Leading Indicator (CLI). Similar to the indicators developed by the NBS and the Conference Board, the OECD's statistical gizmo brings together a set of other indicators that the analysts in Paris believe should move ahead of the growth cycle. Keeping an eye on the CLI should give markets a clue to when growth in the Chinese economy is about to dive into a dip or surge toward a peak.

How Is the Data Calculated?

The CLI consists of indicators chosen because they tend to move ahead of the industrial output growth cycle. When the index was launched in 2006, just six indicators were in the mix: M2, cargo handled at ports, chemical fertilizer production, enterprise deposits, imports from Asia, and nonferrous metals production. Unfortunately, that set of indicators didn't do a great job of predicting either the downturn in the Chinese economy in 2008 or the rebound in 2009. The OECD itself acknowledges that the original selection produced more of a coincident than a leading index. In 2010, Paris found itself the site for another revolution, several of the old indicators were guillotined, and a new group stepped forward to fill the ranks. The enfant terribles of the indicator world are listed here:

- **M2:** A monthly indicator of growth in broad money supply published by the PBOC. Growth in money supply has a good record of predicting changes in growth and is also a component in the NBS leading indicator.

- **Chemical fertilizer production:** A monthly indicator produced by the NBS. There's no economic intuition for including this as a leading indicator, but the OECD's econometric evidence suggests that it does a good job of moving ahead of the industrial output growth cycle.

- **Production of crude steel:** A monthly indicator produced by the NBS. Steel accounts for a fair chunk of China's industrial output and is a key input in the manufacturing and construction sectors, giving it strong leading properties.

- **5,000 Industrial Enterprises: overseas order level:** A quarterly indicator produced by the PBOC. Overseas orders should be a leading indicator for the export sector. Because this is a quarterly indicator, the OECD must make estimations for the months when data is not available.

- **Real estate under construction:** A monthly NBS indicator. The real estate sector accounts for 20% of investment in the Chinese economy, and the amount of floor space under construction should be a leading indicator of demand for building materials.

- **Production of motor vehicles:** A monthly NBS indicator. Domestic vehicle production has rocketed in the last decade, from a few hundred thousand cars a year at the beginning of the 1990s to more than a million cars a month in 2010. Motor vehicle output is also a driver of demand for steel and other industrial products.

- **Shanghai stock exchange turnover:** Chinese investors have taken to equity markets like a Peking duck to hoisin sauce, and investor sentiment is extremely sensitive to changes in the economic outlook. Turnover on the mainland's main equity market fell some months ahead of the 2008 downturn in industrial output and then picked up some months ahead of the rebound in 2009.

The OECD gives equal weight to each of the six components but also accounts for volatility, so that volatile components don't throw the reading off and components that typically move within a smaller range have an equal impact on the result. Components are seasonally adjusted, smoothed, and detrended before they are included in the calculation. Smoothing means looking at a moving average of an indicator instead of the latest reading. Detrending is an unfamiliar term, but it basically means that the OECD attempts to separate out movements that are in line with the long-term trend from movements that are distinct from it.

The OECD has a rolling approach to the calculation and publication of its indicator. So a reading for the CLI will be published in the following month, based on available data, and recalculated and republished a month later when the complete data is available. Because each new set of monthly data also affects the OECD's estimate of past trends, the historical data undergoes frequent minor revisions.

Interpreting the Data

The first challenge in interpreting the data is finding it on the OECD's rather clunky and not particularly user friendly website. A Google search for "OECD CLI" is a quicker route to the relevant part of the website than an attempt to get there from the home page.

Happily, interpreting the data is more straightforward than finding it. The China CLI is published alongside CLIs for the OECD's member countries, and for five other emerging market economies that the OECD think are relevant for understanding the global outlook.

Table 2.13 *OECD Composite Leading Indicators*

Subject	Normalized (CLI)			
Frequency	Monthly			
Country	Australia ▲▼	Austria ▲▼	[...]	China ▲▼
Time	i	i		i
Sept-2008	100.0	98.8		97.5
Oct-2008	99.6	98.3		97.1
[...]	[...]	[...]		
Nov-2009	99.7	99.8		101.8
Dec-2009	100.0	100.1		101.9
Jan-2010	100.3	100.4		101.8
Feb-2010	100.5	100.7		101.8
Mar-2010	100.7	101.0		101.6
Apr-2010	100.7	101.2		101.5
May-2010	100.8	101.5		101.3
Jun-2010	100.8	101.8		101.1

Source: Adapted from OECD

At first sight, the CLI as originally designed did a decent job of anticipating the 2008 crisis. The OECD flagged a 0.7-point downturn in the index in December 2007 as a sign of a possible slowdown ahead. In fact, if growth in industrial value added is detrended in the same way the components of the CLI are, it also turned down at the beginning of 2008. The fact that the CLI as originally designed proved more of a coincident than a leading indicator was one of the reasons for the extensive revisions at the beginning of 2010.

The new CLI certainly does a decent job of anticipating changes in the growth cycle in the period before 2010. In the period since 1990, the CLI has turned an average of 3 to 4 months ahead of peaks and troughs in industrial value added growth. But that's no surprise: Hindsight is 20–20, and the CLI is designed based on data for that period. The real question is how well the CLI will do in anticipating future trends in growth.

The data series in the time since the launch of the reworked CLI is too short to give a clear indication of its leading properties. But it does serve as a useful illustration of the difficulty of gazing into the future of the Chinese economy. A reading of 101.1 for the CLI in June 2010 was down from 101.3 in May and 101.9 in December 2009, suggesting that industrial output growth would continue to slow moving into the second half of 2010. As it happened, a slowdown in June 2010 proved short-lived, as the government opened the liquidity taps to buoy growth in the final months of the year.

A significant role for policy in determining the pace of growth in the Chinese economy is one of the reasons for caution in reading too much into the leading indicators produced by the OECD, the NBS, or the Conference Board. A decision by the government like that in summer 2010 to speed up or slow down the approval of investment projects, allow the banks to lend more, or force them to lend less, can have a major impact on the growth rate. But until policy decisions are made, the impact doesn't show up anywhere in the data and thus cannot be reflected in the leading indicators.

Market Impact

With all the component data available in advance and too short a track record to judge the forecasting ability of the new index, the OECD's China CLI is not currently a focus of attention for the markets. But the OECD's CLIs for other major economies do get some attention, and if the new China indicator demonstrates a track record in forecasting turning points in the economic cycle, it will, too.

CHAPTER 3

Investment and Real Estate

FIXED ASSET INVESTMENT

Market sensitivity: Medium
What is it? Report on investment in fixed assets, broken down by type of investment and by sector, published for the year-to-date in current CNY100 millions and nominal MoM % and YoY %
Chinese news release on the Internet: www.stats.gov.cn/
English news release on the Internet: www.stats.gov.cn/english/
Release time: 10 a.m. on the 11th day of the following month. March, June, September, and December data is released later, to coincide with the quarterly GDP data
Frequency: Monthly; data for January and February is released together
Source: National Bureau of Statistics (NBS)
Revisions: No

Why Is It Important?

Countries that want to grow have only three options: increase the stock of capital, increase the stock of labor, or improve the technology that brings the two together. In Beijing, this basic precept of development theory is well understood. A demographic bulge has taken care of increasing the stock of labor. To increase the capital stock, China has followed the path blazed by its Asian neighbors Japan and Korea, with a deliberate policy of encouraging saving and increasing investment:

- Weak public services and the fear of poverty in old age reinforce a cultural tendency toward thrift and generate high levels of household saving.
- State-owned banks work hand-in-glove with state-owned enterprises and local government to channel those savings toward priority projects.
- Artificially low deposit and lending rates compel households to save even more and keep the cost of capital for investment at bargain-basement prices.
- If funds from the household savings piggy bank are not enough, state-owned firms can also fall back on their monopoly profits.

The result of this heady policy mix has been three decades of breakneck investment in the industrial base and public infrastructure, with a heavy dose of real estate investment thrown in for good measure. China's households might still be poor, but rapid growth in fixed asset investment (FAI) has transformed the mainland from an impoverished backwater to a powerhouse of the global economy.

For those concerned about China's unbalanced growth model (an excessive reliance on red-blooded investment as a driver of growth and a more anemic performance from consumption), the FAI data makes uneasy reading. In 2009, urban FAI came in at a palpitation-inducing CNY19.3 trillion, up more than 30% from a year earlier and equal to 56% of GDP. But before concluding that China is an overinvested bubble waiting to implode, naysayers should consider the limitations of the FAI data as a measure of additions to China's capital stock. FAI is a gross measure of investment spending. If company A invests in a machine and then sells it to company B, the addition to China's stock of machines is just 1. The expenditure-side GDP data on capital accumulation would include only the initial investment. But the FAI data includes both the initial investment by company A and the transfer to company B. As Figure 3.1 shows, that difference in approach means the level and growth rate of FAI is consistently higher than the level and growth rate of capital accumulation. The expenditure-side GDP data shows that additions to the capital stock in 2009 added up to CNY15.7 trillion, up 22% year-on-year (YoY) and equal to 45% of GDP. The expenditure-side GDP data is the more accurate gauge of changes in China's capital stock. But because it is available only on an annual basis, the markets use the monthly FAI data as a decent proxy and a useful measure of the strength of overall investment activity.

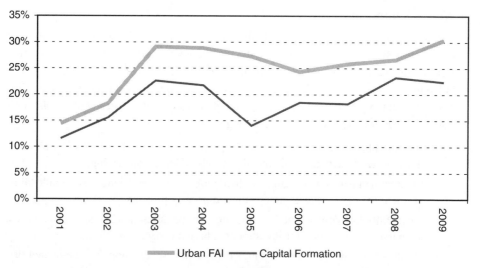

Urban FAI ▬▬▬ Capital Formation

Source: National Bureau of Statistics, author's calculations

Figure 3.1 *Urban FAI versus capital formation (YoY%)*

How Is the Data Calculated?

For the purposes of data collection, the National Bureau of Statistics (NBS) divides investment into two categories: investment by the real estate sector and investment by everybody else.

For the real estate sector, the 8,000 largest real estate developers in the country report their investment spending directly to the NBS in Beijing. Smaller firms report to the local statistics bureau, which then passes the information up through the provincial office to headquarters in Beijing.

For everybody else, investment projects above a threshold of CNY5 million are included in the survey. Projects that fall under the jurisdiction of the national government, such as railways built by the Ministry of Railways, are reported direct to the NBS in Beijing. Data on local-level projects is collected by the local statistical bureau and reported up the administrative chain. The trigger for including local projects in the report is administrative approval for the investment by the local government.

In 2011, the NBS made two changes to improve the FAI data:

- The threshold for inclusion in the survey was raised to CNY5 million from CNY500,000. The low threshold had seen the number of projects included in the survey increase to 661,000 in 2010, more than four times higher than 159,000 in 1997. The sheer number of projects, many of them small and with weak data-reporting capacity, made it difficult for the NBS to keep track of what was going on. The new CNY5 million threshold means fewer projects to keep track of and higher quality data.

- Until 2010, the monthly data covered only urban fixed asset investment, which accounts for 80% of total investment. From 2011 on, the scope of the data has been expanded to include investment by rural enterprises, improving the coverage of the survey. That leaves only rural households—which account for only a small share of total investment—out of the loop. Annual data on total investment includes spending by rural households, with data on this group collected in a sample survey.

The new approach should result in improved data quality and coverage. But changing the sample set means comparisons between the pre- and post-2011 FAI data need to be treated with caution.

Interpreting the Data

Table 3.1 *Fixed Asset Investment (June 2010)*

	Actually Completed		Proportion (%)	
	Accumulated from January (100 million Yuan)	Growth Rate over Same Period of Previous Year	Accumulated from January	Same Period of Previous Year
1 ▶ **I. Total amount of investment in fixed assets (100 million yuan) o/w:**	**98,047.38**	**25.5**	**100.0**	**100.0**
2 ▶ State-owned and state-controlled o/w:	40,453.61	21.5	41.3	42.6
3 ▶ Housing	19747.12	38.1	20.1	18.3
1. By Industry				
Primary Industry	1682.03	17.8	1.7	1.8
Secondary Industry	41517.94	22.3	42.3	43.5
Tertiary Industry	54847.41	28.4	55.9	54.7
2. By Jurisdiction of Management				
Central Investments	7443.24	13.0	7.6	8.4
Local Investments	90604.14	26.7	92.4	91.6
3. By Type of Construction o/w:				
New Construction	47067.07	28.8	48.0	46.8
Expansion	14362.35	11.6	14.6	16.5
Reconstruction	12283.23	21.1	12.5	13.0
4. By Structure				
Construction and Installation Work	60364.85	24.2	61.6	62.2
Purchase of Equipment and Instruments	20150.52	21.2	20.6	21.3
4 ▶ Other Expenses	17532.00	36.1	17.9	16.5
II. Housing Area (10,000 square meters)				
Floor Space Under Construction o/w:	500319.21	24.0		
Residential Buildings	278874.24	23.0		
Floor Space Completed o/w:	43443.71	13.6		
Residential Buildings	24684.14	17.0		

Source: Adapted from National Bureau of Statistics

1. The main focus of the markets is the YoY growth figure. This is the number that says whether China's investment program is stop or go. But the headline growth figure needs to be interpreted with caution, for several reasons:

   - It is published on a nominal basis, which means it does not take price changes into account. Many of China's data series are published in nominal terms. But this is a particular problem for the FAI data because prices for the land and raw materials that are inputs into the investment process are quite volatile. Between the peak of the commodities boom in summer 2008 and the trough at the beginning of 2009, China's steel prices fell by 40%. There is no easy way around the problem of changing prices. One practical, if imperfect, way out of the perplexity is to use the monthly producer price index to deflate the headline FAI growth number. That exercise reveals a real investment growth series with considerably higher peaks and lower troughs than the nominal data suggests.

- The data is published on a year-to-date basis. That doesn't make much difference in the opening months of the year, but by the time November rolls around, work could grind to a halt on every construction site in the country without denting the growth figures. Backing out the monthly data from the year-to-date figures is quite simple and reveals a lot more volatility than is evident in the published series. Two reasons explain that volatility. First, investment is volatile by nature. Major projects starting or ending can have a major impact on the data. Second, the government uses approval of investment projects as a valve to control the pace of growth. If growth is too fast, the valve is tightened to slow the flow of new projects. If growth is too slow, the valve is opened to allow a few more through. The result is a flood of investments in some months that can dry to a trickle in others. At the beginning of 2011, the NBS began publication of the growth rate of FAI on a month-on-month (MoM) basis. MoM data gives a better sense of the current momentum of the economy than the year-to-date data and will likely become a focus of market attention.

- A strong seasonal pattern in the data is not necessarily reflective of actual changes in the level of investment. According to the official data, investment growth tends to make a quick start to the year, hold steady through the spring and summer, and begin to decelerate around September. December typically sees a sharp falling-away in investment, although this is hidden by publishing the data on a year-to-date basis. One possible explanation is that the seasonal pattern is due not to a change in investment, but to a change in reported investment. At the end of the year, enterprises are pushing up against the limits of their investment quotas. But instead of slowing the pace of investment, they simply don't wait for approval from the government to start new projects. When January rolls around and they have a fresh investment quota, they report all the activity that took place in the last few months, as if they had just broken fresh ground. This assessment is borne out by data on newly started projects, which typically falls implausibly sharply at the end of the year and rebounds implausibly strongly at the beginning.

As Figure 3.2 shows, the year-to-date, nominal data published by the NBS presents a misleading picture of sedately undulating movements in investment growth. The reality, shown by calculating the current month, inflation-adjusted data, is a considerably more volatile series, with sudden starts and violent stops the norm.

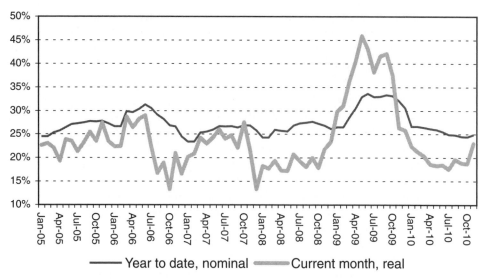

Source: National Bureau of Statistics, author's calculations

Figure 3.2   *FAI: year-to-date nominal versus current month real (YoY%)*

2. Fat profits, easy credit, and access to public finances mean the state sector can always find funds for investment. In the first half of 2009, with the government pushing the big red stimulus button, state-sector investment soared to more than 41% year-on-year growth, substantially higher than overall FAI growth of 33%.

3. The largest single contributor to investment is the real estate sector, accounting for about 20% of the total. In addition to the headline figure on real estate investment published with the FAI data, the NBS publish a more detailed breakdown, including information on construction and sales. That data is covered in the section on Real Estate Prices, Investment, Sales, and Construction.

4. Land purchases are included in the monthly FAI data, and with land prices high and volatile, they can have a marked impact on the level and growth rate. Investment in land shows up in the "other expenses" row of the FAI data.

Table 3.2   *Investment in Fixed Assets by Industry (June 2010)*

	Investment		Proportion (National Total=100)	
	Accumulated (100 million yuan)	Growth Rate over Previous Year	Accumulated	Same Period of Previous Year
[...]				
Manufacturing o/w:	**31108.58**	**24.9**	**31.7**	**31.9**
Smelting and Pressing of Ferrous Metals	1538.28	9.4	1.6	1.8
Smelting and Pressing of Non-Ferrous Metals	1255.02	34.2	1.3	1.2
Manufacture of General Purpose Machinery	2268.00	18.3	2.3	2.5
Manufacture of Special Purpose Machinery	1780.20	28.2	1.8	1.8
Manufacture of Transportation Equipment	2721.67	25.4	2.8	2.8
Manufacture of Electrical Machinery and Equipment	2006.40	37.2	2.0	1.9
Manufacture of Communication Equipment, Computers and Other Electronic Equipment	1508.85	44.1	1.5	1.3
[...]				
Transportation, Storage and Post o/w:	**10265.69**	**25.1**	**10.5**	**10.5**
Railway Transport	2244.50	22.5	2.3	2.3
Road Transport	5067.83	27.1	5.2	5.1
Urban Public Transport	861.29	7.1	0.9	1.0
Water Transport	756.99	23.9	0.8	0.8
Air Transport	372.36	43.4	0.4	0.3
[...]				

1▶ (labels the Manufacturing block)
2▶ (labels the Transportation block)

Source: Adapted from National Bureau of Statistics

1. Not everyone is optimistic about the China growth story. One of the things that keeps China bears up at night, other than the fear of golden-haired children breaking into their house, is the fear that massive investment spending has resulted in production capacity far in excess of demand. The result, the bears maintain, will be worse than cold porridge. In China, a flood of surplus production will mean depressed prices, lower profits, and a shakeout in the industrial sector, with bankruptcies inevitable. Abroad, excess capacity will mean China continues to take global market share at the expense of every other country in the world, with the result a rise in trade tensions that dents the prospects for global growth. If the bears are right and there is a problem with overcapacity, it will be at the sector level that it is most evident. That makes the industry-level investment data a focus for attention. A surge in investment in nonferrous metals could mean China is adding to its already formidable array of aluminum smelters, which would not be good news for next year's global aluminum prices. A surge in investment in ferrous metals might mean the world's largest producer of steel is adding a few more blast furnaces, trouble down the line for global steel prices.

2. The breakdown by sector also provides a way to keep track of China's infrastructure spending. Pouring concrete has been an important part of the mainland's development story, and the transport, power, and water infrastructure for much of the country is top of the emerging market class. Infrastructure projects are also an area over which the

government enjoys a high degree of control, so the level of investment can be used as a lever to control the pace of growth. In 2009, a massive program of infrastructure investment kept the wheels of the economy turning. Urban fixed asset investment as a whole grew 30.5% for the year, but investment in railways (up 67.5%), roads (40.1%), and urban transport (59.7%) led the pack.

Market Impact

Equities: Investment is the most important driver of growth in the Chinese economy, so the equity markets like to see strong investment numbers. But in the NBS monthly release, it plays second fiddle to the industrial value-added data as a guide to the momentum of the economy.

Commodities: Investment is the main source of Chinese demand for metals and is also closely linked to demand for energy. Commodity markets pay close attention to the investment data.

Currency: Strong growth at home can encourage the government to allow more rapid appreciation of the yuan, especially if imported commodity prices are high. But investment is not the main variable affecting decisions on the exchange rate. Strong growth in Chinese investment can be a plus for commodity currencies like the Australian dollar.

REAL ESTATE PRICES, INVESTMENT, SALES, AND CONSTRUCTION

Market sensitivity: High

What is it? Monthly report on prices (current month, YoY %, MoM%), investment (year to date, nominal, CNY100 million, YoY %), sales (year to date, nominal, CNY100 million, 10,000m², YoY %), and construction in China's property markets

Chinese news release on the Internet: www.stats.gov.cn/

English news release on the Internet: www.stats.gov.cn/english/

Release time: Investment, construction, and sales data released at 10 a.m. on the 11th of the month; price data released on the 18th of the month

Frequency: Monthly; data on investment, sales, and construction for January and February is released together

Source: NBS

Revisions: No

Why Is It Important?

On Wednesday evenings in 2009, one show kept China's work-weary professionals glued to their television screens: *Woju* (蜗居, dwelling narrowness). Every week, millions of young teachers, journalists, and lawyers returned from work, kicked off their shoes, collapsed on the sofa, and watched the trials and tribulations of *Woju*'s hapless cast as they struggled through 35 episodes to realize an ambition that seemed at once utterly mundane and, in the context of modern China, completely out of reach: to own a home.

China's fascination with the property sector is easy to understand. Since the liberalization of the housing market at the end of the 1990s, house prices have soared. For those lucky enough to be given a house when public ownership was transferred to private, or smart enough to buy when prices were on the way up, that has meant a tidy profit. For those trying to enter the housing market late, it's a different story. Rapid rises in prices meant that anything but the oldest, smallest, and most inconveniently located accommodation is out of reach. In a country as large and diverse as China, it is difficult to talk about average prices and average incomes. But in Beijing, a small, no-frills, secondhand apartment located a gridlocked commute from the center of town might set you back a cool CNY1 million, 30 times the average annual income for the city. That is substantially higher than a ratio of around 8 times the average income for an apartment in New York.

High prices have meant fat profit margins for China's property developers. China's real estate bubble has fueled a building boom, with developers across the country scrambling to bring bigger and better properties to the market. Years of breakneck investment have made the real estate sector the biggest single domestic contributor to economic growth. Investment in real estate accounts directly for 10% of GDP—and considerably more if the indirect contribution from demand for steel, cement, and other building materials is factored in. China's real estate build is the single largest global driver of demand for iron ore. A real estate boom in the mid-2000s pushed GDP growth comfortably into double digits and iron ore prices to record highs. A real estate bust in the second half of 2008 was the domestic complement to the global financial crisis, kicking the floor out from under global metals prices and crunching GDP growth to a 10-year low of 6.6% YoY in the first quarter of 2009.

The 2008 bust, induced by the government's attempt to control bubble prices, illustrates the key role of policy in shaping developments in China's real estate sector. An ongoing process of urbanization, with the government aiming to take the 49.6% of the population that live in the cities at the end of 2010 up to something closer to 60%, drives demand for more urban housing. Rapid increases in wages, even if they are not as rapid as the NBS data suggest, drive demand for higher-quality housing. But neither urbanization nor increasing wealth alone account for the 10-year boom in China's housing market. Fundamental demand might have baked the cake, but the search for returns generated by China's repressed financial system put the cherry on the top. With little to get excited about in low or negative returns on savings in the Chinese banking system, and too much excitement on the mainland's roller-coaster equity markets, the property sector looks like a good bet. With savers using the real estate market as a substitute for an investment plan, prices have soared—and higher prices have sucked in even more capital. Prices in major cities have now reached crazed multiples of average household income. For speculators, that does not matter. The only constraint on how high prices can go is how much capital is available. But for the government, bubble prices come at the cost of rising discontent from the *woju qun* (蜗局群, narrow dwelling class) as the dream of home ownership slips further beyond their grasp. The government's calculation of the benefit of real estate's contribution to growth versus the cost of high prices' impact on social stability is the arbiter of developments in China's property sector.

How Is the Data Calculated?

China's house price data is the subject of some controversy. It is widely believed that the official data understates the true extent of increases in house prices. The announcement by the NBS that the average increase in house prices in 2009 was just 1.5% sparked a firestorm of irate commentary from China's citizens. Data from private research institutes and the reality evident to would-be home buyers suggested prices had risen at a considerably faster rate. Calculations based on data from the China Real Estate Index System (CREIS)—a comprehensive dataset compiled by a firm called Soufun—showed average prices for new commercial residential property in nine of China's largest cites up 9.4%. In defense of the NBS, the annual increase in prices covers changes over the course of the entire year, and in the first five months of 2009, prices had actually been falling, dragging down the change for the year as a whole. In addition, angry commentators typically focus on the gleaming east coast hot spots, where speculation is rife and price increases are rapid. The 1.5% figure is an average for the country as a whole, including Central and Western provinces where there is less speculative activity and increases in prices are smaller. But even in the East coast cities, the gap between the change in prices recorded by the NBS and those recorded by private research agencies remains significant. For Beijing, the NBS data shows prices up 5.7% for the year in 2009. The CREIS data suggests prices rose by 26.5%. It is difficult to avoid the conclusion that the official data is systematically downward-biased.

The NBS has not been blind to the public mood on in its house price index. In 2010, Ma Jiantang, the head of the NBS, promised far-reaching reforms. At the beginning of 2011, the statisticians rolled out a new system for collecting and reporting house price data. But the new approach raises as many questions as it answers. The most controversial aspect is the end to publication of a figure for the national average change in house prices. The justification offered by the statisticians is that a national average smoothes away important regional differences. That is certainly true, but the national average was also the most straightforward and widely watched measure of developments in China's housing market. Cynics concluded that the real aim was to do away with a controversial number that had been the basis of both rumblings of social discontent and questions about the statisticians' professional integrity.

Other changes rolled out at the beginning of 2011 are more technical and should, if properly implemented, improve the quality and detail of the data:

- For new property, the NBS is shifting from a system where local officials conducted a survey of a sample of house prices to a system where transaction data captured by local property bureaus is used as the basis of the calculation. The old system was based on a sample that was slow to reflect the impact of newer, more expensive property on average prices. The discretion for local officials to pick representative transactions also raised suspicion that meddling hands were downward-biasing the data to disguise the extent of price increases. By capturing 100% of transactions and taking discretion for local officials out of the picture, the new system should provide a more accurate reading on the extent of price increases. As of February 2011, the new approach has been rolled out in 54 of the 70 cities covered in the data, with the remaining 16 cities still making the necessary preparations. Data on secondhand property prices will continue to be collected through a survey, with city data covering a minimum of 75% of transactions.

- The data is published in more granular detail. Data for the 70 cities is published for new residential property, for new commercial residential property, and for secondhand property. The difference between *new residential property* and *new commercial residential property* is that the former includes social housing—which is cheaper and biases down the growth rate. For new commercial residential and secondhand property, the NBS publishes the change in prices for properties below 90m^2, between 90-144m^2, and above 144m^2. The choice of 90m^2 and 144m^2 as thresholds is based on government regulations that encourage development of apartments below these sizes, on the basis that smaller apartments are more affordable.

Interpreting the Data

Table 3.3 *Sales Price Indices of Newly Constructed Residential Buildings (January 2011)*

Cities	Price Indices of Newly Constructed Residential Buildings			Cities	Price Indices of Newly Constructed Residential Buildings		
	Pd. Ago	Y-O-Y	Fixed Base Index		Pd. Ago	Y-O-Y	Fixed Base Index
Beijing	100.8	106.8	102.4	Tangshan	100	103.8	101.1
Tianjin	100.9	106.7	103.1	Qinhuangdao	100.8	110.4	105.8
Shijiazhuang	100.8	111.5	106.3	Baotou	100	108	103.9
Taiyuan	100.2	102.1	100.8	Dandong	100.5	112.3	108.2
Hohhot	100.1	106.8	102.8	Jinzhou	100.8	108.1	103.6
Shenyang	100.4	108.8	104.2	Jilin	101.7	109.2	105.7
Dalian	100	106.6	103.3	Mudanjiang	101.5	109.9	106.4
Changchun	100.4	106.9	102.6	Wuxi	100.8	103.4	101.9
Harbin	100.2	107.3	103.6	Yangzhou	101	104.9	102.8
Shanghai [...]	100.9	101.5	100.8	Xuzhou	101	103.4	101.8
Xi'an [...]	101.1	105.6	102.2	Sanya	100.4	119.1	100.8

Source: Adapted from NBS

1. The problems of the hapless cast of *Woju* were not brought on by moderate increases in house prices or price increases lower than the increases in average income. But as Figure 3.3 shows, moderate rises in house prices, and prices rising more slowly than average income, are exactly what the official statistics suggests. When the NBS still published a national average price index, the official data purported that average house prices rose 23% in the period of 2006–2010. Over the same period, the NBS figures show urban disposable income per capita up more than 43%.The CREIS data, in contrast, shows the average price in nine of China's largest cities up 63%. The reality disguised by the NBS data but revealed by the CREIS data is that in China's biggest cities house prices are rising considerably faster than incomes.

   The new data collection system the NBS has in place since the beginning of 2011 is intended to provide a more accurate reading on the change in prices. As of February 2011, only two months of data produced using the new system are available—not enough to form a detailed view on its accuracy. But the early signs are not promising. For January 2011, the first month of data using the new system, the NBS reports prices for Shanghai and Guangzhou up 1.5% and 0.1%, respectively, on the previous year.

Data from the CREIS shows prices up 23% in Shanghai and 31% in Guangzhou. The continued discrepancy might be because, in the opening months of 2011, the NBS relied on a hybrid of data collected under the old and new systems. A comparison of NBS and CREIS data from the beginning of 2012 will provide a clearer picture of whether the official data under the new system remains downward-biased or not.

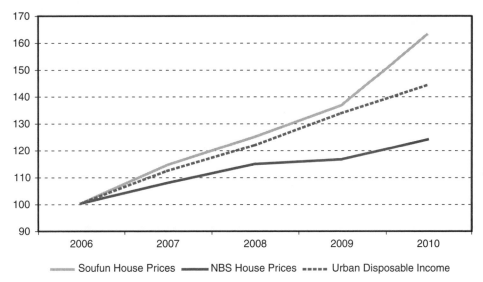

Source: National Bureau of Statistics, Soufun, author's calculations

Figure 3.3 *Change in house prices versus urban per-capita disposable income (Index: 2006 = 100)*

2. In a country as large and diverse as China, there are many different local property markets. The price of a luxury apartment in Shanghai has no more relation to the price of a hovel in Gansu than that of a penthouse apartment in the Upper Eastside of New York has to a trailer park in Kentucky. The 70-city breakdown shows the variation in changes in house prices across the country. That data feeds into the debate on whether China has a national property bubble or a bubble confined to certain categories of property and certain cities. In Table 3.3, the data for January 2011 shows that prices for Sanya on holiday hotspot Hainan island were up 19.1% YoY. In industrial and coal mining center Tangshan, meanwhile, speculators were understandably thin on the ground, and prices rose just 3.8%.

Table 3.4   *Sales Price Indices of Newly Constructed Commercial Residential Buildings (January 2011)*

Cities	Sales Price Indices of Newly Constructed Commercial Residential Buildings			Cities	Sales Price Indices of Newly Constructed Commercial Residential Buildings		
	Pd. Ago	Y-o-Y	Fixed Base Index		Pd. Ago	Y-o-Y	Fixed Base Index
Beijing	101	109.1	103	Tangshan	100	104.1	101.2
Tianjin	101	107.6	103.5	Qinhuangdao	100.9	111.5	106.5
Shijiazhuang	100.8	111.7	106.5	Baotou	100	108.1	103.9
Taiyuan	100.2	102.2	100.8	Dandong	100.6	112.3	108.2
Hohhot	100.1	107	102.9	Jinzhou	100.8	108.1	103.6
Shenyang	100.4	109.8	104.6	Jilin	101.7	109.5	105.9
Dalian	100	106.6	103.3	Mudanjiang	101.5	110	106.5
Changchun	100.4	107.1	102.7	Wuxi	100.9	103.6	102.1
Harbin	100.2	107.6	103.7	Yangzhou	101.1	104.9	102.9
Shanghai	101.1	101.8	101	Xuzhou	101	103.5	101.9
[...]							

Source: Adapted from NBS

For China's property speculators, not all apartments are created equal. For those who can afford it, the most desirable investment properties are new high-end apartments in first-tier and rising second-tier cities. With speculators focusing their attention on the high end of the market, it is here that the increase in prices is most rapid. In Table 3.4, the data for January 2011 shows the price of a new commercial residential apartment in Beijing up 9.1% YoY. That contrasts with an increase of just 6.8% for new residential apartments shown in Table 3.3. The reason for the difference is that the *new residential* data includes low price social housing—which tends to bias down the change in prices. The *new commercial residential* data does not include social housing and so provides a more accurate read on the price of housing in the private market.

The NBS also publishes data on the change in the price of secondhand homes. The secondhand home series for January 2011 shows prices in Beijing up a mere 2.6%. Chinese families have a cultural aversion to living in secondhand homes. Tiled-roof hutongs might be nice to visit, but no one likes living in an apartment with no central heating and medieval plumbing. With the focus for buyers who can afford it on new commercial residential apartments, secondhand prices tend to increase much more slowly.

Table 3.5 *Investment in Real Estate Development (February 2011)*

Indicators	February		Jan-Feb	
	Absolute Magnitude	Increased YoY (%)	Absolute Magnitude	Increased YoY (%)
[...]				
Investment in Real Estate Development				
Investment in Real Estate (100 million yuan) o/w:	...	...	4250	35.2
1▸ Residential Buildings	...	...	3014	34.9
Floor Space under Construction (10,000 sq.m) o/w:	...	...	291473	39.0
2▸ Residential Buildings	...	...	224049	38.9
Floor space of houses newly started (10,000 sq.m) o/w:	...	...	19083	27.9
3▸ Residential Buildings	...	...	14838	25.4
Floor Space of Buildings Completed (10,000 sq.m) o/w:	...	...	6952	13.9
Residential Buildings	...	...	5366	12.1
Floor Space of Commercial Buildings Sold (10,000 sq.m) o/w:	...	...	8143	13.8
4▸ Residential Buildings	...	...	7282	13.2
Office Buildings	...	...	192	26.4
Buildings for Commercial Business	...	...	478	8.7
Sales of Commercial Buildings (100 million yuan) o/w:	...	...	5242	27.4
Residential Buildings	...	...	4471	26.2
Office Buildings	...	...	244	46.3
Buildings for Commercial Business	...	...	435	22.1
Sources of Funds for Real Estate Development Enterprises (100 million yuan) o/w:	...	...	12173	16.3
Domestic Loans	...	...	2679	7.7
Foreign Investment	...	...	86	61.5
Self-raising Funds	...	...	4184	21.4
Other Sources	...	...	5223	16.6

1. Real estate investment is a key driver of growth in the Chinese economy, accounting directly for 10% of GDP and more if demand for steel, cement, and other raw materials is taken into account. Within real estate investment, it is residential investment that is the most important category—accounting for more than 70% of the action in 2010. It is easy to see why this data point gets a lot of attention. But coming from the same stable as the fixed asset investment data, it needs to be treated with caution:

   • Real estate investment data is published on a year-to-date basis. At the beginning of the year, that doesn't matter much. But by the end of the year, even if a nuclear strike obliterated China's entire east coast, any surviving members of the NBS could still crawl out of their radiation bunker to inform the mutant remnants of the financial press that growth in real estate investment year-to-date was little changed. Backing out the monthly data from the year-to-date figures can reveal a markedly different rate of growth.

- The data is published on a nominal basis and thus does not take price changes into account. Changes in the cost of raw materials and land that are key inputs into real estate construction can be extreme.

2. Data on the surface area of housing under construction provides a way of thinking about the supply–demand balance in the property market. As Figure 3.4 shows, there is a close relationship between movements in sales, prices, and construction. When sales volumes and prices start to rise, construction activity picks up. That results in new supply coming onto the market, putting a lid on rising prices. In Table 3.5, the data shows residential floor space under construction in the first two months of 2011 up 38.9% YoY. Coming after a year of super-fast investment, continued rapid growth in construction suggested oversupply might start to bring property prices down. Source: NBS

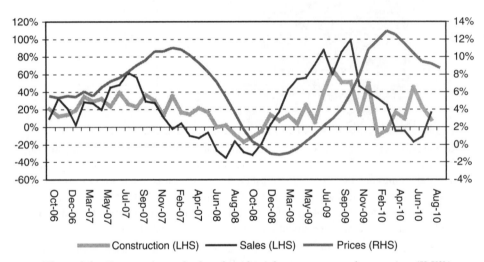

Figure 3.4   *Construction and sales of residential property versus house prices (YoY%)*

3. Data on floor space newly started provides an insight into developers' outlook for the future. As an illustration, in Table 3.5, the data for the first two months of 2011 showed newly started construction of floor space up 25.4%. A slower rate of growth for new construction than for construction as a whole suggested developers might be starting to take notice of concerns about oversupply and going slow on breaking new ground.

4. China's real estate developers aren't building property out of the goodness of their hearts. They are building property because they expect to sell it at a profit. Property sales are a key leading indicator of changes in both prices and investment. As Figure 3.4 shows, in the first half of 2007 and again in 2009, a sharp increase in sales drove prices higher and encouraged developers to ramp up their investment spending. At the end of 2007 and the beginning of 2010, falling sales anticipated the end of rising prices and slower growth in investment.

Market Impact

Equities: The real estate sector is a key driver of growth in the Chinese economy, so it is no surprise that it is also a major influence on equity markets. But with policy a key determinant of changes in the sector, and developers slow to respond to changes in policy, equity markets often react to the policy change rather than waiting for the actual move in prices, sales, and construction. In August and September 2007, the government announced a series of measures aimed at controlling runaway house prices. Valuations for the mainland's property developers, and for the Shanghai Composite Index as a whole, start to fall more or less immediately, but not until the beginning of 2008 did increases in house prices start to trend downward.

Commodities: Changes in house prices are a major determinant of changes in investment by Chinese property developers, the world's largest single source of demand for steel and cement and a major source of demand for copper. Investors in commodity markets pay close attention.

Currencies: On the exchange rate, movements in house prices and investment pull China's policymakers in two different directions. On one hand, rapid increases in house prices and growth in investment are signs of overheating and might encourage Beijing to slam on the brakes by allowing a more rapid appreciation of the yuan. On the other hand, the lessons of the Japanese experience in the 1980s, when an appreciating currency led to inflows of speculative capital that fueled a real estate bubble, left a marked impression on the Chinese government. With arguments in both directions, changes in house prices are not a key influence on government thinking in managing the exchange rate.

CHINA REAL ESTATE INDEX SYSTEM

Market sensitivity: Medium
What is it? Weekly report on change in house prices (current prices, CNY/m^2, week-on-week %) and transaction volumes (units and 10,000 m^2) in China's major cities
Chinese news release on the Internet: www.soufun.com
English news release on the Internet: n/a
Release time: Monday of the following week
Frequency: Weekly
Source: Soufun
Revisions: No

Why Is It Important?

Soufun, a real estate website whose name translates as "Search House," maintains an elaborate database of prices and transactions in China's property sector, called the China Real Estate Index System (CREIS). Its weekly data on transaction volume, floor space sold, and average prices for new and secondhand property across China's first- and second-tier cities is the single best source of information on the property sector. The entire data set is available to subscribers. A more limited data set covering transactions in new property in ten major cities—including the four first-tier cities Beijing, Shanghai, Guangzhou, and Shenzhen—is available for free.

How Is the Data Calculated?

For new property, local government property bureaus collect data on all transactions that take place. In cities where Soufun has developed a strong relationship with the property bureau, that information forms the basis of the data set and Soufun captures 100% of all transactions. Coverage is 100% in all China's first-tier cities and most second-tier cities. For some smaller cities in which the property bureau is not playing ball, Soufun has more difficulty collecting the data, and coverage can be as low as 30% to 40%. Local property data is supplemented by information collected from property developers and agents.

Only projects above a certain size are included in the calculation. For residential projects in Beijing, Shanghai, Guangzhou, and Shenzen, the cut-off is 50,000 m^2 (about 550 apartments); for other cities, the cut-off is 30,000 m^2 (about 330 apartments). The calculation of the average price is weighted, so projects with a larger surface area sold receive a correspondingly larger weight in the calculation. Soufun also make adjustments to account for changes in the quality of apartments sold, so the index should measure genuine changes in price.

For secondhand property, Soufun again relies on local government property bureaus and real estate agents for its primary data. For first-tier cities, monthly data is based on more than 20,000 transactions per city per month; for smaller cities covered by the secondhand survey, the minimum sample size is 7,000 transactions.

Interpreting the Data

Table 3.6 *China Real Estate Index System House Prices, Week of September 20, 2010*

城市 City	供应情况 Supply		完成交易情况 Trading [2]			成交价格 Trading Price [1]	
	可售套数 Units For Sale	可售面积 Area For Sale	成交套数 Actual Trading Units	成交面积 Actual Trading Area	环比 Week-on-week %	Average Price	环比 Week-on-week %
	套 Units	万平米 10,000m²	套 Units	万平米 10,000m²		元/平米 yuan/dollar	
北京 Beijing	100206	1270.93	2083	24.53	12.48%		
北京（不含保障性住房）Beijing (Excluding low-income housing)			2068	24.39	14.33%	20039	-7.38%
上海 Shanghai	46396	652.81	3824	41.51	-2.40%	14500	11.88%
天津 Tianjin			2073	22.36	6.37%	9612	2.19%
重庆 Chongqing	93944	925.50	7576	65.97	29.18%	6409	5.77%
深圳 Shenzhen	26790	266.28	1266	10.63	-1.27%	19715	0.72%
广州 Guangzhou	41625	519.77	2806	27.31	0.04%	12450	-3.69%
杭州 Hangzhou	19511	279.15	1299	14.34	-1.68%	23177	11.10%
南京 Nanjing	29380	344.53	1061	10.98	-20.91%	14800	-0.55%

Source: Adapted from China Real Estate Index System

1. The CREIS data provides a more timely, reliable and detailed guide to price developments than the NBS data. It makes for alarming reading. In 2009, the NBS claims house prices increased an insignificant 1.5% YoY. A calculation based on the CREIS data for nine of China's largest cities shows prices rising 9.4%. That difference helps explain the public frustration with the official house price data and the government's concern about housing affordability.

Data on the level of prices also illustrates the reason for concern about a housing bubble in China and the popular discontent about rising house prices. In Table 3.6, the average price of a square meter of property in Beijing in September 2010 is recorded as CNY20,039. In 2009, average income in Beijing was CNY30,673. Assuming an apartment size of 90 square meters, which is fairly typical in big Chinese cities, that means an average apartment costs CNY1.8 million. To buy an average-priced new apartment in Beijing, an average earner would have to save his or her entire income for 59 years.

The ratio between prices and incomes is not an entirely straightforward guide to affordability. The average price is distorted upward by a few high-priced transactions. Smaller, cheaper apartments are available for those willing to buy secondhand, live on the edge of the city, and commute for hours each day to and from work. Most players in the property market are not earning average incomes, and a ratio based on incomes for the top 10% looks more reasonable. When average earners do reach for the bottom rung of the property ladder, they rely on not just their own income, but also their partner's income, and the savings of both sets of parents. But even with these allowances, the Soufun data shows the enormous gap that has opened between average incomes and house prices, which is the basis of popular discontent about China's property bubble.

The Soufun price data is the best on the block. But it still needs to be interpreted with some caution, for two reasons:

- The weekly price data is volatile. In the middle of April 2010, the government announced a move against the speculative purchases in the property market that had pushed house prices to record highs. In the first week of May, the Soufun data showed house prices in Beijing dipping from CNY19,146/m^2 to CNY15,707/m^2, a 17.9% fall in a single week. Had the government's policy change worked faster than anybody expected, driving speculators out and prices down within days of the initial announcement? Not really. The next week, prices were back up to CNY21,406/m^2, close to the level before the government's crackdown. That volatility reflects shifts in the kind of property—high end or low end—bought and sold each week. When a big project comes onto the market, hundreds or even thousands of units can be sold at the same price point in a single week, affecting the average price.

- Part of the government's response to the housing bubble has been a massive investment in affordable housing. For some cities, sales of affordable housing drag down the average and create a misleading impression of low prices. The problem is particularly marked in Shanghai, China's wealthiest city and one of the hot spots for property speculation. According to the data in Table 3.6, property prices in Shanghai in September 2010 were just CNY14,500/m^2, considerably lower than prices in Beijing and also in nearby Hangzhou and Nanjing, satellite cities that revolve in Shanghai's orbit. In its monthly data release, Soufun is able to separate out the affordable housing transactions from the rest and show a price for Shanghai property excluding affordable housing of CNY23,000/m^2 — among the highest in the country. But in the weekly data, the affordable house prices are jumbled in with the rest of the transactions, so the average for some cities needs to be treated with caution.

2. Data on transaction volumes provides further insights into the dynamics of China's housing markets. The housing market sometimes seems like a game of chicken between buyers and sellers, with the government acting as referee. If the government decides prices are rising too fast, it will intervene with new controls—trying to squeeze speculators out of the market. Buyers then step back, waiting to see if the policy change will bring about a fall in prices. Developers sit tight, hoping that buyers will chicken out and return to the market before reduced revenue forces them to lower prices. Transaction volumes fall, but prices stay stable. The outcome depends on who chickens out first. If the buyers come back, prices will resume their upward march. If the developers crack under the pressure, prices might start to fall.

In summer 2010, after the government acted to quell speculation, transaction volumes plummeted. In Beijing, a high of 3,084 transactions covering more than 380,000 m^2 of property in the last week of March collapsed to a low of 564 transactions and 67,000 m^2 in the second week of June, a fall of 82% in terms of square meters sold. But as Figure 3.5 shows, as the summer wore on and developers showed no sign of lowering prices, buyers were the first to swerve. Transaction volumes surged and prices began to rise again, forcing further intervention from the government. Another point to note about the transaction data is that it is affected by seasonal variations. As Figure 3.5 shows, no one buys houses in Chinese New Year in February, but the National Day holiday in October is a peak time for purchases.

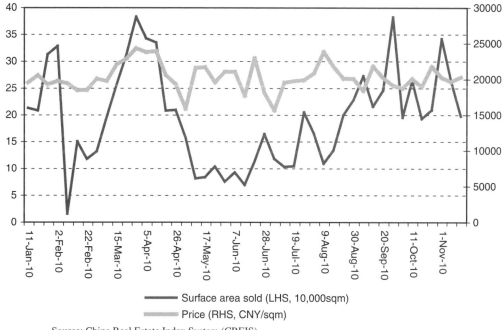

Source: China Real Estate Index System (CREIS)

Figure 3.5 *Beijing: weekly floor area sold versus average price*

Market Impact

The Soufun data is a more timely, accurate, and detailed guide to developments in China's housing market than the NBS data. Its capacity to move markets should be correspondingly greater. The only reason it is not yet a market mover is that it is relatively new, available only in Chinese, and available in its entirety only to paying clients.

CHAPTER 4

Household Sector

Market sensitivity: Medium
What is it? Monthly report on retail sales, published in nominal terms for the current month, CNY100 million, YoY %, and MoM %
Chinese news release on the Internet: www.stats.gov.cn/
English news release on the Internet: www.stats.gov.cn/english/
Release time: 10 a.m. Beijing time, usually on the 11th day of the following month. March, June, September, and December data is released later, to coincide with the quarterly GDP data
Frequency: Monthly; data for January and February is released together
Source: National Bureau of Statistics (NBS)
Revisions: No

Why Is It Important?

China's consumers have a tough time. Companies' profits are high and workers' wages are low. A weak social safety net means that a high proportion of meager wages has to be saved to insure against accident, illness, or old age. In the United States, household consumption accounts for 70% of all economic activity. In China, the share of household spending in GDP is 35%, and that moved in the wrong direction for most of the last decade. With China's hard-pressed households preferring to stuff their cash under the mattress rather than spend it at the shops, investment and exports have been the main drivers of GDP growth.

The government has recognized that this unbalanced growth model cannot be sustained forever. There is a limit to the investments that can be made without building bridges to nowhere and factories whose production lines will never run at full capacity. After more than a decade of breakneck growth in investment, many commentators believe that limit is about to be reached. At the same time, in the wake of the global economic crisis, consumers in the United States and Europe have already taken a pair of scissors to their credit cards and can no longer be relied upon to drive China's growth. The Chinese government wants domestic consumption to pick up the slack. The monthly retail sales data is not a perfect guide to the strength of household consumption, but among the high-frequency data, it's the best guide there is.

How Is the Data Calculated?

The NBS has a three-track approach to measuring retail sales. First, for about 5,000 super-size enterprises, data is reported directly to the NBS headquarters. Second, for about 130,000 large enterprises (wholesalers whose annual operating income is more than CNY20 million, retailers whose annual operating income is more than CNY5 million, and hotels and restaurants whose annual operating income is more than CNY2 million), local statistics bureaus collect the data and report it up the administrative chain. Third, for the 28.4 million small firms that are below the threshold, the NBS conducts a sample survey. For many of the small firms in the sample survey, accounting is not a strong point. The NBS divides firms in the sample survey into two groups: those that can be trusted to submit reliable numbers themselves and those that require an interview from the survey team.

Interpreting the Data

Table 4.1　*Retail Sales of Consumer Goods (September 2010)*

Indicators	September		Jan.-Sep.	
	Absolute Magnitude	Increased YoY (%)	Absolute Magnitude	Increased YoY (%)
[...]				
1 ▶ Total Retail Sales of Consumer Goods (100 million yuan) o/w:	13537	18.8	111029	18.3
[...]				
2 ▶ Grain, Oil, Foodstuff, Beverages, Tobacco, and Liquor	702	31.9	5248	22.3
Garments, Footwear, Hats, Knitwear	459	26.7	4000	24.0
Cosmetics	78	16.7	635	16.3
Gold and Silver Jewelry	109	54.9	897	43.4
Articles for Daily Use	183	28.9	1467	24.9
Sports and Recreation Articles	26	24.9	214	18.0
Household Appliances and AV Equipment	334	28.5	2907	28.1
Traditional Chinese and Western Medicines	279	20.6	2151	22.4
Cultural and Office Appliances	101	31.3	799	23.1
Furniture	65	39.6	479	38.4
Communication Appliances	69	14.8	564	17.9
Petroleum and Related Products	937	29.3	7454	35.0
3 ▶ Automobile	1480	29.7	11659	34.9
4 ▶ Building and Decoration Materials	75	39.0	502	31.6

Source: Adapted from NBS

1. The main takeaway from the data is the headline growth in retail sales for the current month. This is the number that reflects the strength of retail activity and provides a clue to whether households are hitting the shops. Until 2011, the main focus of attention was the year-on-year (YoY) growth rate. From 2011 on, the NBS has begun publishing a figure for month-on-month (MoM) growth. The MoM data is a better guide to the current momentum of growth and will take some of the limelight from the YoY figure.

In Table 4.1, the data for September 2010 shows retail sales growing 18.8% YoY. That seems pretty fast. It would be tempting to conclude that the domestic consumption engine is finally roaring to life, ready to propel the Chinese economy forward. But the retail sales data is not entirely straightforward as a guide to the strength of household demand. Before jumping to any conclusions, a few caveats have to be considered:

- To most people, retail sales means spending by households at the shops. In China, this is only part of the story. The retail sales figure includes not just spending by households, but also spending by government departments and business-to-business sales. If the People's Liberation Army (PLA) decides that March is a good time to buy new uniforms for each of its 2.3 million soldiers, that will mean a surge in spending on clothing. But unless the PLA decides that spring camouflage colors simply will not do for summer and uniforms need to be updated every season, it is a surge that is not likely to be sustained.

- The published figure is in nominal terms. Taking account of a reading of 3.6% on the Consumer Price Index (CPI) in September 2010, real growth was a less impressive 15.2%.

- Retail sales figures do not include spending on services. According to the NBS, 60% of household spending is on goods. The 40% that is spent on haircuts, school fees, and medical expenses does not show up in the retail sales data.

- There are larger structural trends at work that mask cyclical movements in retail sales growth. China's households are getting richer, moving to the cities, and spending more. The NBS has said that this process tends to add about one percentage point a year to growth in retail sales. That long-term structural trend obscures shorter term cyclical movements in retail sales growth, creating the illusion of cheerful households continually increasing their consumption spending.

The more accurate guide to the strength of household spending is the household consumption component of the expenditure-side GDP data. This data set has the advantage of excluding spending by government and business and including spending by households on services. As Figure 4.1 shows, for every year in the last decade, growth in retail sales has been faster than growth in household consumption. The contrast between the two data series illustrates the deficiency of the retail sales data as a guide to the strength of household consumption, and the distance left to travel before China's consumers can play a central role in driving growth. Where the gap between the two is large, as it was in 2008 and 2009, that suggests a large share of retail sales represents spending by the government (perhaps those new summer uniforms for the PLA). With the expenditure-side GDP data available only once a year, and then with a considerable delay, the household income and expenditure data (which is published quarterly) provides a more timely cross-check against the retail sales data. That comparison also indicates household consumption is growing at a slower rate than the retail sales data suggests.

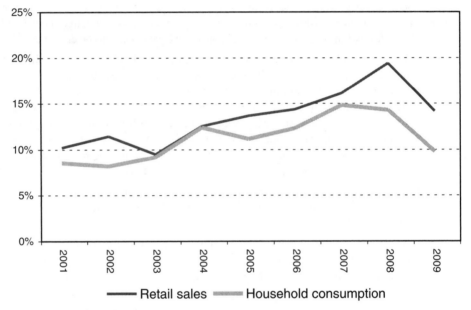

Source: National Bureau of Statistics, author's calculations

Figure 4.1   *Retail sales versus household consumption (YoY%)*

2. A substantial component of retail spending is nondiscretionary. Purchases of food, clothes, and other essentials are not much affected by the economic cycle. This makes growth in retail sales considerably more stable than industrial value added, and a less sensitive indicator of changes in the economy. Changes in purchases of automobiles and household appliances are a better indicator of fluctuations in demand than the headline growth rate, although these, too, have their idiosyncrasies.

3. In November 2007, in Chongqing, China's largest city, 3 people died and 31 were injured in a stampede at a Carrefour supermarket. The reason? A promotion offering CNY11.5 (USD1.5) off the price of a CNY51.4 (USD6.9) bottle of cooking oil. Chinese people like a bargain, and incentives to spend can have a marked impact on the retail sales data. In 2009, the government offered tax breaks to anyone buying a fuel-efficient car. Those incentives tipped the balance for consumers. Despite stagnant wages and uncertainty about the outlook for employment, sales of cars soared 33% YoY, compared to overall growth in retail sales of just 15%. That meant car sales contributed around 1.5 percentage points to headline growth in retail sales. Like the "cash for clunkers" scheme in the United States, the tax break helped keep retail sales strong through the crisis, but created a misleading impression of the underlying strength of household demand. The wider point is that government schemes and incentives can have a material impact on the growth rate of retail sales.

4. An additional oddity of China's retail sales data is that it includes spending on building and decoration materials. Spending on bricks and mortar is normally regarded as investment spending. In China's GDP calculation, it shows up in the investment category. Including it in retail sales is another factor pushing up the headline figure. With spending on building and decoration materials small as a percentage of total retail sales, the distortion is not significant. But when growth is rapid, as in the data for September 2010 shown in Table 4.1, that can add an extra half-percent to headline growth.

Market Impact

Equities: It doesn't matter whether households, the government, or businesses are hitting the shops; higher sales mean higher profits and point to strong economic activity. Robust growth in retail sales is a positive for equities.

Commodities: Retail sales is a second-order indicator for commodity markets, behind industrial value added and fixed asset investment. But cars and household appliances require metal and plastic when they are made and energy when they are used, which means retail sales also earns some attention from commodity markets.

Currency: For currency markets, retail sales is also a second-order indicator. A figure that surprises on the up- or the downside by a significant margin might get the attention of traders. But generally the focus of the currency markets in the NBS monthly release is elsewhere.

URBAN AND RURAL HOUSEHOLD SURVEYS

Market sensitivity: Low
What is it? Quarterly report on income of urban and rural households, published for the year-to-date in current prices and nominal YoY %
Chinese news release on the Internet: www.stats.gov.cn/
English news release on the Internet: www.stats.gov.cn/english/
Release time: Midway through the following quarter
Frequency: Quarterly
Source: NBS
Revisions: No

Why Is It Important?

How fast is China's household income growing? The answer to that question is important for two reasons:

- Households whose income is growing are happy households, and households whose income is shrinking are not. The average urban household is more than seven times better off in real terms than it was 30 years ago. That level of growth buys a lot of social stability. But in the years when income has grown more slowly, or even fallen in real terms, the gloves have come off with destabilizing speed. It is no coincidence that 1988 and 1989, the years when students and workers took to the streets in Beijing, were also the only years in the reform era when China's households saw their real income fall.

- Households that enjoy rapid increases in their income have more money to spend at the shops, and households suffering stagnant wages do not. With limits to China's capacity to tap foreign consumers as a source of demand, the government wants domestic households to move to center stage as the main drivers of growth.

As the basis of social stability and the fulcrum of economic growth, understanding China's household income has taken on a new importance. The NBS quarterly surveys of urban and rural income tell the story.

How Is the Data Calculated?

The urban and rural household surveys are carried out separately. For the urban survey, the NBS has a sample of 476 cities and 65,000 households. Households that participate in the survey are expected to keep a daily record of their income and expenses on a standard form provided by the NBS. Local NBS survey teams collect the completed forms from the households and are responsible for an initial check. The verified data is then transmitted up the chain from the county to the provincial and national NBS. Every year, a third of the houses in the sample are rotated out, so the entire sample is refreshed once every three years.

Checks are in place, but that does not mean the survey is free of problems. First among them is the unwillingness of China's highest earners to disclose details of their income to the survey teams. The NBS is not the State Administration of Taxation or the Public Security Bureau. But with China's elite earning a large portion of their income—or even a majority of their income—from sources that are at best dubious, and at worst illegal, they are naturally disinclined to provide the details to anyone wearing an official badge. In all probability, income levels for high earners are grossly understated. The result is that the survey understates the average income level and the extent of the divide between the haves and the have nots.

For the rural surveys, the NBS sample covers 68,000 households around the country. As is the case with the urban survey, households complete forms each day detailing their income and expenses. This information is collected on a monthly basis by local survey teams and transmitted back up the statistical hierarchy to the NBS headquarters in Beijing.

Treating urban and rural households separately makes sense. Conditions in China's town and country are very different. But it also makes sense to have a single number to represent the country as a whole, not least to facilitate international comparison. From 2010 on, the NBS has been experimenting with a unified approach, although the results haven't yet been published.

Interpreting the Data

Table 4.2   *Income of Urban Households by Region (1st and 2nd Quarters 2010)*

	Number of Households	Average Household Size (Person)	Average Number of Persons Engaged Per Household	Average Total Income Per Capita (Yuan)	Disposable Income Per Capita (Yuan)
National Total	65607.2	2.88	1.49	10699	9757
Beijing	5000.0	2.79	1.58	16864	14750
[...]					
Shanghai	999.7	2.9	1.6	18273	16360
[...]					
Hunan	1250.0	2.91	1.41	8967	8438
[...]					
Sichuan	2650.0	2.87	1.51	8941	8168
[...]					
Gansu	880.0	2.76	1.37	7016	6447

Source: Adapted from NBS

1. Average total income per capita for urban households shows income before tax and national insurance payments are made. Chinese households have four main sources of income. Wages account for around two-thirds of the total. The next-largest contributor is transfers, which includes welfare payments from the government. This accounts for about a quarter of household income. Operating income, income from any household-run enterprise, accounts for around 8%. Income on investments includes rent from property, profit from equity investments, and interest on deposit accounts. For the average family, this accounts for slightly more than 2% of income. At different times, different components contribute more or less to changes in income. In 2009, the increase in wages was lackluster, but a substantial increase in the state pension provided a boost to income from transfers, and a strong year for equities and real estate boosted income from capital investments.

2. Disposable income shows income after taxes and national insurance have been paid. In Table 4.2, in the first half of 2010, the average urban resident had a disposable income of CNY9,757 (USD1,434), up 10.1% from the same period in 2009. Taking into account changes in consumer prices, which rose 2.6% YoY in the first half of 2010, real urban incomes rose 7.5%.

   As Figure 4.2 shows, the urban disposable income data tells a different story than the retail sales data about the strength of household consumption. In the first half of 2010, retail sales in urban areas grew 18.6% YoY. If urban income was growing by just 10.1%, it is difficult to believe that China's households, with their famous preference for saving over spending, could be hitting the shops hard enough to generate an 18.6% increase in retail sales. That suggests spending by government and firms was playing a big part in driving retail sales growth.

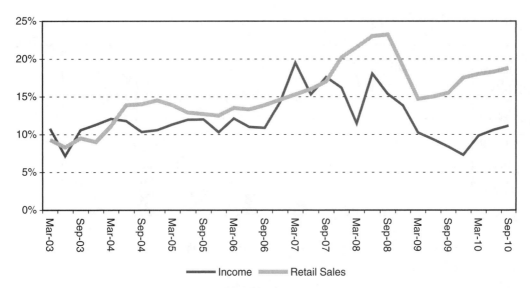

Source: National Bureau of Statistics, author's calculations

Figure 4.2 *Urban per-capita disposable income versus retail sales (YoY%)*

The urban disposable income data is a useful guide to the growing spending power of 665 million urban Chinese residents. But it also needs to be interpreted with caution, for several reasons:

- Chinese households systematically understate their income, with the missing income for the richest households especially significant. A survey conducted by Professor Wang Xiaolu of the China Reform Foundation discovered that, in 2008, for the top 10% of the population, gray income added CNY95,000 (USD13,970) to per-capita income, taking the total to CNY139,000 (USD20,441). As Figure 4.3 shows, this is three times the level reported in the official data. Vastly higher incomes for the top tier drag up the average. According to Professor Wang's estimates, the average in 2008 was CNY32,154 (USD4,728), 90% more than the official figures suggest. Professor Wang's methodology is less than perfect, with a small and unrepresentative sample set. But Gucci, Louis Vuitton, and Bentley are not making China the center of their global growth strategy because the top tier is making the CNY43,613 (USD6,413) figure that the official data suggests. Professor Wang might not be right on the money, but his numbers make more sense than those of the NBS.

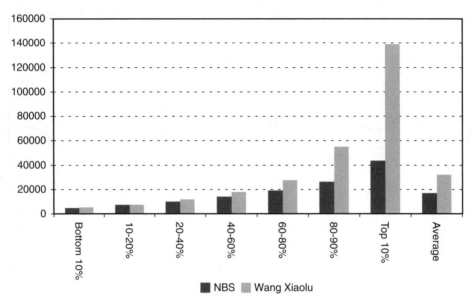

Source: National Bureau of Statistics, Wang Xiaolu

Figure 4.3 *Household income by percentile: NBS versus Wang Xiaolu estimates (2008, CNY)*

- The simple average published by the NBS in the quarterly data disguises the wide variations in income between different sections of the population. Annual data from the NBS does provide the breakdown of income for the richest and poorest households in the country. Data for 2008 shows that the richest 10% of households had a per-capita disposable income of CNY43,613 (USD6,413), more than nine times the CNY4,753 (USD698) a year allotted to the poorest 10%. That distribution of income gave China a gini coefficient of around 0.45, close to that of the United States. But if Professor Wang's research is to be believed, the gap between the haves and the have nots is even wider than the official data suggests, with the top 10% pulling in a socially destabilizing 25 times more than the bottom 10%.

- With many hidden taxes on Chinese families, the term "disposable income" is something of a misnomer. The official tax rate might be low. But with public services and welfare provision weak and patchy, Chinese households are forced to save a high proportion of their income to pay for children's education, guard against the risk of ill health, and prepare for old age. The inordinately high cost of property is also a hidden tax on Chinese households. Average earners who want to get a foot on the bottom rung of the housing ladder have no option but to save thriftily for many years. Urban households' disposable income is not entirely at the disposal of urban households.

3. The breakdown by province gives a sense of the enormous differences in income between the glittering east coast and the more backward central and western hinterland. Per-capita income in Shanghai in the prosperous East is more than two and a half times as high as in lowest-income Gansu in the impoverished Northwest.

Table 4.3   *Per-Capita Cash Income of Rural Households by Region (CNY, First Quarter, 2010)*

Region	Cash Income								
	Cash Income Total	Income from Wages and Salaries	Income from Household Operations					Income from Property	Income from Transfer
			Total	Agriculture	Forestry	Animal Husbandry	Fishery		
National Total	1814.3	761.6	855.2	360.8	15.5	228.2	29.1	59.4	138.0
Beijing	4308.5	2684.8	673.8	77.5	12.9	302.6	9.9	357.6	592.4
[...]									
Shanghai	5671.1	3989.7	290.3	95.5	0.0	39.1	21.5	420.6	970.5
[...]									
Tibet	563.5	154.7	308.2	60.7	20.2	98.6	0.6	11.4	89.2

Source: Adapted from NBS

1. China's 674 million peasants are poor. Cash income in 2009 was just CNY6,270 (USD922) per capita. The inclusion in the sample of family members who live away from home for substantial periods of time—husbands or adult children who leave the farm for the factory for several months a year—means even that low figure may be upward-biased. Average rural incomes are some way above the World Bank's USD1/day measure of absolute poverty, but they are a long way below the CNY18,858 (USD2,773) average annual income enjoyed by China's urbanites. Low levels of education, low investment in rural areas, and barriers to labor mobility all conspire to keep China's rural incomes down. With rural incomes growing at a lower rate than urban incomes, the gap between China's town and country mice is also getting wider. China's rural majority are a lot better off in absolute terms than they were at the beginning of the reform era. But in relative terms, their position is considerably worse. Rising inequality is one of the major threats to social stability on the mainland.

2. The largest source of income for rural households comes from their own enterprise, otherwise known as the family farm. Operating income accounts for around 50% of rural households' income. Income from employment is the second-largest source of cash, accounting for about 40% of the total. For rural households near big cities, that ratio can be reversed as laborers find more profitable ways to employ their time on construction sites, in street-side trade, and in informal work in the service sector. In the vicinity of Beijing, rural households earn almost two-thirds of their income from employment. Income on investments, which for rural households normally means renting out a portion of their land, comes in at around 3% of the total. Transfers reflect agricultural subsidies and welfare payments, and account for around 7% of total income.

3. Rural income is also highly variable between provinces. Peasants living in the vicinity of big, rich eastern cities benefit from superior employment opportunities and higher incomes. Peasants living in less developed central and western provinces do not. The benighted inhabitants of rural Tibet get by on less than a tenth of the cash income of those living in the vicinity of Shanghai. The gap in income between the richest and poorest villages is much greater than that between the richest and poorest cities.

Market Impact

Ten years ago, the urban and rural household survey was of interest mainly to sociologists and political scientists. Now, with China's households moving to center stage as a driver of growth, the survey is getting increased attention from investors as well. But the data comes out too infrequently, with too long a delay, and too many questions about accuracy to move the markets.

NATIONAL BUREAU OF STATISTICS CONSUMER CONFIDENCE INDEX

Market sensitivity: Low
What is it? Survey of consumer confidence
Chinese news release on the Internet: www.stats.gov.cn/
English news release on the Internet: www.stats.gov.cn/english/
Release time: Late the following month
Frequency: Monthly
Source: NBS
Revisions: No

Why Is It Important?

In the United States, consumer confidence matters. Confident consumers are good for business; they are more likely to buy a new automobile, computer, or washing machine. Insecure consumers are bad for business; they are more likely to use their cash to pay off credit card bills than spend it at the shops. With household consumption accounting for 70% of GDP, changes in consumer confidence do not just *predict* shifts in U.S. growth and employment; they *cause* shifts in U.S. growth and employment. That makes consumer confidence a focus for the markets.

In China, where household consumption is equal to just 35% of GDP, consumer confidence still matters, but until now it has not mattered that much. China's consumers do not have the spending power to move the big economic aggregates the way their cousins in the U.S. do. But that might be about to change. Incomes are rising, and discretionary spending is rising with them. Chinese firms are starting to pay as much attention to the domestic as to the international market.

If the Chinese consumer moves to center stage as the new idol of economic development, polling consumer sentiment will take on a new importance. Two organizations are already betting that interest in Chinese consumer confidence is set to increase. The NBS has been conducting a survey of consumer confidence since 1991. In 2007, private research firm INTAGE entered the fray with its own independent survey.

How Is the Data Calculated?

The NBS survey started life humbly enough, with a sample based on just 6 cities. But over the years, it has expanded to cover 14 more, for a total of 20 cities. The powers-that-be do not disclose information about the exact size and composition of the sample, but they do maintain that it is a representative cross-set of China's 665 million urban residents.

The **Consumer Confidence Index (CCI)** is the combination of two separate indexes, one covering consumer satisfaction and one covering consumer expectations:

- The **Consumer Satisfaction Index (CSI)** assesses households' views on the current situation. Participants are asked for their views on the current condition of the economy, wages, and quality of life.

- The **Consumer Expectations Index (CEI)** assesses households' views on future conditions. Participants are asked about their expectations for the year ahead on the economy, labor markets, quality of life, and purchases of consumer durables.

When calculating the indexes, if positive and negative answers are equally balanced, the score would be 100. A score above 100 means households have a positive view; a score below 100 means they have a negative view.

The CCI combines the CSI and CEI into a single indicator. The two indexes are given slightly different weights, with the CEI (60%) weighted slightly more heavily than the CSI (40%). A higher weight for expectations gives the CCI a forward-looking tilt.

Interpreting the Data

Table 4.4   *Consumer Confidence Index (CCI, August 2010)*

Date	Consumer Expectation Index (CEI)	Consumer Satisfaction Index (CSI)	Consumer Confidence Index (CCI)
[...]			
2009.12	104.0	103.8	103.9
2010.01	104.6	104.8	104.7
2010.02	104.5	103.7	104.2
2010.03	108.2	107.5	107.9
2010.04	106.8	106.2	106.6
2010.05	108.2	107.7	108.0
2010.06	108.9	107.8	108.5
2010.07	108.6	106.4	107.8
2010.08	107.9	106.2	107.3

Source: Adapted from NBS

The highlight of the data set is the latest reading for the CCI. In Table 4.4, a score of 107.3 for the index in August 2010 suggests that consumers continued to have a positive outlook (the score was above 100), but slightly less positive than earlier in the summer (107.3 in August was down from 107.8 in July and 108.5 in June).

In theory, consumers should be sensitive to changes in the economy, and consumer confidence should move ahead of key measures of economic activity, such as industrial value added and retail sales. In practice, as Figure 4.4 shows, the NBS CCI does not provide a consistent guide to the outlook for the economy. In 2003, a glance at the CCI in May suggested the world was about to end, as households reacted to the threat from severe acute respiratory syndrome (SARS). Retail sales also fell, but they rebounded just as quickly. At the end of 2007, a year ahead of the financial crisis, Chinese consumers started to lose confidence, and the downturn in the index was a leading indicator of the coming calamity. But in 2009, the rebound in consumer confidence lagged behind the rebound in the real economy.

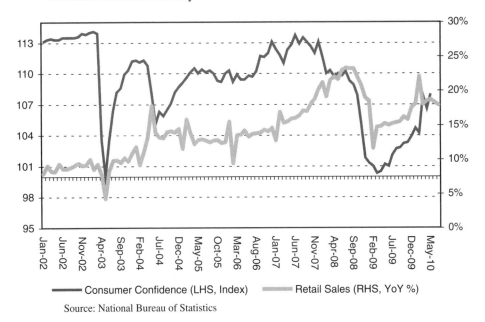

Source: National Bureau of Statistics

Figure 4.4 *Consumer confidence index versus retail sales*

Why does the CCI not do a better job of predicting movements in the economy? Several factors are at work:

- The most obvious reason is that consumers are not a particularly important part of China's growth story. The industrial sector is geared to provide investment goods such as steel and cement, which are not high on consumers' shopping list. The manufacturing sector makes goods for export to foreign consumers. The firms that produce the majority of China's output do not care whether domestic consumers are confident.

- Even with retail sales, household consumers are not the only source of demand. The retail sales data includes not just spending by households, but also spending by government and businesses. Consumer confidence might be moving up and down, as the NBS CCI suggests. But with the government playing a countercyclical role, spending when households are saving and saving when households are spending, the impact of consumer confidence on the retail sales figures is obscured.

- A large part of household spending is nondiscretionary. Confident or not, households will still be buying food, clothes, and other essentials. Only spending on luxury items and expensive consumer durables is dictated by changes in confidence. With the average income in China still low, that discretionary spending makes up a relatively low percentage of the total.

- Finally, policy plays an important role in shaping household spending decisions. If the government decides to offer a substantial tax break on the purchase of cars, as it did in 2009, that changes consumers' outlook and generates more sales in a way that the consumer confidence survey could not have anticipated. The CCI does not capture the decisive role of policy in shaping spending decisions.

Market Impact

The results of the NBS consumer confidence survey appear late in the month, after indicators for retail sales, industrial output, and an alternative measure of consumer confidence from INTAGE have already been published. An inconsistent record of predicting changes in economic activity is also not an attraction. As incomes rise and discretionary spending increases, this indicator may gain increased prominence, but for now, it is not a focus of attention for the markets.

INTAGE CHINA CONSUMER SENTIMENT SURVEY

Market sensitivity: Low
What is it? Survey of consumer confidence, indexed to 100 in April 2007
Chinese news release on the Internet: www.intage-china.com
English news release on the Internet: www.intage-china.com
Release time: Paying subscribers receive the complete data set on the final work day of the month; the headline data is available for free on the company's website 14 days later
Frequency: Monthly
Source: INTAGE China
Revisions: No

Why Is It Important?

The INTAGE consumer sentiment survey is a latecomer to the economic indicators party. The NBS CCI has been around since 1991. INTAGE arrived only in 2007 (at that time, under the *ezidata* brand). But it did not come empty-handed. A more detailed data set and a sample skewed toward the high earners that account for the bulk of China's discretionary spending mean INTAGE has something to offer in addition to the official NBS data.

How Is the Data Calculated?

Every month, INTAGE conducts around 1,000 telephone interviews with residents of China's 30 most developed cities. Interviews last around 10–15 minutes and include 30 questions. Interviewees are 18–64 years old, are responsible for household decisions on finance and investment, and are chosen at random from a stratified sample.

The consumer sentiment index is based on answers to five questions:

1. Would you say that the financial situation of your family is better or worse than it was a year ago?

2. Looking ahead, do you think that a year from now the financial situation of your family will be better or worse?

3. And how about a year from now—do you expect, in the region as a whole, business conditions will be better or worse than they are at present, or just about the same?

4. What about the outlook for business conditions in the region over the next 5 years? Do you think business conditions will be better, about the same, or worse 5 years from now?

5. About the big consumer durables people buy for their homes, such as furniture, appliances, computers, and TVs, do you think it is a good time or a bad time now for people to buy such major household items?

All responses to the index questions are classified on a five-point scale as Very Favorable (VF), Favorable (F), Neutral, Unfavorable (U), Very Unfavorable (VU), and Don't Know/Refused. The percentage of each of the responses is first calculated and then weighted using the following formula to score each question:

Score = $100\% + 1.0 \times \%VF + 0.5 \times \%F - 0.5 \times \%U - 1.0 \times \%VU$

The score shows the difference between the percentages of positive and negative answers. If positive and negative answers are equally balanced, the score is 100. If the percentage of positive answers is larger than that of negative ones, the score is above 100. If the percentage of positive answers is smaller than that of negative ones, the score is below 100.

To arrive at the consumer sentiment index, INTAGE adds up the scores of all five questions and divides by the score in the base month, currently April 2007.

A key difference between the NBS survey and the INTAGE approach is that whereas the NBS tries to sample a representative cross-section of the population, the INTAGE sample is slanted toward a higher income bracket. At first sight, a skewed sample set does not sound like a big selling point. But the gap between the haves and the have nots in China is so great, and the spending power of the have nots is so limited, that a sample set skewed toward the haves makes a certain amount of sense. There is no point in asking a street cleaner in Lanzhou if he's planning to buy a car when his monthly income is barely enough to keep him clothed and fed. If spending by China's affluent middle class is moving the retail sales data, then China's middle class should be the target of the survey.

Interpreting the Data

Table 4.5 *Consumer Sentiment Index and Components (September 2010)*

		Nov 2009	Dec 2009	Jan 2010	Feb 2010	Mar 2010	Apr 2010	May 2010	Jun 2010	Jul 2010	Aug 2010	Sep 2010
2▶	Personal Finance: Current	121.9	125.7	109.9	129.8	115	117.6	118.3	126.2	124.4	121.6	131.7
	Durable Buying Conditions	115.1	113.1	114	115.3	109.2	107.4	105.5	111.4	109.2	107.9	116.5
	Current Index	104.3	105.1	98.6	107.9	98.7	99	98.5	104.6	102.8	101	109.3
	Personal Finance: Expected	128.1	129.7	123.5	135.1	126.3	126.4	129.5	129	126.7	126.8	132.6
	Business Condition: 1 Year	127.3	127.2	128.4	132.1	130.8	126.5	125.7	130.2	127.3	122.3	134
	Business Condition: 5 Years	143.5	138.9	146.2	146.9	146.9	141.6	144.3	150.4	150.2	136.5	144.3
	Expectations Index	96.6	95.8	96.4	100.3	97.8	95.5	96.7	99.2	97.9	93.4	99.5
1▶	**Total Index**	**99.3**	**99.1**	**97.2**	**103**	**98.1**	**96.8**	**97.4**	**101.1**	**99.6**	**96.1**	**103**

Source: Adapted from INTAGE

1. The main takeaway from INTAGE's monthly data release, and the only takeaway that
    is available to nonsubscribers, is the headline reading for the index. A rise in the index
    means consumers are more confident this month than in the previous month. A fall in
    the index means that consumers are less confident this month than in the previous
    month. In Table 4.5, the data for September 2010 shows the index rising sharply to
    103.0 from 96.1 in August, the highest level since February of that year. A sharp rise
    in the index suggests that, after an uncertain start to the third quarter, consumers were
    increasingly confident about the outlook.

    In theory, the index should be a good way to anticipate movement in retail sales.
    Confident consumers tend to buy more; consumers who are uncertain about the future
    buy less. In practice, the same problems that bedevil the NBS consumer confidence
    survey are at work in the INTAGE index. The countercyclical role of government pur-
    chases in smoothing out the impact of changes in purchases by households, low per-
    centage of discretionary household spending, and role of policy in shaping the timing
    of big purchases all reduce the reliability of consumer confidence as a forecasting tool.
    For the short period of time in which the INTAGE survey has been in operation, its
    forecasting record is mixed. In 2007, the index turned down in October, almost a full
    year before retail sales started to decline. At the end of 2008, the lead time was rather
    tighter, with the index ticking up in December 2008, 3 months before retail sales
    rebounded in March 2009.

2. For subscribers to the INTAGE service, more detailed data is available. Subscribers get a monthly reading on consumers' estimate of current and future conditions, the current and future state of their personal finances, business conditions in the short and medium term, and whether the time is right to make a purchase of major consumer durable items (such as a computer or a car). Some of these subindexes are well correlated with movements in key components of retail sales. In particular, as Figure 4.5 shows, the index of consumers' attitude on purchases of durable goods tracked the surge in sales of automobiles at the end of 2008.

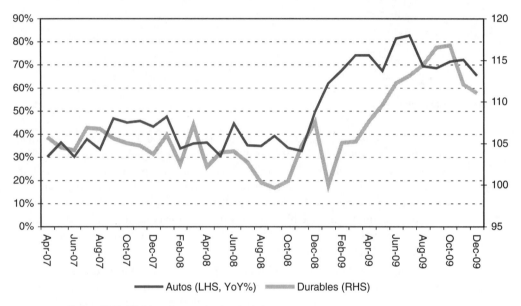

Source: INTAGE, Bloomberg, author's calculations

Figure 4.5   *Durable buying conditions index versus retail sales of autos*

Market Impact

Over time, the importance of households as drivers of growth in the Chinese economy will increase and the markets will pay more attention to measures of consumer confidence. If the INTAGE survey can demonstrate a strong record of predicting changes in retail sales, it will capture some of that attention. For now, it is not a market mover.

CHAPTER 5

External Sector

TRADE

Market sensitivity: High
What is it? Report on exports, imports, and trade surplus, published in current USD100 millions and nominal YoY % for the current month and year-to-date
Chinese news release on the Internet: www.customs.gov.cn/publish/portal0/
English news release on the Internet: http://english.customs.gov.cn/publish/portal191/
Release time: Around 10 a.m. the 10th day of the following month
Frequency: Monthly
Source: General Administration of Customs
Revisions: No

Why Is It Important?

Although it seems difficult to believe these days, large sections of domestic industry bitterly opposed China's entry into the World Trade Organization (WTO) in 2001. China's telecommunications, machinery, and automobile producers and their representatives in government fought tooth and nail against the move. Premier Zhu Rongji, who led the negotiations on WTO entry for China, was vilified as a traitor for selling out the national interest. Ten years later, China is the world's largest exporter, having overtaken second-place Germany in 2009. The low value-added textile, toy, and tool industries that were the mainstay of the export sector in the decades before WTO entry are still there. But as China has moved up the value chain, other industries have risen in prominence. China is the world's biggest exporter of mobile phones, machinery manufacturers are challenging Japanese and Korean firms for a share of global markets, and the docks of Guangzhou and Shenzhen are lined with fleets of Chinese-brand cars. The same industries that fought tooth and nail against WTO entry at the beginning of the century are the biggest winners a decade later. China's exports account for 1 in every 3 yuan of domestic GDP, and 9% of global exports. The export data is an important gauge of not just the state of the Chinese economy, but also the strength of global demand.

WTO entry opened the door to global markets for China's exporters. But the rapid move up the ranks would not have been possible without support from a range of other factors. Low cost of labor, land, and energy has enabled China's exporters to keep prices for their products down. Low cost of capital and a freewheeling approach to intellectual property protection has meant exporters can gain scale in their production and assimilate new technologies quickly. An undervalued yuan has enhanced competitiveness. But the same policies that have resulted in surging exports have also choked off growth in imports. Low wages limit demand for foreign consumer goods. A low cost of capital for domestic industry means that setting up local production is a relatively cheap alternative to sourcing from abroad, and an undervalued yuan tips the balance further in favor of domestic producers. Commodities that feed the industrial engine, a dwindling number of high-technology products that remain beyond the ken of Chinese manufacturers, and intermediate goods that are assembled in factories located near the ports before being re-exported to their final destination make up the vast majority of China's imports. That means the import data reflects the strength of demand from China's industrial sector and exporters' estimation of the outlook for overseas demand, but not the strength of domestic consumption.

The Exchange Rate: A Drama in Four Acts

The difference between surging exports and stunted imports has made the Chinese trade surplus the stuff of high political drama. According to the economics textbooks, a country with a trade surplus should see an appreciation in its currency, making exports more expensive and imports cheaper until the surplus has been eradicated. In the years leading up the financial crisis, China's trade surplus ballooned in size. But the policymakers in Beijing had not read their economics textbooks, or perhaps had read them but formed a different view. The result has been a drama of epic proportions, played out on a global stage:

- In Act I, instead of allowing the yuan to float upward to correct the trade imbalance, Beijing kept the exchange rate under tight control. Between WTO entry in 2001 and July 2005, the yuan remained pegged at 8.27 to the dollar.

- Act II was more exciting and even included a small amount of dialogue. From July 2005 to August 2008, the yuan rose 21%, to end the period at around 6.83 to the dollar. Despite that appreciation, the trade surplus continued to grow, rising from 4.5% of GDP in 2005 to around 7.7% in 2007. "That's because you're not allowing the yuan to appreciate enough," said Washington, D.C. "No," said Beijing, "it's because the exchange rate is not the main factor determining the trade balance."

- In Act III, the economic crisis changed the dynamic of the drama. The yuan's 3 years of appreciation came to an end. A collapse in foreign demand at the same time as the domestic stimulus drove a surge in imports resulted in a contraction of

China's trade surplus. The United States, chastened by the role of Wall Street and the Federal Reserve's lax monetary policy in allowing the crisis to take shape, fell silent. But at the beginning of 2010, with the origins of the crisis fading into memory and unemployment in the United States high, the chorus of disapproval from Washington, D.C., began to increase in volume.

• In June 2010, it was time for Act IV. Beijing declared that a new stage in exchange rate management had begun, with the peg to the dollar over and a greater role for the markets in determining the value of the yuan.

The question now is, what will happen in the final act? The view from Beijing is that the shift to a smaller surplus is structural and there is no basis for significant appreciation of the yuan. The view from Washington, D.C., is that China's surplus is still plenty large, and significant appreciation of the yuan is a necessary condition to restore balance to the relationship. Who is correct? The monthly trade data will reveal all.

How Is the Data Calculated?

China's exports to the United States in 2009 as recorded by China's General Administration of Customs added up to USD220 billion. U.S. imports from China as calculated by the U.S. Census Bureau were USD296 billion, USD76 billion more than the total recorded by the Chinese side. In the same year, China's Custom's bureau reported a trade deficit with Japan of USD32 billion, making Japan the only member of the G8 to boast a trade surplus with China. But according to the Japanese data, the situation was reversed and China enjoyed a bilateral surplus of USD12 billion. What's going on? Another case of statistical sleight of hand? An attempt to hide the enormity of China's trade surplus and deflect criticism of its exchange rate regime? The real explanation is far more mundane.

Detailed work by the U.S. Department of Commerce and the Chinese Ministry of Commerce (MOFCOM) has traced the discrepancy in the trade data to two sources. First, the territorial basis of the figures produced by the General Administration of Customs is the Chinese mainland, with Hong Kong and Macao operating separate regimes. Many of China's exports stop off in Hong Kong before heading on to their final destination. These goods are recorded as exports to Hong Kong by the Chinese side, but imports from China by the United States. Goods channeled through Hong Kong account for about 25% of the discrepancy between the United States and Chinese data. Exports from China channeled through other third countries to the United States account for another 25%. What about the remaining 50%? The explanation for the remainder of the discrepancy lies in the practice by trade intermediaries of buying cheap in China and selling at a mark-up in the United States. The low price at which goods are bought in China is the one reported to Chinese Customs; the high price at which goods are sold in the United States is the price reported to U.S. Customs. Statistical anomaly, not communist conspiracy, explains the mismatch between China's import and export data and the data of its trade partners.

Detailed data on the value, product category, customs regime, company ownership, origin, and destination is collected on all imported and exported goods and verified by Customs officials. For exports, the goods are valued on a "free on board" (f.o.b.) basis, which includes the costs to deliver goods onto vessels but no other costs. For imports, the basis for valuation is "cost, insurance, and freight" (c.i.f.). As the name suggests, this also includes insurance and freight charges. The General Administration of Customs has statistical offices around the country in each of the customs districts. These offices are responsible for the initial collection and verification of data, before it is transmitted to the headquarters in Beijing.

Interpreting the Data

Table 5.1   *Trade Summary Table (July 2010)*

2010年7月全国进出口总值表
July 2010 Whole Country Import and Export Tables

单位：亿美元 Units: USD100mln

项目 Item	当月 Current Month	1至当月累计 Year to Date Total Value	当月 Current Month		1至当月累计 与去年同期比±% Year to Date YoY % Change
			与上月环比±% Month on Month % Change	与去年同期比±% YoY % Change	
进出口总值 Total Imports and Exports	2,623.08	16,170.47	3.00	30.8	40.9
1 ▶ 出口总值 Total Exports	1,455.19	8,504.90	5.90	38.1	35.6
2 ▶ 进口总值 Total Imports	1,167.89	7,665.57	-0.40	22.7	47.2
3 ▶ 进出口差额 Trade Surplus	287.3	839.33	-	-	-

注释：1、进出口差额，+为出大于进；-为进大于出；
Note: 1. Regarding the trade surplus, "+" means surplus; "-" means deficit;
2、经季节调整后，今年7月份进出口总值同比增长33.7%；其中出口增长39.4%，进口增长27.3%。
2. After seasonal adjustment, July imports and exports rose 33.7% YoY, among which exports rose 39.4%, imports rose 27.3%.
进出口总值环比下降1.9%；其中出口增长1.2%，进口下降5.6%。
Total imports and exports fell 1.9% MoM, among which exports rose 1.2%, imports fell 5.6%.

Source: Adapted from General Administration of Customs

1. The first focus for the markets is the year-on-year (YoY) growth of exports. In the bubble years before the crisis, the markets became accustomed to turbo-charged growth. From 2003 to the end of 2007, YoY growth in exports between 20% and 30% was the norm. In 2008, the collapse in external demand in the face of the global financial crisis brought that story to an end; in 2009, China's exports actually shrank. In 2010, the growth came back. But with Europe and the United States—the main markets for China's exports—dialing down growth expectations, a return to the go-go years before the crisis is not in the cards. The outlook depends on exporters' ability to find new product markets by pushing into higher value-added segments of the global supply chain, and new geographical markets by capturing a share of demand in faster-growing South America, Eastern Europe, and emerging Asia.

A few words of warning on interpreting the export data:

- Exports are reported in current prices. That means export growth can appear misleadingly high when inflation is high and misleadingly low when inflation is low. One imperfect way out of the problem is to use the monthly Producer Price Index (PPI) to deflate export growth. In Table 5.1, the data shows China's exports for July up 38.1% YoY in nominal terms, an impressive rate of growth. But taking into account a 4.8% YoY increase in producer prices in July, real exports grew by a slightly less elevated 33.3%. A more laborious but rewarding approach that some analysts favor is to use the price index data that the Customs Bureau publish for specific products to deflate the growth rate.

- The headline data is not corrected for seasonal variation. The Custom's Bureau does publish seasonally adjusted growth figures in a footnote to its data release. But correcting for seasonal variations around Chinese New Year, a week-long holiday that falls in January some years and February in others, and the October holiday remains fraught with difficulty.

- Export orders are typically placed sometime ahead of shipment. That means strong growth in exports reflects strong demand at the time when the export order was placed, not necessarily at the point when it ships. In October 2008, exports recorded 19.2% YoY growth. But that's not because global demand in October 2008 was strong; it's because, in July and August 2008, China's trade partners failed to anticipate the collapse in demand that would follow from the eruption of the Lehman volcano and continued to increase their orders for Chinese goods.

2. After headline exports, the next port of call is the import data, an important register of the strength of demand in China's industrial and export sectors. A few points to keep in mind when reading the import data:

- Imports are reported on the basis of current prices. With commodities accounting for a substantial chunk of the import bill and prices volatile, the headline import growth figure needs to be interpreted with caution. Think about crude oil as an example. In June 2008, international oil prices pushed past USD140 per barrel. In February 2009, they were below USD60 per barrel. With China importing around 100 million barrels of crude every month, that change in prices has a marked impact on the total import bill. With prices for imported iron ore, copper, and other commodities similarly volatile, and China's demand relatively unresponsive to changes in price, changes in commodity prices can have a marked impact on China's import bill. The Customs Bureau publishes price indexes for import products that can be used to calculate the real growth rate.

- Chinese firms protect themselves against the impact of volatile commodity prices by stockpiling—buying large volumes of crude oil and iron ore when prices are low and depleting their stock piles when prices are high. Sharp movements in imports sometimes reflect stockpiling behavior rather than changes in underlying demand.

- Seasonal variations also affect imports, with a particularly marked impact on the month-on-month (MoM) change in imports around Chinese New Year and the October holiday.
3. Exports minus imports add up to one of the biggest sources of controversy in the world economy: China's trade surplus. In the wonder years before the crisis, a monthly trade surplus above USD20 billion was nothing out of the ordinary, and when China's exports held up a month or two longer than imports at the end of 2008, the trade surplus pushed past USD40 billion. In 2009 and 2010, with China's recovery leading the world, imports bounced back faster than exports. The result was a smaller surplus in most months and even a surprise deficit in March 2010.

    The surplus is significant for two reasons. First, in the expenditure-based approach to calculating GDP, net exports (another way of saying the trade surplus) are part of the arithmetic. A growing surplus adds a few decimal points to GDP growth; a shrinking surplus pulls in the other direction. Second, the trade surplus is exhibit A in the case against China's exchange rate regime. A bumper trade surplus is evidence that the yuan remains undervalued and a stick China's trade partners can use to beat Beijing. China's leaders point to a shrinking surplus as evidence that there is no fundamental imbalance in the mainland's trade account, and no basis for significant appreciation of the yuan. The surprise trade deficit in March 2010 was one factor contributing to the delay in resuming appreciation of the yuan against the dollar. Premier Wen Jiabao thought the March deficit was so significant that he announced it himself, ahead of the release of the Customs data.

Table 5.2   *Imports and Exports by Customs Regime (October 2010)*

2010.10进出口贸易方式总值

Total value of import and export trade by regime

单位：亿美元，% Units: USD100mln, %

出口 Exports	当月 Current month		一至当月累计 Year to date total value	
	金额 Value	同比 YoY %	金额 Value	同比 YoY %
总值 Total value	1359.8	22.9	12705.9	32.7
其中：o/w:				
1▶ 加工贸易 Processing trade	658.7	15.6	5975.1	28.4
一般贸易 General trade	600.1	30.5	5791.1	36.5
[⋯]				

进口 Imports	当月 Current month		一至当月累计 Year to date total value	
	金额 Value	同比 YoY %	金额 Value	同比 YoY %
总值 Total value	1088.3	25.3	11228.1	40.5
其中：o/w:				
一般贸易 General trade	571.9	28.0	6127.1	43.6
2▶ 加工贸易 Processing trade	354.3	18.6	3413.9	34.3
[⋯]				

Source: Adapted from General Administration of Customs

1. An important part of China's exports is made up of "processing trade," which refers to the practice of importing components, assembling them, and then exporting the finished product. In the early days of its development, a low skilled workforce, low capital stock, and limited access to technology confined China to the lowest-value links of the global supply chain. Work to assemble parts imported from Korea, Japan, and Taiwan was the norm. Between 1996 and 2000, processing trade accounted for 55% of total exports. An aggressive policy of import substitution has meant that China can now make more of the inputs into the manufacturing process itself, and the share of processing trade has declined. But in 2010, it still accounted for 47% of total exports.

2. The growth of processing trade imports is a leading indicator of the outlook for exports. A high number means that China's exporters are anticipating strong demand for their finished goods; a low number points in the opposite direction. In addition to the data shown in Table 5.2, which aggregates processing trade into a single category,

the Customs Bureau also publishes a detailed breakdown that includes imports of machinery to be used by export processors and imports of parts and raw materials.

Table 5.3　*Exports by Product (July 2010)*

2010年07月全国出口重点商品量值表
July 2010 Whole Country Export Volume and Value Table

单位：千美元 Accounting Unit: USD1000

商品名称 Item	计量单位 Accounting Unit	当月 Current Month		1至当月累计 Year to Date Total Value		2009年同期累计 Year to Date Total Value in 2009		累计比去年同期比±% Year to Date Year on Year % Change	
		数量 Volume	金额 Value	数量 Volume	金额 Value	数量 Volume	金额 Value	数量 Volume	金额 Value
[...]									
成品油 Refined Petroleum Products	万吨 10000 tons	254	1,596,646	1,689	10,852,691	1,257	5,387,223	34.4	101.5
塑料制品 Plastics Products	吨 tons	703,517	1,760,427	4,210,802	10,179,088	3,663,439	7,816,672	14.9	30.2
[...]									
2▶ 服装及衣着附件 Garments	-	-	13,603,910	-	66,827,181	-	56,924,729	-	17.4
鞋类 Shoes	-	-	3,803,492	-	19,419,738	-	15,717,485	-	23.6
[...]									
3▶ 钢材 Steel	万吨 10000 tons	455	4,010,632	2,813	22,683,583	1,116	11,790,907	152.1	92.4
未锻压铝 Aluminum	吨 tons	68,786	139,947	419,008	826,561	107,325	181,000	290.4	356.7
手持无线电话机及其零件 Cell Phones and components	-	-	5,476,567	-	33,065,595	-	27,683,059	-	19.4
彩色电视接收机 Color TV sets	万台 10000 sets	570	1,323,175	3,442	7,347,944	2,492	5,029,370	38.2	46.1
集成电路 Integrated Circuit	万个 10000 units	780,291	2,543,802	4,696,682	16,225,444	2,735,702	11,594,764	71.7	39.9
[...]									
玩具 Toys	-	-	1,034,150	-	4,754,681	-	3,658,183	-	30.0
自动数据处理设备及其部件 Automatic Data Processing Machines and Components	万台 10000 sets	15,070	14,290,848	90,488	87,898,486	65,055	60,627,812	39.1	45.0
电动机及发电机 Electric Motors and Generators	万台 10000 sets	34,828	698,530	201,759	4,071,132	139,891	2,776,199	44.2	46.6
家具及其零件 Furniture	-	-	2,907,705	-	18,543,425	-	13,744,658	-	34.9
[...]									
1▶ *机电产品 Mechanical and Electrical Products	-	-	83,830,271	-	500,694,976	-	367,713,578	-	36.2
*高新技术产品 High-tech Products	-	-	42,675,409	-	260,086,519	-	187,184,280	-	38.9

注：＊“机电产品”和“高新技术产品”包括本表中已列名的有关商品，请读者使用时注意。

Note: * "Mechanical and Electrical Products" and "High-tech Products" include some items listed in the table.

Source: Adapted from General Administration of Customs

The monthly breakdown of important export products, as shown in Table 5.3, covers 33 different categories of product:

1. In terms of value, the most important product category is electrical goods, which account for around 60% of the value of China's total exports. The data release provides an aggregate figure for electrical goods and a breakdown by category of product. Computers, mobile phones, and televisions are among the most important categories.

2. Less glamorous than semiconductors and smartphones, but still an important contributor to total exports, are the low value added goods where China's exporters have traditionally excelled: clothes, textiles, shoes, toys, and tools. Higher costs for factor inputs

are eroding China's competitiveness in these product categories, but they still make up a significant share of China's exports and employ a large number of workers. Taken together, China's exports of clothes and textiles is still worth more than its exports of computers. The textile sector employs 4.5 million workers, more than all the computer and mobile phone manufacturers combined. Profit margins in many of these traditional export sectors are razor thin. The risk of mass unemployment and social unrest if the factories of the Pearl and Yangtze River Deltas are driven into bankruptcy is an important consideration for Beijing in deciding on its exchange rate policy.

3. China is the world's largest producer of steel and aluminum. Most of it is intended for home consumption. But when domestic demand dries up, China's surplus production can flood world markets, depressing prices. The export numbers are a focus of attention for international metal markets.

Table 5.4 *Imports by Product (July 2010)*

2010年07月全国进口重点商品量值表

July 2010 Whole Country Import Volume and Value Table

单位：千美元Accounting Unit: USD1000

商品名称 Item	计量单位 Accounting Unit	当月 Current Month		1至当月累计 Year to Date Total Value		2009年同期累计 Year to Date Total Value in 2009		累计比去年同期比±% Year to Date Year on Year % Change	
		数量 Volume	金额 Value	数量 Volume	金额 Value	数量 Volume	金额 Value	数量 Volume	金额 Value
[...]									
3 ▶ 大豆 Soybean	万吨 10000 tons	495	2,091,050	3,076	13,502,286	2,648	11,170,987	16.2	20.9
[...]									
2 ▶ 铁矿砂及其精矿 Iron Ore	万吨 10000 tons	5,120	7,238,833	36,041	41,803,779	35,511	26,865,293	1.5	55.6
1 ▶ 原油 Crude Oil	万吨 10000 tons	1,900	10,276,344	13,697	77,029,029	11,027	40,890,982	24.2	88.4
成品油 Refined Petroleum Products	万吨 10000 tons	278	1,596,011	2,132	12,547,746	2,339	9,393,215	-8.9	33.6
肥料 Chemical Fertilizer	万吨 10000 tons	32	113,883	404	1,453,106	294	1,517,319	37.0	-4.2
[...]									
钢材 Steel	万吨 10000 tons	140	1,788,422	983	11,752,144	987	11,053,195	-0.4	6.3
未锻造的铜及铜材 Copper	吨 tons	342,901	2,413,863	2,574,929	19,015,979	2,643,419	11,953,592	-2.6	59.1
废铜 Scrap Copper	万吨 10000 tons	38	1,029,696	241	6,631,125	219	2,329,330	10.2	184.7
氧化铝 Alumina	万吨 10000 tons	27	94,178	262	906,652	329	781,882	-20.4	16.0
未锻造的铝及铝材 Aluminum	吨 tons	67,462	309,855	587,093	2,309,148	1,611,359	3,351,998	-63.6	-31.1
废铝 Scrap Aluminum	万吨 10000 tons	27	393,966	165	2,453,507	121	1,105,274	36.6	122.0
[...]									
汽车和汽车底盘 Motor Vehicles and Chassis	辆 Unit	71,417	2,513,602	458,885	16,985,972	181,666	6,521,853	152.6	160.4
飞机 Aircraft	架 Unit	34	1,312,041	193	6,195,538	164	4,616,623	17.7	34.2
*机电产品 Mechanical and Electrical Products	-	-	57,706,157	-	360,281,039	-	252,364,350	-	42.8
*高新技术产品 High-tech Products	-	-	35,992,880	-	224,781,746	-	157,367,047	-	42.8

注：* "机电产品" 和 "高新技术产品" 包括本表中已列名的有关商品，请读者使用时注意。

Note: * "Mechanical and Electrical Products" and "High-tech Products" include some items listed in the table.

Source: Adapted from General Administration of Customs

The product breakdown for imports, as shown in Table 5.4, reflects China's continued dependence on foreign supplies of commodities and some high-technology products:

1. The largest single category of imports is oil. China consumes more than 8 million barrels a day of oil and produces less than half of that itself. The remainder has to be made up with imports. Most of those barrels come from Saudi Arabia, but significant quantities imported from pariah states such as Iran, Sudan, and Angola have become a bone of contention in international relations. Chinese demand is relatively inelastic: Even at the peak of USD140 / barrel oil in summer 2008, imports continued to grow. But international markets are extremely sensitive to the suggestion of changes in China's purchases. Back in summer 2008, the government's announcement of a hike in the regulated price for gasoline and diesel was enough to knock several dollars off the international price of a barrel of oil. In 2010, record levels of oil imports from China, despite evidence of slowing global growth, helped put a floor under international oil prices.

   China's oil imports sometimes move in ways that have little obvious relation to the strength of underlying demand. In September 2010, despite expectations of a slowdown in industrial production, oil imports hit a record high. To understand why requires a brief excursion into China's price-setting mechanism for gasoline and diesel. China's gasoline and diesel prices are set not by the market, but by a powerful government planning agency: the National Development and Reform Commission (NDRC). The NDRC sets prices in reference to the average of a basket of international oil prices. When the average price moves by more than 4% in a 22-day period, that is a signal to the NDRC to consider adjusting domestic prices. Players in the domestic gasoline and diesel markets are well aware of the trigger for adjustment in prices. When they see international prices moving in a direction that suggests an adjustment is on the horizon, they act accordingly. If prices are expected to rise, they buy now at the lower price, hoping to make a profit by selling after the hike. If prices are expected to fall, they hold off on purchases and draw down their reserves, hoping to be able to buy later at a lower price. In August and September 2010, international oil prices were sharply up. The domestic market was anticipating a price hike and buying large quantities of gasoline and diesel, driving stronger demand for imported crude. This quirk in the pricing system, not a surge in underlying demand, drove September 2010 imports to record levels.

2. After crude oil, the next commodity on China's shopping list is iron ore. China is the world's largest producer of steel, but domestic supplies of iron ore are inadequate in quantity and quality to meet demand. More than 70% of China's iron ore is imported, mainly from Australia and Brazil, with India in third place. As is the case with crude oil, China's dependence on imports of iron ore means that it is not sensitive to changes in price. Even as iron ore prices surged in Summer 2008, China's imports continued to grow. Conversely, global prices are extremely sensitive to Chinese demand. China's

investment-driven stimulus, which triggered a surge in iron ore imports, was the catalyst for prices to touch record highs in April 2010. The threat of a slowdown in China's investment boom was enough to bring prices back down to earth. Elsewhere in the metals, Chilean mines benefit from China's demand for copper, Australia sells large volumes of alumina to China's aluminum smelters, and Korean and Japanese producers of high-quality steel still benefit from the gap in the market left by China's relatively low-quality producers.

3. Self-sufficiency in the production of food is a priority that the Chinese government has pursued with almost paranoid determination. Despite a small area of agricultural land, a very low water endowment, and the world's largest population, the government has more or less achieved its objective. The only agricultural product that looms large on the list of China's imports is soybeans. Soybeans are the main input into feed for the commercial rearing of pigs, poultry, and fish. As China's rising wealth translates into demand for a higher-quality diet, and as China's meat industry transitions from hogs raised on scraps from the farmyard to commercial production, demand for soybeans is projected to grow. That's good news for the soybean producers in the United States, Brazil, and Argentina who compete for a chance to get their nose in the Chinese trough.

Table 5.5 *Exports and Imports by Country (July 1010)*

2010年07月进出口商品主要国别（地区）总值表
July 2010 Whole Country Import and Export Table By Country

单位：千美元 Units: USD1000s

进口原产国（地）Imports From 出口最终目的国（地）Exports To	进出口 Exports and Imports		出口 Exports		进口 Imports		累计同比（±%） Year to Date %		
	当月 Current month	1至当月累计 Year to Date Total Value	当月 Current month	1至当月累计 Year to Date Total Value	当月 Current month	1至当月累计 Year to Date Total Value	进出口 Export and Imports	出口 Exports	进口 Imports
总值 Total Value	262,308,256	1,617,047,178	145,519,322	850,489,914	116,788,934	766,557,264	40.9	35.6	47.2
其中：香港 HongKong	19,883,847	118,999,674	18,998,146	112,514,173	885,728	6,485,502	34.2	33.8	42.2
印度 India	5,058,167	35,462,345	3,685,927	22,143,451	1,372,240	13,318,894	51.6	40.1	75.3
日本 Japan	25,213,037	161,705,210	10,047,510	64,145,985	15,165,527	96,559,224	34.9	24.7	42.8
韩国 Korea	17,937,243	115,833,972	6,042,675	38,456,458	11,894,568	77,377,514	42.6	36.5	45.8
台湾 Taiwan	12,538,608	81,912,826	2,614,010	16,264,354	9,924,598	65,648,472	55.9	62.6	54.3
东南亚国家联盟 ASEAN	24,507,961	161,002,465	12,142,203	76,735,896	12,365,758	84,266,569	49.6	43.2	56.1
其中：印度尼西亚 Indonesia	3,697,819	23,212,829	2,163,107	11,998,164	1,534,712	11,214,665	60.8	60.8	60.7
[…]									
欧洲联盟 EU	43,789,386	263,155,472	28,673,916	169,366,907	15,115,471	93,788,565	36.6	36.4	36.9
其中：英国 UK	4,544,683	26,635,676	3,546,777	20,537,204	997,907	6,098,472	32.1	28.6	45.5
德国 Germany	12,774,001	78,030,554	6,348,874	37,046,944	6,425,127	40,983,610	40.9	42.5	39.5
法国 France	4,184,417	25,516,615	2,384,294	15,607,564	1,800,122	9,909,051	38.9	38.5	39.5
[…]									
俄罗斯联邦 Russia	5,007,677	30,704,415	3,212,391	15,008,768	1,795,286	15,695,648	49.6	70.7	33.7
南非 South Africa	2,234,570	13,045,249	975,152	5,766,026	1,259,418	7,279,223	56.2	50.9	60.7
巴西 Brazil	6,127,833	32,509,907	2,600,809	12,917,054	3,527,024	19,592,853	54.6	102.1	33.9
加拿大 Canada	3,524,737	20,191,630	2,285,235	12,218,967	1,239,502	7,972,663	23.7	27.8	18.0
美国 US	35,269,750	207,230,861	27,350,019	151,840,139	7,919,731	55,390,722	30.6	29.4	34.0
澳大利亚 Australia	8,209,653	46,141,163	2,478,732	14,156,467	5,730,921	31,984,697	46.3	36.4	51.1
新西兰 New Zealand	606,192	3,662,564	263,390	1,418,262	342,801	2,244,302	46.6	29.9	59.4

Source: Adapted from General Administration of Customs

Finally, the Customs data provides a breakdown of trade by country, shown in Table 5.5. The country breakdown explains a lot about the focus in the United States on the iniquities of China's exchange rate regime. In 2008, China's trade surplus with the world was almost USD300 billion, and its trade surplus with the United States was USD170 billion. In 2009, China's trade surplus with the world collapsed to less than USD200 billion, but the bilateral surplus with the United States remained robust, at USD143 billion. The cruel reality for Washington, D.C., is that demand for the kind of consumer basics that U.S. households buy from China is inelastic. Whatever the weather or the economic climate, U.S. households will always be shopping at Walmart, and that means they will always be buying goods made in China. In contrast, even when China's imports boom, as they did in 2009, the commodity exporters in Australia and Brazil, not the creaking manufacturers of the U.S. rust belt, are the main beneficiaries. The country data tells the tale of China's surplus with the United States and Europe; its complex interrelationship with its East Asian neighbors; and its dependence on the commodity exports of Saudi Arabia, Australia, and Brazil.

Market Impact

Equities: Exports are a key driver of growth in the Chinese economy, and a high number for exports is also an indicator that global demand is robust. Strong growth in exports is positive not just for domestic markets, but also for global equities markets. Beyond the headline data, equity investors dig into the detail to see what is happening at a country and sector level.

Commodities: A strong import number often reflects robust demand for raw materials, a bullish signal for commodities markets. Commodity investors also dig into the detail to see what is happening to China's imports of oil, iron ore, copper, and soybeans.

Currency: The trade surplus is the focus of attention for international critics of China's exchange rate regime. An expanding surplus is a ratchet that Washington, D.C., can use to increase the pressure on Beijing to allow more rapid appreciation. A contracting surplus supports the argument from Beijing that there is no fundamental misalignment in the exchange rate. The trade data also has implications for broader currency markets, with a strong set of import numbers a positive for commodity currencies such as the Australian dollar and proxies for China's growth in the Korean won and Singapore dollar.

U.S. IMPORT PRICE INDEX

Market sensitivity: Low

What is it? Measure of change in the price of U.S. imports from China, indexed to 100 in December 2003

Chinese news release on the Internet: n/a

English news release on the Internet: www.bls.gov

Release time: 8:30 a.m. Eastern Standard Time (EST) around the middle of the following month

Frequency: Monthly

Source: U.S. Bureau of Labor Statistics (BLS)

Revisions: Monthly releases can contain revisions and corrections stretching back 3 months

Why Is It Important?

In the period from July 2005, when the People's Bank of China (PBOC) announced the beginning of yuan appreciation, to August 2008, when the global financial crisis brought that appreciation grinding to a halt, the yuan gained 21% against the dollar. A higher value for the yuan was meant to make Chinese exports more expensive to U.S. consumers and make U.S. exports cheaper to Chinese households. The result should have been a more equal trade relationship, with China enjoying a smaller surplus and the United States laboring under a smaller deficit. U.S. exports to China certainly grew, rising from USD48 billion in 2005 to USD81 billion in 2008. But they did not grow as fast as China's exports to the United States, which exploded from USD162 billion to USD252 billion during the same period. With U.S. export growth playing Mark Hazinksi (U.S. top-ranked table tennis player, world ranking #427) to China's Ma Lin (China's top-ranked table tennis player, world ranking #1), China's trade surplus with the United States grew from USD114 billion in 2005 to more than USD170 billion in 2008.

How could the trade balance have moved further in China's favor even as the appreciation of the yuan cut the competitiveness of China's exporters? The answer is that the exchange rate is only one factor at work in determining the competitiveness of China's exports. With many different influences at work, the number that captures the changing competitiveness of China's export sector isn't the exchange rate, but the change in the actual price of export goods. Happily, it is not necessary to take a clipboard down to the docks at Shanghai to keep track of the price of goods as they are loaded onto the boat. The U.S. BLS is there already, clipboard in hand, and the results of their work are published in the monthly index of import prices.

How Is the Data Calculated?

Every month, the BLS collects data on import and export prices of more than 20,000 products from more than 6,000 companies. The China index, which is one of several indexes covering different products and trade partners, is based on a subset of around 3,500 to 3,750 of these products.

Weights of products in the index are based on dollar value of imports from China. That means a high weight for computers, electronic appliances, machinery, clothing, and other manufactured goods. The weights of products in the index are recalculated in January every year based on trade data from 2 years ago, so index weights in 2010 reflect trade weights in 2008.

Import prices are normally reported on a "free on board" (f.o.b.) basis, reflecting the value of imports at the port in China. This means that the prices do not include either the cost of transport, which can be quite volatile, or the margin added by wholesalers or retailers when the product reaches the United States. The index is based on prices in December 2003.

Interpreting the Data

Table 5.6 *U.S Import Price Index (September 2010)*

Description	Percent of U.S imports	Index				Percentage Change				
		June 2010	July 2010	Aug. 2010	Sept. 2010	Annual	Monthly			
						Sept. 2009 to Sept. 2010	May to June 2010	June to July 2010	July to Aug. 2010	Aug. to Sept. 2010
[...] China (Dec. 2003=100)	16.449	100.4	100.5	100.5	100.3	-0.2	-0.2	0.1	0.0	-0.2

Source: Adapted from BLS

The data shows the change in the price of a representative basket of U.S. imports from China. In Table 5.6, which covers the 4 months to September 2010, the data shows the price of U.S. imports from China down 0.2% on a YoY and MoM basis. At first sight, that fall in import prices presents something of a puzzle. In September 2010, the pace of yuan appreciation picked up considerably, with the Chinese currency gaining more than 1.5% against the dollar over the course of the month. The fact that import prices continued to fall points to an inconvenient truth for the United States: The pass-through of movements in the exchange rate to movements in the import prices is incomplete. As Figure 5.1 shows, movements in the exchange rate are not reflected immediately, and never reflected fully, in movements in import prices.

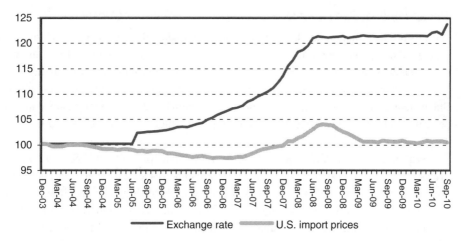

Source: BLS, China Foreign Exchange Trading Center, author's calculations

Figure 5.1 *Yuan–dollar exchange rate versus U.S. import prices from China (Index: Dec 2003–100)*

Appreciation of the yuan against the dollar began in July 2005. But not until August 2007 did U.S. import prices from China rise above their July 2005 level. By August 2008, when appreciation had come grinding to a crisis-induced halt, the cost of China's exports to the United States had risen just more than 5%. What explains the extraordinary stability of China's export prices, in the teeth of sharp yuan appreciation? One reason is that China exports mainly finished goods, and the price of finished goods is inherently more stable than the price of raw materials. Japan also exports mainly finished goods to the United States, and the BLS data shows that the price of imports from Japan is also stable, despite wide fluctuations in the dollar–yen exchange rate.

But the stability in the price of imports from China demands further explanation. A continued low cost for labor and capital, improvements in productivity that enabled firms to do more with less, and a willingness to accept lower margins to protect market share are all part of the picture. These factors conspired to delay and curtail the pass-through of a more expensive yuan to more expensive export prices. For the currency boosters on Washington, D.C.'s Capitol Hill and the workers in the industries of the U.S. rust belt, the depressing reality is that even if the yuan rises further, the impact on the competitiveness of China's exports will be limited.

Cheap Imports: Bad News for Producers, Good News for Consumers

With its producer hat on, the United States sees an undervalued yuan as an evil that bankrupts U.S. companies and forces U.S. workers into unemployment. One of the submissions to a 2010 hearing of the House Ways and Means Committee hearing on the exchange rate described China's currency manipulation as a worse attack on the United States than Pearl Harbor. But when it dons its consumer hat, the United States enjoys the benefits of cheap Chinese electronics, clothing, and other goods on sale at Walmart, Target, and Kmart.

With imports from China accounting for more than 16% of total U.S. imports, low prices are not just a boon for consumers—they also help keep inflationary pressure under control. Since December 2003, when the BLS started publishing its index, the price of U.S. imports as a whole has risen more than 30%, compared to an increase of less than 1% in the cost of imports from China. Limited changes in the price of imports from China is a countervailing force that helps contain inflationary pressure from higher-cost imports of oil and other raw materials. But this cannot be relied on forever. If yuan appreciation and higher input costs for Chinese firms erode the competitiveness of China's exports, the flip side of that process is a more expensive shopping basket for U.S. consumers and higher levels of imported inflationary pressure.

Market Impact

This is more a data point to muse over than trade on. The main interest so far has been in the limited pass-through from movements in the exchange rate to prices. Over time, a more expensive yuan and higher costs for labor and capital might have a more marked impact, with implications for the competitiveness of China's export sector and for inflation in the United States.

FOREIGN DIRECT INVESTMENT

Market sensitivity: Medium
What is it? Data on the inflows and outflows of direct investment, published in current USD100 millions and nominal YoY % for the current month and year-to-date
Chinese news release on the Internet: www.mofcom.gov.cn/
English news release on the Internet: http://english.mofcom.gov.cn/
Release time: Normally the 15th day of the following month
Frequency: Monthly
Source: Ministry of Commerce (MOFCOM)
Revisions: No

Why Is It Important?

In the early days of the reform era, China was hungry for foreign capital and expertise. At the same time, foreign investors wanted to benefit from China's low production costs and get a foot in the door of China's massive domestic market. The solution was obvious, and when Deng Xiaoping instituted the famous open door policy the result was a torrent of inbound foreign direct investment (FDI). At its peak in the mid-1990s, FDI accounted for around 11% of total Chinese investment spending and played a crucial part in establishing a modern industrial base. Any sector you care to name benefited from an influx of foreign capital and expertise. From the Hong Kong-owned textile sweatshops that line the coast of Guangdong, to Volkswagen's partnership with Shanghai Automotive Industry to build China's iconic taxi cabs, and Morgan Stanley's partnership with China Construction Bank to form China's first investment bank, foreign firms and foreign capital have a foundational role in China's development story.

More than 30 years later, the door for foreign investors remains open. But with Chinese firms now in possession of the resources and the expertise to run the show themselves, the welcome mat is no longer rolled out with quite the same degree of enthusiasm. In 2008, a series of new laws and regulations equalized the tax rates for foreign-invested and domestic enterprises, introduced strict new protections for workers rights, and added more sectors to the list that is off-limits to foreign investment. For foreign investors, the dream of tapping the demand of China's 1.3 billion customers remains. A change to the rules to allow foreign firms to set up shop on their own, free from the old joint venture straitjacket, has also been welcomed. But with higher regulatory barriers to jump over, less favorable tax treatment, and higher costs for labor, the dream has lost a lot of its luster. Throw in the usual problems dealing with China's complex and opaque bureaucracy, and it was enough for the CEO of General Electric to wonder whether the Chinese government wanted foreign firms to make any money on the mainland at all. With the door swinging closed, FDI as a share of total investment fell from a peak of around 11% in the mid-1990s to less than 2% in 2009.

The same abundance of domestic capital that has made foreign investors surplus to requirements has also left China's homegrown enterprises flush with funds and ready to spend overseas. The financial crisis has cast once-mighty corporations in the United States and Europe in the role of damsels in distress, with Chinese firms as white-knight investors ready to ride a wave of capital to the rescue. The white knight might have bumped into a few villains along the way. Audacious bids by Aluminum Corporation of China for a share in Australian mining giant Rio Tinto, and Huawei for U.S. networking company 3Com ran into tough political opposition. But a string of smaller acquisitions testifies to the strength of Chinese investors and their interest in acquiring the natural resources, technology, and brand names they need to fuel the next stage of China's development. As Figure 5.2 shows, the door to inbound investment might be swinging slowly closed, but the door to outbound investment is now firmly open.

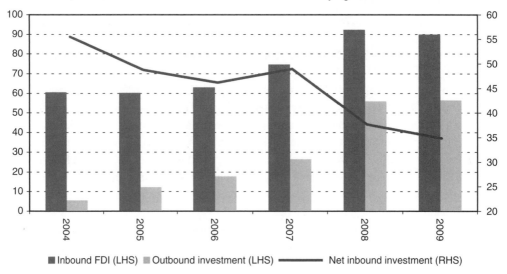

■ Inbound FDI (LHS) ■ Outbound investment (LHS) ▬▬▬ Net inbound investment (RHS)

Source: MOFCOM, NBS, author's calculations

Figure 5.2 *Inbound versus outbound investment (USD, billions)*

How Is the Data Calculated?

Responsibility for collecting and publishing China's monthly FDI data falls to the MOFCOM, which relies in part on data provided by provincial governments. According to the Organization for Economic Cooperation and Development (OECD), FDI should be measured as soon as there is a 10% foreign stake in a project. In China, the threshold to begin counting FDI is a 25% foreign stake. That starting point means the Chinese data understates the level of FDI that would be captured if the international standard was used.

In addition to the higher-than-usual threshold, three problems make collecting accurate FDI data rather complicated and suggest that the MOFCOM data should be taken with a grain of salt:

- Local governments in China have a well-known propensity for playing fast and loose with the statistical truth. With inbound investment a key metric by which the success of local officials is judged, governments have an obvious incentive to exaggerate the real level of investment. This was a particularly serious problem before 2006, when MOFCOM reported "contracted" FDI as well as "utilized" FDI. Contracted FDI numbers were often grossly exaggerated and bore little relation to the reality. From 2007 on, MOFCOM publishes only utilized FDI numbers, reducing some of the scope for local exaggeration.

- The majority of FDI goes to genuine investment projects. But a substantial share is actually disguised speculative inflows. For speculators who want to place a bet on the mainland's bubbly real estate and equity markets, and make a few percent from yuan appreciation along the way, FDI projects are an obvious cover for moving funds into and out of the country. It is impossible to differentiate between genuine FDI and inflows of speculative capital.

- Until a change to the law in 2008, foreign-invested enterprises benefited from a lower tax rate than domestic enterprises. That meant domestic investors had an incentive to take their capital offshore and then bring it back disguised as foreign capital so their investment could benefit from the tax break. It's unclear how much of this round-tripping went on—and how much still goes on after the tax rates for foreign and domestic firms were equalized. But the large volumes of capital flowing in from Hong Kong, which accounts for almost 50% of total FDI in some years, and from offshore financial centers such as the Virgin Islands suggests that a fair chunk of FDI is actually just domestic investment back from a vacation. A 2004 study by the Asian Development Bank estimated round-tripping at 30% to 50% of total FDI.

The State Administration of Foreign Exchange (SAFE) publishes an alternate set of FDI data in its balance of payments report. The SAFE data is based on a broader definition of FDI and also benefits from use of records of actual capital flow into and out of the country (instead of reports from local governments) as the basis of its data. That means there's less scope for local exaggeration to impact the numbers. The gap between the MOFCOM and the SAFE numbers can be substantial. In 2008, the MOFCOM data shows USD92.3 billion in FDI. In the same year, SAFE recorded USD147 billion in inflows. The SAFE data certainly wins on accuracy, but it loses on timeliness: The MOFCOM data is available every month. The balance of payments report appears once a quarter.

Interpreting the Data

The data appears on the MOFCOM website in two different statements. One deals with inward investment, and the other deals with outward investment. The statement dealing with inward investment is slightly more detailed, including the number of inbound investment projects, the total value of inbound investment, and a breakdown of investment by continent and country of origin.

Inbound Investment

The level of FDI says a lot about the strength of investor sentiment. A high number means that investors see opportunities to earn a buck, either in the long term with a genuine project or in the short term by making a bet on yuan appreciation or a run on the equity or property markets. A low number may mean that investors have a dim outlook on the Chinese economy. It is difficult to know what percentage of inflows represents speculative capital instead of long-term investment. But with the property sector a focus for investors looking to make a quick profit, investment in the real estate sector might be a decent proxy. In 2009, FDI targeted at the real estate sector amounted to USD16 billion, or 18% of the total.

The monthly data is valuable for what it says about investor sentiment, but it also needs to be treated with caution. A major project one month can lead to a surge in FDI that disappears completely if there are no major projects in the next month. YoY growth in FDI was down 2% in September 2007. Four months later, in January 2008, it was up more than 100%. By February, it had fallen back to 38% growth. That doesn't mean that investor sentiment was swinging wildly from freezing cold to raging hot and back to lukewarm, all in a five-month period. It means that investment projects are lumpy and are not evenly distributed across months. Looking at several months of data to get a sense of the trend, instead of reading too much into sharp rises or precipitate plummets in FDI in individual months, makes a lot of sense.

Outbound Investment

The statement on outward flows is shorter and simply mentions the number of countries and projects in which Chinese firms have invested overseas, as well as the total value of investment in the year so far. As with the inbound figures, the outbound figures are lumpy; viewing several months of data together gives a better sense of the trend. For a breakdown of outbound investment by country and sector, investors have to wait for the annual data. The annual sector breakdown shows that raw materials and financials have so far been the major focus of China's investment.

Market Impact

Equities: Inbound FDI is now too small a part of total investment spending to impact the growth trajectory of the economy. But the FDI data remains important as a gauge of international investors' views. Hot money flows disguised as FDI can also give an upward boost to equity markets on the way in and a downward blow on the way out.

Commodities: Strong FDI inflows is a bullish sign for the Chinese economy and can also signal positive investor sentiment on the property sector, both good news for commodities. But the relationship between the FDI data and commodities prices is not a strong one.

Currency: With an unknown but substantial proportion of FDI disguised as hot money inflows, and even genuine investments influenced by the outlook for yuan appreciation, a strong reading for inward FDI suggests that investors have a bullish outlook for the yuan.

BALANCE OF PAYMENTS

Market sensitivity: Medium
What is it? Measure of China's international trade and capital flows, published in current USD100 millions
Chinese news release on the Internet: www.safe.gov.cn/model_safe/index.html
English news release on the Internet: www.safe.gov.cn/model_safe_en
Release time: Initial release around 6 weeks after the end of the quarter, final data released several months later.
Frequency: Semiannually until 2009; quarterly from 2010 on
Source: State Administration of Foreign Exchange (SAFE)
Revisions: Substantial revisions from the initial estimate to the final release, historical revisions on the basis of changes to methodology

Why Is It Important?

The balance of payments report is a comprehensive record of all of China's transactions with the rest of the world. If it is traded, invested, or transferred across China's border, it should be in the report. With trade and investment flows both grossly one-sided, the balance of payments report has become home to one of the most controversial numbers in world politics: China's current account surplus.

How Is the Data Calculated?

SAFE is in the lead in compiling the balance of payments report and follows the international standard approach set out in the International Monetary Fund's (IMF) *Balance of Payments Manual*. Data comes from a combination of other government departments, SAFE's own transaction recording system (which is based on data collected from banks), and, for some items, sample surveys.

The largest part of the current account reflects trade in goods. Data for this part of the report comes from the Customs Bureau's records. The slight difference is that the Customs Bureau measures the value of exports on an f.o.b. basis and imports on a "cost, insurance, freight" (c.i.f.) basis. SAFE measures both imports and exports on an f.o.b. basis. Before crying foul, it's worth noting that f.o.b. actually gives a lower value to imports than c.i.f. (because it excludes the cost of insurance and freight), so the SAFE approach records a larger current account surplus than the Customs approach.

SAFE's calculations are subject to revisions, which can be substantial. SAFE's initial data on 2009 put the current account surplus at 5.8% of GDP, down considerably from 9.6% in 2008 but still meaty enough. It was not until 2011 that SAFE quietly announced a revision of the 2009 surplus down to 5.2% of GDP, based on a change in the accounting treatment of companies' retained earnings. That change might be legitimate and based on an improvement in SAFE's methodology, but cynics noted that it was convenient that the technical improvement had the effect of reducing the current account surplus for the year—and indeed all the historical data back to 2005—at a time when China was under pressure to bring its account with the rest of the world into balance.

Interpreting the Data

Table 5.7 *Balance of Payments Report (2009)*

中 国 国 际 收 支 平 衡 表 China International Balance of Payments

2009年 **2009**

单位:亿美元 **Units, USD100mlns**

	项 目 Item	行次 Number	差额 Net Position	贷 方 Credit	借 方 Debit
1▶	一. 经常项目 Current Account	1	2,971	14,846	11,874
	A.货物和服务 Goods and services	2	2,201	13,333	11,132
2▶	a.货物 Goods	3	2,495	12,038	9,543
3▶	b. 服务 Services	4	-294	1,295	1,589
	[...]				
4▶	B.收益 Income	18	433	1,086	653
	1.职工报酬 Compensation of employees	19	72	92	21
	2.投资收益 Investment income	20	361	994	632
	C. 经常转移 Current transfers	21	337	426	89
	1.各级政府 General government	22	-2	0	3
	2.其它部门 Other sectors	23	340	426	86
	二.资本和金融项目 Capital and financial account	24	1,448	7,464	6,016
	A. 资本项目 Capital account	25	40	42	2
	B. 金融项目 Financial account	26	1,409	7,422	6,014
5▶	1. 直接投资 Direct investment	27	343	1,142	799
	1.1 我国在外直接投资 Outward investment	28	-439	42	481
	1.2 外国在华直接投资 Inward investment	29	782	1,100	318
	2. 证券投资 Portfolio investment	30	387	981	594
	[...]				
	3. 其它投资 Other investment	41	679	5,299	4,620
	[...]				
	三. 储备资产 Reserve assets	64	-3,984	0	3,984
	3.1 货币黄金 Monetary gold	65	-49	0	49
	3.2 特别提款权 Special drawing rights	66	-111	0	111
	3.3 在基金组织的储备头寸 Reserve position in the International Monetary Fund	67	-4	0	4
6▶	3.4 外汇 Foreign exchange	68	-3,821	0	3,821
	3.5 其它债权 Other claims	69	0	0	0
7▶	四.净 误差与遗 漏 Errors and omissions	70	-435	0	435

Source: Adapted from SAFE

1. Why is China's current account surplus the cause of so much controversy and resent-
ment? The macroeconomics textbooks define GDP as the sum of domestic consumption, investment, and net exports—with the last item approximating the current
account. A current account surplus in one country has to be matched by a deficit in
another. If China is enjoying a surplus, that can only be because some other country is
suffering a deficit. Stated simply, China's current account surplus adds to China's own
GDP, but only at the expense of subtracting from GDP in the rest of the world.

   In 2001, the year China joined the WTO, China's GDP was an insignificant fraction of
the global total and, as Figure 5.3 shows, China's current account surplus came in at an
inoffensive 1.3% of GDP. By 2007, China had burst into the top 5 in the global economic rankings and the current account surplus had ballooned in size to 10.1% of
GDP. In a discussion in the U.S. Senate in 2010 on a proposal for legislation aimed at
China's exchange rate regime, one outspoken senator accused Beijing of "international
banditry" that had cost the United States 2.3 million jobs. If the current account surplus represents demand stolen from the rest of the world, in the space of a few short
years, China moved from a little light pick-pocketing to grand larceny.

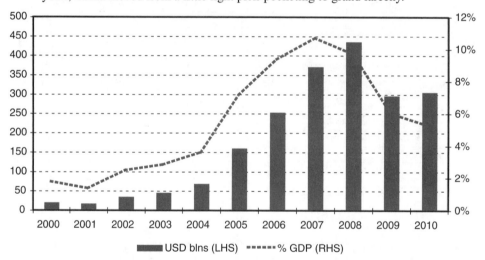

Source: SAFE, IMF, author's calculations

Figure 5.3 *Current account surplus: absolute value and percentage of GDP*

In Table 5.7, the data for 2009 shows the current account surplus coming in at
USD297.1 billion, or 5.8% of GDP. (It was later revised down to USD261 billion and
5.2% of GDP as a result of a change in SAFE's methodology.) A substantially smaller
surplus as a percentage of GDP in 2009 than in the years before the financial crisis
reflects two factors. First, a sharp contraction in global demand as a result of the crisis
meant China's exports collapsed. Second, an investment-led domestic stimulus meant
China's imports of raw materials and machinery surged. Lower exports and higher
imports naturally resulted in a contraction of the surplus.

As the world economy shifts out of crisis mode, the question puzzling policy makers is what happens next? According to the financial crime squad in Washington, D.C., China has shown no sign of a reformed character. The IMF believes that with the effect of China's stimulus fading, global demand back on an even keel, and the yuan still significantly undervalued, the current account surplus will rebound to around 8% by the middle of the decade. The government in Beijing swears that it has turned over a new leaf and that the surplus will sink back to around 4% of GDP, with no need for major policy adjustment. The balance of payments report will show who is right.

2. China's reputation as the factory of the world is well deserved. Almost the entire current account surplus comes from trade in goods. Mobile phones, computers, televisions, cars, tools, furniture, clothes, toys, and shoes manufactured or assembled along China's east coast and shipped through the ports of Shanghai, Shenzhen, and Ningbo to Europe and the United States account for the bulk of the action.

3. When China joined the WTO, other members were resigned to the fact that the mainland's manufacturers would take a larger share of global goods markets. But governments in the United States and Europe reasoned that their own business sector would make up some of the difference with a competitive advantage in the services. China's balance of payments report shows that they were half right. China does have a deficit in its services account. But the services deficit is tiny compared to the size of surplus China enjoys in the goods account. In Table 5.7, the 2009 data shows a surplus of USD249.5 billion on the goods account and a deficit of just USD29.4 billion on the services account. One reason is that services are inherently harder to trade than goods: Few people buy haircuts from overseas. But another reason is that in the financial, telecom, and logistics sectors, where foreign firms have a competitive advantage, the door to the mainland's markets has been kept firmly closed.

4. Definitely second fiddle to trade, but still an important part of the current account, is the income account. The income account is divided into income from foreign investments and income from wages earned overseas, with by far the largest contribution coming from the investment side. Income on foreign investments has grown with China's Foreign Exchange (FX) reserves, and SAFE has acknowledged that the famous stash— which grew to more than USD3 trillion in the first quarter of 2011— is the main source of foreign investment income. Putting together the data on investment income and the size of China's FX reserves, it is possible to make a rough calculation of the return SAFE receives on its investments. In 2009, China earned USD99.4 billion in income on its foreign investments. FX reserves at the end of 2008 were USD1.9 trillion. If most of that income came from interest payments on China's FX reserves, that suggests SAFE is earning about 5% return on investment—a number that is probably at the high end of the range of possibilities.

5. The capital and financial account is where flows of portfolio and direct investment appear. In the United States, this would be a lively category, with tens of billions of dollars of capital flows moving in and out of the country every quarter. In China, the

lessons of the Mexican peso crisis in 1994 and the Asian financial crisis in 1997 continue to die hard. In 1997 in particular, China's leaders saw governments in neighboring countries brought to their knees by sudden and destabilizing outflows of foreign capital. The same kind of thing could not be allowed to happen to them.

The mainland's capital account is not completely closed. Households, enterprises, and investors can all move capital in and out of the country, with a certain amount of difficulty. The government's push to make the yuan an international currency may result in accelerated moves toward capital account convertibility. The effectiveness of the controls that remain is also open to question, with the trade and direct investment channels widely abused to bring speculative capital in and out of the country. But despite incremental moves toward opening the capital account and imperfections in the existing controls, flows of portfolio investment remain extremely limited. For now, the main transactions to show up in the capital account are direct investments.

6. The current account surplus is not the only controversial number in the balance of payments report. The report also includes data on exhibit B in the case against the exchange rate: China's FX reserves. Data on the headline growth in FX reserves is actually published by the PBOC before the balance of payments report is available. So what is the added value in the balance of payments report? To answer that question, we need to take a detour in the accounting methods for China's FX reserves.

The value of China's FX reserves can change in two ways. Either SAFE can engage in transactions, buying or selling assets to add or subtract to the value of reserves, or movements in markets and exchange rates can change the value of assets SAFE already holds. The PBOC figure on total FX reserves includes the contribution of both transactions and valuation changes, without distinguishing between the two. From the beginning of 2010, SAFE's balance of payments report includes the change in the value of FX reserves from transactions, without including the impact of movements in market value and exchange rate. As Figure 5.4 shows, the two numbers can be quite different.

Table 5.7 shows that, in 2009, transactions added USD382.1 billion to the value of China's FX reserves. That contrasts with the PBOC data, which shows China's FX reserves growing USD449.0 billion over the same period. The difference between the two figures means that valuation adjustments from movements in exchange rates and market prices must have added USD66.9 billion to the value of China's FX reserves (USD449.0 billion – USD382.1 billion = USD66.9 billion). That makes some sense. The dollar fell against the euro over the course of 2009, so exchange rate movements would have added slightly to the dollar value of China's euro-denominated reserves.

All this is rather arcane. But knowing how much of FX reserve growth is due to transactions and how much is due to valuation adjustments is rather useful. SAFE is a major player in the U.S. Treasury and other sovereign debt markets. Investors in these markets want to know how much money SAFE is throwing around. That means looking at the change in reserves from transactions, not the addition or subtraction from valuation adjustments. Knowing how much of the change in reserves came from valuation adjustments also helps analysts with one of their favorite parlor games:

guessing the currency composition of SAFE's stash. This can get pretty complicated, but in brief, higher valuation adjustments imply that a large portion must be invested in riskier asset classes and nondollar assets (because these are the assets whose dollar value would be most affected by movements in markets and exchange rates); lower adjustments suggest that the share of investment allocated to dollar-denominated sovereign debt is larger.

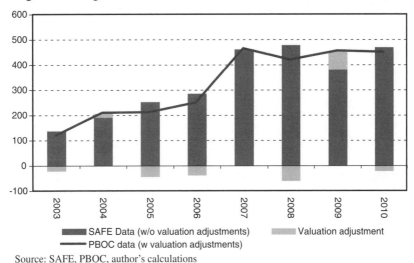

Source: SAFE, PBOC, author's calculations

Figure 5.4   *FX reserve growth: SAFE versus PBOC data (USD billions)*

7. The final entry in the balance of payments report is errors and omissions. The value of errors and omissions can be substantial, and some analysts believe it is here that SAFE accounts for hot money inflows. Given what we know about the motivations of investors, the pattern of hot money flows suggested by the errors and omissions category makes some sense. Positive errors and omissions in 2007 and the first half of 2008 suggested capital inflows as investors aimed to benefit from rapid appreciation of the yuan and the sharp rise in the mainland's equity and property markets. A shift to negative errors and omissions in the second half of 2008 suggested capital outflows—which makes sense given the collapse of Lehman Brothers and the descent of the U.S. financial system into crisis. Table 5.7 shows errors and omissions staying negative in 2009—outflows continued, but much less negative than in 2008—as the recovery gathered pace and international capital renewed its interest in the Chinese economy.

Market Impact

The balance of payments report comes out too late, and with too little new information, to move equity or commodity markets. But the size of the current account surplus has become a key factor shaping the debate on the exchange rate, so currency markets pay close attention.

FOREIGN EXCHANGE AND GOLD RESERVES

Market sensitivity: Medium
What is it? Quarterly report on change in China's FX reserves (current USD100 millions) and holdings of gold (10,000 troy ounces)
Chinese news release on the Internet: www.pbc.gov.cn
English news release on the Internet: www.pbc.gov.cn/publish/english/963/index.html
Release time: Between the 10th and the 15th of the first month of the following quarter
Frequency: Quarterly
Source: PBOC
Revisions: No

Why Is It Important?

How much FX reserves does China need? Enough to cover the cost of imports for a few months? Enough to provide Chinese firms with the foreign currency they need to finance overseas acquisitions? Enough to provide a buffer against financial turmoil and speculative attacks on the exchange rate regime? Against any of these criteria, FX reserves above the USD3 trillion mark at the beginning of 2011 are surplus to requirements. China's FX reserves could cover the total cost of imports for two and a half years. They could pay back every foreign dollar invested in China in the reform era. They could buy a substantial chunk of the Fortune 500. China's closed capital account is already proof against speculative attacks of the sort that brought Indonesia, Thailand, and South Korea to their knees in the Asian Financial Crisis. But even if it were not, the world's largest FX reserves would prove a formidable deterrent.

The irony of China's massive accumulation of FX reserves is that it has occurred more by accident than design. Throughout the reform era, China has pursued an export-driven growth strategy. As part of that strategy, Beijing has maintained the value of the yuan at an artificially low level relative to the dollar, using the exchange rate to support the competitiveness of China's exports. But maintaining a stable exchange rate in the face of a burgeoning current account surplus requires continuous intervention in FX markets. The change in China's FX reserves maps closely to the change in China's current account surplus, and this is no accident. Only by buying up the proceeds of the surplus at their target exchange rate can China keep the yuan from appreciating. The dollars that the PBOC buys in FX markets are the basis of China's FX reserves. But the export-driven growth strategy and political resistance to change, not some desire to build up a massive store of foreign assets, is the driving force behind China's accumulation of reserves.

How Is the Data Calculated?

To calculate the value of FX reserves, SAFE uses the method set out in the IMF's *Balance of Payments Manual*. But the adoption of international standards has not done much to improve transparency, and as with much about China's FX reserves, the exact calculation method is shrouded in secrecy. Determining the value of additions or subtractions to FX reserves from transactions is relatively straightforward. If SAFE buys USD10 billion in U.S. Treasuries, that adds USD10 billion to the value of reserves. The main question is the approach SAFE takes to making valuation adjustments from movements in the market value of reserve assets and the impact of movements in exchange rates.

On the exchange rate issue, the PBOC reports the value of FX reserves in dollars, but reserves are held in a variety of currencies. That means movement in exchange rates should affect the dollar value of reserves. Let's assume for simplicity that 70% of China's FX reserves are held in dollar assets, and the remaining 30% are held in euro assets. Say the dollar appreciates 10% against the euro; the dollar value of the euro-denominated portion of reserves should go down by 10%. That means the overall dollar value of reserves should fall by 3% ($-10\% \times 30\% = -3\%$). Conversely, if the dollar falls against the euro by 10%, that should add 3% to the total dollar value of its reserves. Without knowing the exact currency composition of the reserves, it is impossible to know whether SAFE is making systematic adjustments for movements in exchange rates, but most analysts assume they are.

On the market value issue, the value of an asset today is not necessarily the same as its value when it was purchased. A private investment fund reporting on the current value of its portfolio would "mark to market"—that is, it would report the current market value of its investments, not their value at the time they were made. SAFE claims that it also follows this practice, at least for the trading part of its portfolio. Exactly what practice SAFE is using is not clear. Given what is known about the composition of China's FX reserves, if they are marking the value of all their investments to market, some of the numbers make little sense. One way out of the complexity is to assume that SAFE has a small trading portfolio consisting of equities and higher risk assets and that this portion of its portfolio is being marked to market. The larger part of the reserves composed of U.S. Treasuries and other sovereign debt is not traded, so SAFE does not feel an obligation to mark to market. This explanation fits with SAFE's data on the extent and direction of valuation adjustments in 2008 and 2009.

Interpreting the Data

Table 5.8 *Gold and Foreign Exchange Reserves (2010)* 黄金和外汇储备

项目 Item	Jan. 2010	Feb. 2010	Mar. 2010	Apr. 2010	May 2010	Jun. 2010	[...]
国家外汇储备（亿美元）							
Foreign Exchange Reserves (100 million USD)	24152.21	24245.91	24470.84	24905.12	24395.06	24542.75	[...]
黄金储备（万盎司）							
Gold (10,000 Fine Troy Ounce)	3389	3389	3389	3389	3389	3389	[...]

Source: Adapted from PBOC

At the most straightforward level, interpreting China's FX reserve data is extremely simple. The PBOC data shows the total value of China's FX reserves, in dollars, at the end of each month. In Table 5.8, at the end of June 2010, China's FX reserves added up to USD2.45 trillion. Going a step further and working out what the data means is more difficult.

For starters, the headline number for FX reserves does not provide the complete picture on how much FX reserves China has accumulated. At the end of 2007, USD200 billion was shaved off China's FX reserves and given to the China Investment Corporation, China's sovereign wealth fund, to play with. "Other foreign assets" on the PBOC balance sheet and foreign currency swaps the PBOC has engaged in with commercial banks are part of China's FX reserves, although they are not included in the official figure. Taken together, as of the end of 2010, these additional sources add several hundred billion dollars to the total.

Next, the official data is completely silent on where China's FX reserves are invested. This is for good reason. When you are managing the world's largest single investment fund, telegraphing your intentions to the markets can make anything you want to buy terribly expensive and anything you want to sell awfully cheap. Hints from SAFE and guesstimates from China-watchers suggest that China's FX reserves are mainly invested in sovereign debt, with around 70% invested in U.S. dollar debt, mainly U.S. Treasuries, 20% in Eurozone debt, 5% in Japanese debt, and the rest in other currencies. At the end of June 2010, the last time for which high-quality data exists, the U.S. Treasury's own data suggests that China holds at least USD1.6 trillion in dollar debt—of which USD1.1 trillion is in Treasuries, and a further USD359 billion in agencies, debt issued by government-sponsored enterprises such as Fannie Mae and Freddie Mac. At the time, that was equal to 65% of China's total FX reserves.

Hot Money Shuffle

FX reserve data provides a means of quantifying one of the most important but least visible factors affecting the Chinese economy: hot money. Hot money is speculative capital that moves in and out of markets in search of super-normal returns. The risk for the host market is that large volumes of capital moving quickly and in tandem can result in speculative bubbles when the capital moves in and spectacular busts when it moves out. Massive outflows of foreign capital was one of the factors that crippled the economies of China's neighbors in the Asian Financial Crisis. For China, a partially closed capital account has drastically reduced the potential for speculative flows to destabilize the economy. But for much of the period between 2005 and 2008, and again from 2010, the possibility of high returns on the mainland's equity and property markets, plus a few extra percent from appreciation of the yuan, was enough of an incentive for investors to circumvent capital controls and sneak hundreds of billions of dollars into the country. Because hot money flows are illegal, they are not recorded and there is no way to measure them with any accuracy. With a little manipulation, however, FX reserve data can offer up a rough estimate.

The basic reasoning—shown graphically in Figure 5.5—is that, after known flows into the FX reserves from the trade surplus, net FDI, interest income, and the impact of valuation adjustments is accounted for, the unexplained remainder must be hot money flows. In May 2010, for example the PBOC data shows FX reserves shrinking by USD51 billion. In the same month, Customs data shows a trade surplus of USD20 billion and MOFCOM data shows net FDI inflows of USD5 billion. The second quarter of 2010 was a tough time for the euro, with the European sovereign debt crisis in full swing. A dip in the value of the euro against the dollar probably knocked about USD30 billion off the dollar value of China's reserves. Interest income of about USD8 billion on existing reserves completes the picture of known and estimated contributions. Adding all that together, known flows into reserves come to USD3 billion. With actual reserves shrinking by USD51 billion, that suggests hot money outflows of around USD54 billion (–USD51 billion – USD3 billion = –USD54 billion).

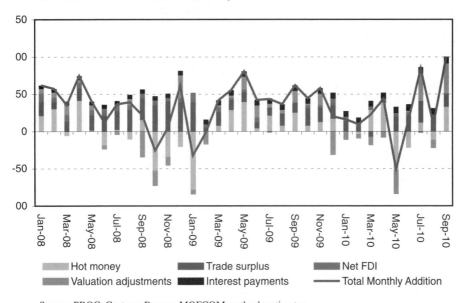

Source: PBOC, Customs Bureau, MOFCOM, author's estimates

Figure 5.5 *Composition and growth of FX reserves (USD billions)*

Why go to all this trouble to guesstimate hot money flows? Hot money flows are a useful indicator of investor sentiment on the Chinese economy. High levels of hot money inflows suggest that investors are bullish, with a positive outlook on China's real estate and equity markets, and expectations of rapid yuan appreciation. Weak capital inflows, or even capital outflows, might reflect a global downturn in risk appetite. For China, it can also mean investors are turning bearish on the real estate and equity markets or that the outlook for yuan appreciation is unfavorable. Hot money flows are also an important variable for the PBOC in setting China's monetary policy. A flood of hot money coming into the country means more liquidity in China's financial system, fueling asset price bubbles and adding to inflationary pressure. Surprise capital outflows can be a drain on liquidity in China's money markets and can cause short-term interest rates to spike. In May 2010, with tens of billions of dollars of speculative capital exiting the country, the interest rate on 7-day loans in China's money markets spiked from 1.6% to 3.2%.

There are problems with using this approach to calculating hot money flows. A part of trade and investment flows—perhaps a large part—is disguised hot money flows. It is common practice for Chinese exporters and their foreign customers to agree to over-invoice for an order as a means of bringing hot money into the country. A portion of the tens of billions of dollars in FDI that flows into China each year is also disguised hot money inflows, destined for the real estate or equity markets. If a part of trade and FDI flows is actually hot money, it makes no sense to subtract the trade surplus and net FDI from the change in FX reserves to arrive at an estimate of hot money inflows. The use of the yuan as a trade settlement currency also complicates the calculation. If importers are paying for their purchases in yuan not dollars, then the addition to FX reserves from trade would be greater than the trade surplus suggests. There are also cross-border flows that are not included in trade or investment, but which do help explain change in reserves without resorting to hot money. In July 2010, USD10 billion in funds from the Hong Kong leg of the Agricultural Bank of China initial public offering (IPO) was brought back into the country, and this, not a sudden surge in hot money, explained a monster USD84 billion addition to reserves.

The approach to estimation is certainly flawed, but it does produce results that make sense, given what we know about the drivers of speculative flows. Sticking with the May 2010 example, in April 2010, the Chinese government cracked down on the real estate sector, the mainland's equity markets were in the doldrums, and expectations for the resumption of yuan appreciation had collapsed. There was little reason to bring funds into China. At the same time, the European sovereign debt crisis resulted in a downturn in global risk appetite, with funds exiting high-risk emerging markets for safer havens. The USD54 billion number for outflows might not be right on the money, but a substantial outflow of capital in May 2010 makes sense.

Gold Bugs Beware

What about China's holdings of gold? Interpreting the data here is a bit more straightforward, but investors should beware one major pitfall. The PBOC publishes data on its holdings of gold every quarter. The snag is that it does not feel obligated to publish information about changes in its holdings on a timely basis. In April 2009, the PBOC announced that its holdings of gold had increased from 19.29 million ounces to 33.89 million ounces, adding more than 75% to the total. Does that mean the PBOC purchased 14 million ounces of gold in April? Probably not. It means that, during the 7 years since it last published a change in the official holdings of gold (December 2002, when it recorded an increase of 3.21 million ounces), the PBOC had at various times purchased more gold but only now decided to tell the world about it. Why so secretive? For the same reason, SAFE is unwilling to tell the world about the composition of its FX reserves: If you have USD3 trillion in your wallet and you tell the world you want to buy gold, gold is going to get very expensive.

Changes in China's holdings of gold have obvious implications for international gold prices. But with the PBOC announcing changes in its holdings at such irregular intervals, and changes in recorded holdings not necessarily signaling current purchases, markets should be leery of interpreting the data as evidence of stronger or weaker demand from China for gold.

Market Impact

Data on FX reserves is published only quarterly and provides a glance in the rear view mirror of China's economy. But that doesn't mean it cannot move the market:

- Monster FX reserves are the most visible sign of the impact of China's continuous and massive interventions in currency markets to maintain the yuan at a stable level. If there is to be a currency war, FX reserves pushing past USD3 trillion hang a target round the neck of China's currency regime. That means the FX reserve data is a focus of attention for the currency markets.

- Information on hot money flows might be dated and imprecise, but it provides an important insight into investors' risk appetites and views on the outlook for both the yuan and the mainland's equity and property markets.

- The PBOC is silent on the composition of China's FX reserves, and for good reason. But in the absence of concrete information, rumor and speculation can move the markets. In May 2010, a story in a major financial newspaper suggesting that SAFE was growing weary of European debt contributed to a sharp fall in the euro. SAFE issued a denial, but not before a 1.5% plunge in the value of the euro against the dollar over the course of a single day following publication of the story.

TREASURY INTERNATIONAL CAPITAL SYSTEM

Market sensitivity: Medium

What is it? Monthly report on cross-border transactions in U.S. securities, published in USD millions

Chinese news release on the Internet: n/a

English news release on the Internet: www.treas.gov/tic/

Release time: 9 a.m. Eastern Standard Time on the 11th business day of each month, with a one and a half month lag

Frequency: Monthly

Source: U.S. Treasury

Revisions: Major revisions to end-of-June totals made once a year, with preliminary results published at the end of the following February

Why Is It Important?

In 2001, the year China joined the WTO, Beijing could lay claim to USD61 billion in U.S. Treasury debt, just 6% of the total held by foreign investors. China was the second-largest foreign holder of U.S. debt, but a long way behind first-place Japan and not a major player in U.S. Treasury markets. Fast-forward to the end of 2008, with the U.S. economy on the brink of collapse and the Obama administration planning the biggest fiscal stimulus in history, and the situation had changed beyond recognition. China had displaced Japan as the U.S. Treasury's biggest single creditor. China's holdings of Treasuries had surged to USD727 billion, equal to 23% of the total held by foreign investors. SAFE, the organization charged with managing China's FX reserves, had become a major player in U.S. Treasury markets.

China's massive accumulation of U.S. Treasury debt is not without controversy. In China, there is growing disagreement over how the national treasure trove should be invested. The irony of a country with average per-capita income of just USD4,000 per year lending hundreds of billions of dollars to a country with an average per-capita income of more than USD46,000 per year has not been lost on China's citizens. Everyone from Beijing taxi drivers to PBOC advisors wonders why FX reserves could not be more profitably invested in gold, land, technology, or other assets that cannot be inflated away by the whirring of the Federal Reserve's printing press. In the United States, China's FX reserves are a fearful symbol of Beijing's growing heft in global affairs and *prime facie* evidence of Beijing's manipulation of the exchange rate. Far from welcoming Chinese investment that keeps the cost of borrowing down, Washington, D.C., worries that Beijing's massive holdings of U.S. Treasury debt provides it with a financial nuclear weapon, with the risk that a sudden sale by China would prompt a collapse in the value of the dollar. That fear might be ill founded, but it is also widespread. In February 2009, when Premier Wen Jiabao hinted that China had other options for the allocation of its FX reserves, the news sent a shock wave through global markets.

As it happened, global markets did not need to worry. SAFE has to find a home for tens of billions of dollars a month in investment. Outside the U.S. Treasury market, precious few are big enough to accommodate that kind of cash. The United States is also China's single largest trade partner. Cutting credit to your best customer is not a good idea. Investment of reserves in dollars also makes sense from the point of view of managing the yuan–dollar exchange rate. A combination of limited alternative investment options, common sense, and self-interest kept the funds flowing across the Pacific. By the end of 2009, China had added another USD167 billion to its stash of Treasuries, taking the total to USD894 billion and retaining its position as the United States' biggest creditor. But Premier Wen's threat was not entirely empty. China might have kept the line of credit open through the financial crisis. But the continual whirring of the Federal Reserve's printing press and additions to the U.S. public debt do not make Treasuries any more attractive. In the last few years, a transfer of USD200 billion from the ultra-conservative SAFE to the free-wheeling China Investment Corporation, the decision by SAFE itself to carve out a chunk of cash for investment in equities and corporate bonds, higher levels of investment in Asian and emerging market debt, and more foreign earnings left in the hands of firms to fund outbound investment, all underline that China has other options for allocating its reserves. The Treasury International Capital (TIC) system provides a means of keeping track of the changing pattern of China's purchases of U.S. securities.

How Is the Data Calculated?

Every month, the U.S. Treasury asks a group of major securities custodians, banks, brokers, and dealers to provide data on cross-border transactions in long-term U.S. securities. (Long-term securities have a maturity of greater than 1 year.) At the same time, the Treasury asks banks to provide data on foreign holdings of short-term securities. It is an impressive and labor-intensive data-collection effort. But it is not perfect, and the results need to be interpreted with caution, especially when it comes to China. In particular, the way the data is collected introduces two important biases:

- The data attributes holdings of U.S. securities to the country where they are held in custody, not to the nationality of the final owner. This custody bias means that if SAFE decided to buy USD10 billion in U.S. Treasuries and hold them with a custodian in London, those Treasuries would show up as an addition to the U.K.'s holdings of Treasuries rather than as an addition to China's holdings.
- The monthly data on transactions in long-term securities attributes holdings to the country where they were purchased rather than the country of ownership. This transaction bias means that if SAFE decided to buy another USD10 billion in U.S. Treasury notes but channeled the purchase through a broker on one of the Caribbean islands, that would show up as an addition to the holdings attributed to the Caribbean, not China.

The result of these biases is that the monthly data consistently understates the actual level of China's purchases of long-term securities and overstates the purchases of major custodian and transaction centers such as the UK, the Caribbean, Belgium, Luxembourg, and Switzerland.

Annual Survey Corrects For Transaction Bias

In addition to its monthly attempt to track securities transactions, the Treasury conducts an annual survey of holdings of long-term securities. By asking custodians, brokers, and other players for an extra level of detail, and collecting data on a security-by-security basis, the annual survey is able to correct for the transaction bias (but not the custodial bias) in the monthly data and provide a more accurate picture of China's total holdings. As Figure 5.6 indicates, the difference in the results is quite striking. In June 2009, the total additions to China's Treasury holdings captured by the monthly survey over the course of the past year suggested that China had purchased just USD241 billion in Treasuries. The annual survey showed that, in fact, in those 12 months, China had racked up some USD380 billion in purchases, more than 50% more than the total captured in the monthly data. The annual survey adds a lot in terms of accuracy, but it loses a lot in terms of timeliness. With the TIC system processing 2.8 million reporting forms to compile the annual survey, it is understandable that it comes out with a lag of 9 months. Data for China's holdings at the end of June the previous year makes its first appearance in February.

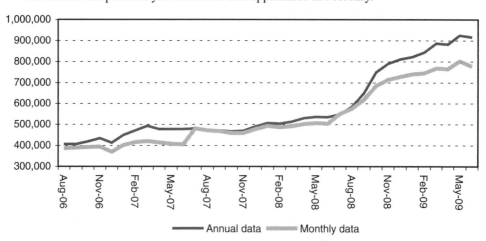

Source: TIC system, author's calculations

Figure 5.6 *China's U.S. Treasury holdings (USD millions)*

The discrepancy between monthly data and annual survey results for China is far greater than that for Japan, the second-largest foreign holder of U.S. Treasuries. The size of the discrepancy suggests that China's FX reserve managers are deliberately taking advantage of the transaction and custody biases in the TIC reporting system to hide their purchases, hoping to create a smokescreen that prevents financial markets from second-guessing their investment decisions.

Interpreting the Data

Table 5.9   *Major Foreign Holders of Treasury Securities (August 2010): Holdings at End of Period (in billions of dollars)*

Country	Aug 2010	Jul 2010	Jun 2010	May 2010	Apr 2010	Mar 2010	Feb 2010	Jan 2010	Dec 2009	Nov 2009	Oct 2009	Sep 2009	Aug 2009
1 ▶ China, Mainland	868.4	846.7	843.7	867.7	900.2	895.2	877.5	889	894.8	929	938.3	938.3	936.5
Japan	836.6	821	803.6	786.7	795.5	784.9	768.5	765.4	765.7	754.3	742.9	747.9	727.5
2 ▶ United Kingdom	448.4	374.3	362.2	350	321.2	279	233.5	208.3	180.3	155.5	108.1	126.8	104.3
Oil Exporters	226.6	223.8	223	235.1	239.3	229.5	218.8	218.4	207.4	208.3	209	205.9	209.8
Brazil	165	162.2	158.4	161.4	164.3	164.4	170.8	169.1	169.3	165.8	164.9	153.6	146
Carib Bnkng Ctrs	159.1	150.7	165.2	165.5	153.4	148.4	144.6	143.8	128.5	123.5	114.4	116.9	125.3
Hong Kong	137.8	135.2	141	145.7	151.8	150.9	152.4	146.6	148.7	142.1	137.8	128	120.5
[...]													

Source: Adapted from TIC System

1. The most important takeaway from the monthly TIC data is China's total Treasury holdings. In Table 5.9, the data shows that, as of August 2010, China held some USD868.4 billion in U.S. Treasuries, up USD21.7 billion from its holdings in July.

    The TIC data does not always show China making such a substantial increase in its Treasury holdings. In some months, meager Treasury purchases stand in contrast to robust growth in China's FX reserves. In other months, the transaction data suggests that China is a net seller of Treasury debt. It is tempting to interpret movements such as this in the TIC data as evidence that China has lost interest in Treasuries and perhaps is even selling down its existing holdings. In fact, the explanation is often more innocent. Normally, the custodian and transaction bias in the TIC data, not a Communist conspiracy to topple the U.S. government, accounts for the occasional fall in China's Treasury holdings recorded by the monthly TIC data.

2. One way to increase the value of the monthly TIC data is to keep in mind the pattern of revisions in past annual surveys. In past annual surveys, a large volume of transactions that were wrongly attributed to the U.K., and, to a lesser extent, other financial centers such as the Caribbean in the monthly data has been deducted from their total holdings and added to China's total. In the 2009 annual survey, the U.K.'s holdings were revised down by USD124 billion, holdings for Caribbean banking centers were dialed down by USD56 billion, and China's holdings were pushed up by USD139 billion. This is not an exact science, but keeping an eye on the purchases attributed to the U.K., the Caribbean, and elsewhere in the monthly data makes it possible to get an idea of whether China is making back-door purchases through these other financial centers.

Table 5.10   *Total Liabilities to Foreigners by Type and Country*

1
▼

Ctry Code	End of Month		Held by foreign official institutions and foreign banks [7]	Held by all other foreigners [8]	o/w: short-term U.S. Treasury obligations [9]	o/w: other short-term negotiable securities excl. CDs [10]	o/w: negotiable CDs [11]	Held by foreign official institutions and foreign banks [12]	Held by all other foreigners [13]	Total liabilities payable in foreign currencies [14]
41408	2010-08	[...]	16,364	521	15,705	1,040	140	7,115	467	n.a.
41408	2010-07		6,787	503	6,145	1,006	139	6,678	94	n.a.
41408	2010-06		4,435	563	3,999	872	127	5,017	371	88
41408	2010-05		7,342	381	6,827	765	131	7,812	446	n.a.
41408	2010-04		42,521	494	42,221	664	130	7,424	148	n.a.
41408	2010-03		41,111	245	40,758	467	131	14,066	79	73
41408	2010-02		42,199	1,052	41,784	709	758	15,561	118	n.a.
41408	2010-01		58,110	982	57,632	706	754	16,166	162	n.a.
41408	2010-00		70,142	998	69,735	639	766	10,089	99	72

Source: Treasury International Capital Reporting System.
Notes: Cntry Code 41408 = China, Mainland; position at end of period in millions of dollars.

1. The TIC data also provides insight into China's changing preference for long- and short-term debt. Purchases of long-term debt indicate a high degree of confidence in the outlook for the U.S. economy and the dollar; China normally focuses its purchases here. But at the end of 2008, when China enjoyed several months of monster trade surplus and needed somewhere to park the cash, SAFE increased its holdings of short-term Treasuries from less than USD20 billion in August 2008 to more than USD210 billion in May 2009. That surge in purchases of short-term debt, at a time when the collapse of Lehman Brothers signaled the U.S. financial system hovered on the brink, suggested that SAFE had understandably lost some of its confidence in the long-term outlook. Table 5.10 shows that as the U.S. economy moved out of crisis, China's appetite for short-term Treasury debt reduced. In August 2010, the China's holdings were down to USD15 billion.

Table 5.11 *Foreign Purchases and Sales of Long-Term Domestic and Foreign Securities, by Type*

| | | <-------- Gross Purchases by Foreigners --------> | | | | | <------------ Gross Sales by Foreigners ------------> | | | | | |
| | | <-------------- from U.S. Residents --------------> | | | | | <---------------- to U.S. Residents ----------------> | | | | | |
Cntry Code	Year-Mo	U.S. Treasury Bonds & Notes	U.S. Gov't Agency Bonds	U.S. Corp. Bonds	U.S. Corp. Stocks	Foreign Bonds	Foreign Stocks	U.S. Treasury Bonds & Notes	U.S. Gov't Agency Bonds	U.S. Corp. Bonds	U.S. Corp. Stocks	Foreign Bonds	Foreign Stocks
41408	Aug-10	20,381	812	261	1,360	175	945	8,257	4,963	445	1,458	256	891
41408	Jul-10	9,970	4,536	419	1,827	139	704	9,097	5,416	369	1,579	326	807
41408	Jun-10	15,541	8,809	538	1,985	426	678	36,764	3,222	401	1,498	356	722
41408	May-10	17,474	7,381	293	2,989	493	953	14,572	2,612	317	1,439	113	1,164
41408	Apr-10	20,750	4,240	448	2,288	534	1,276	17,217	2,408	332	1,570	713	1,122
41408	Mar-10	32,394	2,387	155	1,861	1,908	582	13,683	1,990	289	1,701	75	1,100

Source: Adapted from TIC System
Notes: Cntry Code 41408 = China, Mainland; all amounts in millions of dollars.

As Table 5.11 shows, the TIC data also breaks down China's purchases and sales of long-term U.S. securities by Treasury notes and bonds, agencies, corporate bonds, and stocks. The majority of China's investments are held in Treasury debt (around USD1.1 trillion as of June 2010), but SAFE also has substantial quantities stashed away in agency debt (USD359 billion) and smaller amounts invested in corporate debt (USD11 billion).

Treasuries, agencies, and corporates have different risk profiles. Treasuries are backed by the full faith and credit of the U.S. government and are assumed to have zero risk of default. Agencies are government-sponsored enterprises, but the Treasury does not stand behind them in the same way it stands behind its own debt. In 2008, with the two largest agencies, Fannie Mae and Freddie Mac, at the very center of the subprime mortgage storm, SAFE decided it did not like their risk–return profile. For 20 straight months from July 2008 onward, as the financial crisis deepened, the TIC data showed China selling down its holdings of agency debt.

Market Impact

The main impact of the TIC data is on markets for U.S. Treasury and agency debt. Evidence of strong purchases by China is positive for prices; evidence of fading purchases is negative. The TIC data also plays into the market's views on exchange rates, with strong purchases a sign that SAFE is keeping faith with the dollar as a reserve currency. But with the TIC data delayed by a month and a half, and the reliability of the monthly data for China leaving a lot to be desired, the information informs investors' overall outlook instead of triggering a knee-jerk trading reaction. The annual survey does a lot better in terms of accuracy, but at the cost of almost a year in terms of timeliness.

CHAPTER 6

Labor Markets

URBAN WAGES

Market sensitivity: Low
What is it? Report on the level and change of average wages in urban areas, published in current yuan and nominal YoY % for the year-to-date
Chinese news release on the Internet: www.stats.gov.cn/
English news release on the Internet: www.stats.gov.cn/english/
Release time: Typically with a considerable delay
Frequency: Quarterly data on wages in state-owned and large private-sector firms. From 2010, the results of an annual survey on wages in small private-sector firms are also published.
Source: National Bureau of Statistics (NBS)
Revisions: No

Why Is It Important?

For 30 years, China has benefited from a surplus supply of workers that has kept the bargaining power in labor markets in the hands of employers and wages low. The U.S. Bureau of Labor Statistics estimates that, in 2006, hourly wages in the Chinese manufacturing sector were just 3% of the equivalent wages in the United States and a quarter of wages in competitor countries such as Mexico. But a surplus supply of labor and low wages is not a natural state of affairs; it is the product of three specific factors:

- China has enjoyed the benefits of a demographic dividend. High rates of childbirth in the 1960s and 1970s meant millions of extra workers entering the labor markets in the 1980s and 1990s. With the single-child policy coming into effect at the start of the reform era, the number of births decreased. More than 30 years later, the consequence is a gradual decline in the number of young people entering the labor force. From the end of the decade on, the size of the labor force will start to shrink.

- A mainly rural population at the beginning of the reform era and very low wages in the countryside meant a constant stream of country mice making the trek from the farm to the factory. According to the 2010 population census, 674 million people are still living in the countryside. But that doesn't mean there are 674 million potential workers ready to step up to a place on the production line. The young, educated, able-bodied workers have already made the journey. The joke in China is that the rural population that remains is like the sign asking passengers to give up their seats on the metro: old, sick, disabled, or pregnant.

- China is a communist country. In theory, all things are run *by* the workers *for* the workers. The Communist Party does not see the need for any organizations other than the Party-affiliated All China Federation of Trade Unions (ACFTU) to represent the interests of workers. The ACFTU is famously spineless, with union reps often chosen directly by company management. The lack of effective representation or capacity to organize collective action has also kept a lid on blue-collar wages.

With an aging workforce and a diminishing supply of surplus rural workers, China's labor markets are entering a period of transition. Stories of worker shortages in the second half of 2009 segued rapidly into tales of trouble on the factory floor in the first half of 2010. Workers at a Honda plant in Zhongshan in Guangdong province went on strike for higher wages and won a 24% raise. A wave of suicides at Foxconn's factory in Shenzhen was about more than low salaries, but triggered a promise from management of higher wages and better working conditions. Key export provinces competed to attract workers, with increases in the minimum wage of 28% or more. Against the background of China's demographic shift, many analysts believe these are not isolated incidents. They are the signal of the beginning of a new phase in China's labor markets: the end of surplus labor and the beginning of rising wages.

How Is the Data Calculated?

Getting It Wrong: The Old Approach to Calculating Wages

Wage data should be ground zero for observing the shift in labor markets. But until recently, a legacy data-collection system that covers only a small subset of the labor market meant the official numbers had little reference value. The debacle of the 2009 wage data illustrates the problems in the old system. In 2009, growth in the Chinese economy slowed to its lowest level in 10 years. Corporate bankruptcies, especially in the export sector, were widespread. Many workers came home with redundancy slips. Not many came home with pay raises. The view from the factory floor was bleak. But the view from the NBS was rather different. According to the official data, despite slow growth, widespread bankruptcies, and higher unemployment, average wages continued to climb. The official data showed wages up more than 12% for the year. Taking account of inflation, that was actually a faster rate of increase than in 2008.

For China's workers, the gap between the 12% wage growth reported by the NBS and the reality of their own stagnant incomes was too much to bear. Internet bulletin boards and chat rooms were ablaze with outraged comments. The wage data became a flashpoint for contempt with official statistics. A joke making the rounds on the Internet quipped, "The NBS gave me a pay raise, but they forgot to tell my boss." An article in the NBS magazine *Statistics Education* noted that the incident had shifted the status of China's statisticians from anonymity to notoriety.

How could the NBS wage data have gotten it so wrong? The problem lies in a system for collecting wage data inherited from the days of the planned economy. In the 1980s, the state sector was the economy. The 100 million workers employed in state-owned and collective enterprises accounted for 99% of the urban labor force. A wage data system based on numbers reported up the administrative chain from the state-owned enterprise to the local government made sense. The wage data in the 1980s and 1990s was actually a rather sensitive reflection of changes in the labor market, capturing the boom in real wages in the mid-1980s and the collapse into negative territory that preceded the social unrest at the end of the decade. Fast-forward 30 years, and the 70 million employed in the state and collective sectors make up just 22% of the urban workforce. What's more, the state-sector workers who survived the restructuring at the end of the 1990s are part of a privileged elite, with wages that are higher to start with and that rise more quickly than those of workers in the private sector. A wage data system based on salaries for this happy few is not based on just a small subset of the workforce; it is based on an unrepresentative subset of the workforce. Responding to the 2009 wage data, one online joker commented, "This report includes only the salaries of state-owned employees. If the NBS could calculate the benefits they receive from expensing their every meal, drink, visit to the toilet, and fun with a prostitute, the increase in the average wage would be even higher."

Who was left out by the old wage data system? The most important group is the migrant workers, who are the muscle of China's export and construction sectors. No systematic data is collected on their wages. But no systematic data is required to know that they are the lowest paid of any group in the Chinese labor markets. Beyond the migrant workers, informal workers in the services sector, the self-employed, and large numbers of redundant or retired workers who have been re-employed off the books are also overlooked. Research by academics at the Chinese Academy of Social Science and the University of Michigan suggests that, taken together, these various categories of workers add up to 46% of the urban labor force. The vast majority of these workers have lower wages and less rapid increases in wages than workers in the state sector, so it is clear that the results produced by the old system overstate both the level and the growth rate of wages.

Getting It Less Wrong: The New Approach to Calculating Wages

Within the NBS, the flaws in the old wage data system are well recognized. Public outrage at the 2009 wage data provided a spur to action. In June 2010, the NBS put out a new set of data, sticking with the old quarterly survey as a way of measuring wages in state-owned and large-scale private enterprises, but also including the results of a new annual survey of wages in small-scale private-sector firms. The terminology is a little confusing, with the NBS referring to firms covered in the old survey as "non-private units" (非私营单位, fei siying danwei), even though the survey covers large listed and foreign-invested private-sector firms, and the firms covered by the new survey as "private units" (私营单位, siying danwei). But essentially, the "non-private unit survey" is unchanged from under the old system and covers state-sector and large-scale private sector firms; the "private unit" survey is new and covers small private-sector firms.

The non-private unit survey incorporates 1.56 million firms in urban areas, with a total 118 million employees, 37% of the total urban workforce. Firms report on their total wage bill and number of employees, and this information is reported up the statistical chain from county to province and ultimately to the NBS headquarters where it is verified and aggregated. For the new data on wages in the private sector, the source is a sample survey. The coverage of the survey is 100% for firms with more than 100 workers and 10% for firms with 20 to 99 workers. Firms with fewer than 20 workers are not included directly in the survey, but are covered through information collected from other sources, including the economic census. Because the census is conducted only once every 5 years, this suggests that data on wages in this group is not particularly reliable. In 2009, the survey covered 640,000 private-sector firms, 16.1% of the total. For both surveys, the calculation of wages is based on salary before tax and includes other benefits in cash or kind paid to employees (so if visits to the brothel are indeed expensed, they should show up in the total). The average is a simple average of total wages divided by total employees.

The new approach is better than the old, but it is far from perfect. The problem of partial coverage remains. China's 275 million migrant and off-farm rural workers are still nowhere in the official data. Including small private-sector firms improves the coverage of lower-paid workers, but large numbers of informal workers in the state and private sector, whose salaries are paid off the books, remain uncounted. The continued absence of these two low wage groups from the data means that results almost certainly continue to overstate the level and growth rate of wages. Finally, the extra effort of collecting data on the private sector appears to have exhausted the NBS's reserves of energy. With data on wages in the small-scale private sector published only annually, it is impossible to keep track of developments over the course of the year. The NBS has plans to increase the frequency of its survey of wages in private units, expand coverage, and capture the differences between high and low wage earners.

Interpreting the Data

Non-Private Units

Table 6.1 *Average Wages for Workers in Urban Non-Private Units, According to Region (2009)*

单位：元，% (Unit: yuan, %)

	2008年	2009年	增长率 (% change)
1 ▶ 总计 (Overall)	29229	32736	12.0
2 ▶ 东部地区 (Eastern Region)	34316	38002	10.7
中部地区 (Central Region)	24390	27478	12.7
西部地区 (Western Region)	25602	29120	13.7
东北地区 (North Eastern Region)	25101	28383	13.1
北　京 (Beijing)	56328	58140	3.2
天　津 (Tianjin)	41748	44992	7.8
河北 (Hebei)	24756	28383	14.7
上　海 (Shanghai)	56565	63549	12.3
[...]			
江　西 (Jiangxi)	21000	24696	17.6
[...]			
四　川 (Sichuan)	25038	28563	14.1
河　　南 (Henan)	24816	27357	10.2
[...]			

Source: Adapted from NBS

1. The main takeaway from Table 6.1 is the data point that got the statisticians into hot water: the increase in the average wage. The data for 2009 shows average wages for workers in urban non-private units up 12% YoY to CNY32,736 (USD4,814). In nominal terms, that was a fall from 17.2% YoY wage growth in 2008 and an average growth rate of 13.9% for the last decade, as the financial crisis took a chunk out of wage growth for even the protected state sector. But it was still a substantially bigger increase than workers in small private-sector firms enjoyed.

     The data is published in nominal terms, so to get to real changes in wages, it is necessary to cut out the effect of changing prices. As Figure 6.1 shows, the impact in some years can be quite substantial. In 1994, nominal wages grew 34.6%, but with inflation running at record levels, real wages grew by a less impressive 10.5%. Taking account of inflation makes the buoyancy of non-private unit wages in 2009 even more striking. With inflation in 2008 running at 5.9%, the change in real wages was 11.3%. With prices actually falling in 2009, real wages grew 12.7%. Faster real wage growth in the midst of the crisis rang alarm bells about the official data.

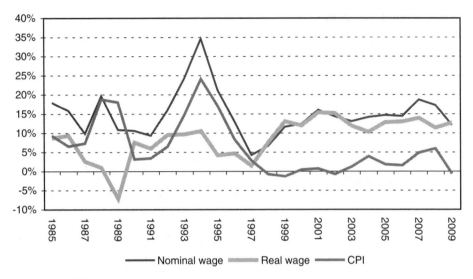

Source: NBS, author's calculations

Figure 6.1 *Real versus nominal wage growth (YoY %)*

2. The breakdown by region and province makes clear that, to paraphrase George Orwell, in Communist China, some workers are more equal than others. Workers in Shanghai are the highest paid in the country, pulling in an average CNY63,549 (USD9,345) a year. The lowest paid are in benighted Jiangxi, where the average worker is bringing in just CNY24,696 (USD3,631). Wages of workers in heavily populated central provinces such as Sichuan and Hunan give a sense of the median wage. In 2009, that suggests a median wage of around CNY28,000 (USD4,117) a year, somewhat lower than the mean.

The NBS also publishes a breakdown of wages by sector. As shown in Table 6.2, the breakdown reveals that workers in finance and IT are the highest paid, with workers in construction and agriculture among the lowest paid. For 2009, the sector breakdown also helps explain some of the controversial 12% increase in overall wages. With part of the government's stimulus package channeled into an increase in wages for public-sector workers, teachers enjoyed a 16.1% pay raise, bumping up the average. Wages in the manufacturing sector, the most important in terms of number of workers and for thinking about the competitiveness of China's exports, increased by a more modest 9.9%. Lower wage growth in manufacturing makes sense, as this is the sector that was hardest hit by the collapse in foreign demand.

Table 6.2 *Average Wages for Workers in Urban Non-Private Units, According to Sector (2009)*

单位：元，% (Units: yuan; %)

	2008年	2009年	增长率 (% change)
总　　计 (Overall)	29229	32736	12.0
(一)农、林、牧、渔业 (Agriculture, Forestry, Animal Husbandry, and Fishery)	12958	14911	15.1
(二)采矿业 (Mining)	34405	38224	11.1
(三)制造业 (Manufacturing)	24192	26599	9.9
(四)电力、燃气及水的生产和供应业 (Production and distribution of electricity, gas, and water)	39204	42668	8.8
(五)建筑业 (Construction)	21527	24625	14.4
(六)交通运输、仓储和邮政业 (Traffic, transport, storage and post)	32796	36224	10.5
(七)信息传输、计算机服务和软件业 (Information transmission, computer services, and software)	56642	59919	5.8
(八)批发和零售业 (Wholesale and retail trades)	25538	29031	13.7
(九)住宿和餐饮业 (Hotels and catering services)	19481	21193	8.8
(十)金融业 (Financial intermediation)	61841	70265	13.6
(十一)房地产业 (Real estate)	30327	32591	7.5
(十二)租赁和商务服务业 (Leasing and business services)	31735	34318	8.1
(十三)科学研究、技术服务和地质勘查业 (Scientific research, technical services, and geological prospecting)	46003	50866	10.6
(十四)水利、环境和公共设施管理业 (Management of water conservancy, environment)	22182	24551	10.7
(十五)居民服务和其他服务业 (Services to households and other services)	23801	25704	8.0
(十六)教育 (Education)	30185	35042	16.1
(十七)卫生、社会保障和社会福利业 (Health, social security and social welfare)	32714	36380	11.2
(十八)文化、体育和娱乐业 (Culture, sports and entertainment)	34494	38319	11.1
(十九)公共管理和社会组织 (Public management and social organization)	32955	36268	10.1

Source: Adapted from NBS

Table 6.3   *Average Wages for Workers in Urban Non-Private Units, According to Ownership Type (2009)*

单位：元，% (Units: yuan; %)

	2008年	2009年	增长率 (% change)
全 部 单 位 (All units)	29229	32736	12.0
内 资 (Domestic invested)	29181	32846	12.6
国 有 (State Owned)	31005	35053	13.1
集 体 Collective)	18338	20958	14.3
股份合作 (Cooperative)	21705	25303	16.6
联营 (Joint Ownership)	27872	29879	7.2
有限责任公司 (Limited Liability)	26376	28965	9.8
股份有限公司 (Share Holding)	35324	40075	13.4
其他内资 (Other domestic)	19668	21702	10.3
港澳台商投资 (Hong Kong, Macao, Taiwan invested)	25335	27433	8.3
外商投资 (Foreign invested)	32653	35555	8.9

Source: Adapted from NBS

The NBS also releases a breakdown of wages in non-private units by enterprise ownership type, shown in Table 6.3. This confirms the picture of privileged workers in state-owned enterprises enjoying higher wages and more rapid increases in wages than most other workers. In 2009, the average worker in the state sector enjoyed a 13.1% pay raise, taking average wages to CNY35,053 (USD5,154).

Private Units

Table 6.4   *Average Annual Wage for Workers in Urban Private Units, by Area (2009)*

单 位：元，% (Units: Yuan, %)

	2008年	2009年	增长率 (% change)
总计 Overall	17071	18199	6.6
东部地区 (Eastern Region)	18980	19840	4.5
中部地区 (Central Region)	13843	15402	11.3
西部地区 (Western Region)	14751	16234	10.1
东北地区 (North Eastern Region)	14933	16414	9.9

Source: Adapted from NBS

Recognizing the problems with partial coverage of the labor force in its existing data series, the NBS has begun collecting and publishing data on wages for workers in urban private enterprises. As shown in Table 6.4, the new data set shows wages for workers in this sector of the economy starting at a lower level and rising less rapidly than those of workers in the state sector. Average wages of CNY18,199 (USD2,676) in 2009 were just over half the level in the state sector, and an increase in wages of just 6.6% YoY was also nothing to write home about.

Wages for China's 275 million migrant workers are not covered in any of the official data. But with migrant workers employed in the least skilled positions, and with minimal protection from the labor laws, it is no surprise that their wages are even lower and more variable than those in small private-sector firms. A large-scale survey conducted by the Center for Chinese Agricultural Policy and Stanford in 2009 found that average wages for migrant workers were slightly more than CNY9,000 (USD1,323) a year, less than 50% of the level in the private unit survey and slightly more than 25% of the level in the non-private unit survey. The survey also showed that wages had actually fallen about 10% from a year earlier, as a result of the collapse in the export sector where most migrants work. The fact that migrant workers were willing to accept a 10% pay cut points to the fact that this group has limited bargaining power. With no welfare system and little social network to fall back on, migrant workers will take whatever salary they can get.

Market Impact

Wages are a key indicator of the competitiveness of exports, the outlook for domestic consumption, and the extent of inflationary pressure. By improving coverage of the private sector, the NBS has taken a significant step toward improving China's wage data. But the official statistics remain too partial in coverage and infrequent in publication to move markets.

UNEMPLOYMENT

Market sensitivity: Low
What is it? Quarterly report on number of registered urban unemployed and unemployed as a percentage of the urban workforce
Chinese news release on the Internet: www.mohrss.gov.cn/
English news release on the Internet: n/a
Release time: Varies
Frequency: Quarterly
Source: Ministry of Human Resources and Social Security (MOHRSS)
Revisions: No

Why Is It Important?

Unemployment is an important—perhaps the most important—indicator of the state of the economy. In the United States, the jobs report, which comes out on the first Friday of every month, is the single biggest focus for attention for investors and policymakers. Unfortunately, anyone seeking enlightenment on the outlook for growth and inflation in China's official unemployment data will search in vain. Even though, or perhaps because, unemployment is such an important indicator, in no aspect of the Chinese economy is the data weaker. Two episodes in China's immediate past illustrate the deep deficiency of the unemployment data.

At the end of the 1990s, the Chinese economy went through a wrenching transition from state to private ownership. The government kept the commanding heights of the economy in state hands. But years of bloodletting left tens of thousands of smaller state-owned enterprises bankrupt and consigned tens of millions of state-owned workers to the scrap heap of unemployment. With jobless workers spitting sunflower seeds on every street corner, it was clear that unemployment had surged. Professor Hu Angang of Tsinghua University estimated that 48 million were unemployed, an unemployment rate of more than 20%. But the Ministry of Human Resources and Social Security (MOHRSS) had misplaced its abacus. MOHRSS could find only 8 million unemployed, an unemployment rate of just 4%. What happened to the other 40 million? The answer for many is that they were lost in a spaghetti soup of administrative definitions that classified away the problem. Millions of workers who were effectively unemployed were classified as shifting to part-time work, retiring early, or on long-term leave. With the jobless lost in a bureaucratic maze, the government could reduce the cost of welfare payments and avoid the embarrassment of announcing a 20% unemployment rate.

Almost a decade later, in the final months of 2008 and the first half of 2009, the global economic crisis resulted in a precipitate collapse in external demand, pushing many of the factories of China's east coast into bankruptcy. This time, it was not the privileged ranks of state-sector workers but the toiling masses of migrant workers who suffered. But the result once again was tens of millions thrown into unemployment. The press was full of stories of factory owners who fled the country, leaving the factory gates bolted shut and back wages unpaid. A national survey conducted by the Center for Chinese Agricultural Policy and Stanford University suggested that, at the end of 2008, as many as 45 million, or 17% of China's 275 million migrant and off-farm rural workers, were out of a job. But MOHRSS was still taking its afternoon nap. The official unemployment rate in the first quarter of 2009 came in at 4.3%, virtually unchanged from the 4% level attained in the boom years of 2006 and 2007.

This time, administrative definitions weren't the problem—the problem was an approach to measuring unemployment that covers only half of China's labor force. The basis of the unemployment data is in reports from local employment bureaus on the number of benefit claimants. Only registered urban residents are eligible for unemployment benefits, so only this group shows up in the unemployment data. In 2009, there were 311 million registered urban workers. That means the official unemployment rate is calculated based on less than 50% of China's 790 million–strong workforce. The most important omission is the 275 million–strong army of migrant workers. Measuring unemployment within this group is, of course, difficult. But the complete absence of migrant workers from the data makes nonsense of China's official unemployment rate.

Interpreting the Data

The first point to understand about China's unemployment data is that it is wrong. According to the MOHRSS data, in the last decade, through the Asian Financial Crisis, the restructuring of the state sector, the bursting of the dotcom bubble, the boom years that followed entry into the WTO, and finally the 2008–2009 crisis, the unemployment rate has varied between a low of 3.1% and a high of 4.3%. Such tiny changes in the unemployment rate when the economy has moved through such rapid and wrenching dislocations defies belief. A more straightforward and thoroughgoing approach to making the calculation would not necessarily show an unemployment rate that is higher on average than the official series. The migrant workers who are the main omission from the official survey have little choice but to work, so in normal times, they have a very low unemployment rate. But the data would certainly show a rate that is more volatile, falling more in the booms and rising more in the busts than the current, rather turgid official data series.

This assessment is borne out by data from a mini-census carried out by the government in 2000 and again in 2005. By adopting a survey approach instead of relying on data provided by local employment bureaus, the census avoids the problem of partial coverage that plagues the official unemployment data. According to the results of the 2000 census, urban unemployment had risen to 8.1%—not as high as Professor Hu's 20% estimate, but more than double the 4% level suggested by the official data. Eight percent unemployment is not good news. But the short-term pain of restructuring the state sector also brought longer-term benefits. The surge in growth that followed entry into the WTO and

the restructuring of the state-owned enterprises created enough jobs to clear the street corners of redundant workers and find employment for the millions of young people entering
the labor market. By the time of the 2005 census, the unemployment rate was back down
to 5.2%—still slightly higher than the official data suggested, but by no means out of
control. In the financial crisis, the Center for Chinese Agricultural Policy survey, which
showed 17% of migrant workers unemployed at the end of 2008, also showed that, by the
third quarter of 2009, almost all of them had found new employment, taking the unemployment rate back down to 4.9%. The official data creates the impression of static labor
markets; the reality is considerable volatility.

What's the Alternative?

With the official data so clearly inadequate, and unemployment such an important indicator of the state of the economy, what is the alternative? The public employment services
data on the labor market supply and demand situation (covered in the next section) is the
best data source on China's labor markets and includes figures on the number of people
who are seeking work through public employment bureaus. This data series tells a more
believable story about the development of China's labor markets than the official unemployment data, showing a rise in unemployment at the beginning of the 2000s, a fall in
the boom years in the middle of the decade, and an uptick in the number of jobseekers in
2009—coinciding with the arrival of the financial crisis.

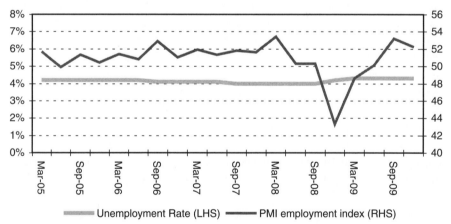

Source: MOHRSS, China Federation of Logistics and Purchasing (CFLP), author's calculations.

Note: PMI readings above 50 show rising employment; readings below 50 show falling employment.

Figure 6.2   *Unemployment rate versus Purchasing Managers Index (PMI) employment index*

The Purchasing Managers Index (PMI) surveys conducted by the China Federation of Logistics and Purchasing (CFLP) and HSBC Markit both ask managers whether the level of employment in their firm is higher or lower than in the previous month. The PMI employment indexes are much more sensitive to changes in the labor market than the official unemployment data. As Figure 6.2 shows, the CFLP series show firms taking on more workers in the boom years from 2005 to 2007, starting to shed workers rapidly as the crisis hit in the second half of 2008, and hiring again as the stimulus took hold in the first half of 2009. The HSBC series follows a similar pattern. That narrative makes a lot more sense than the official data, which shows virtually no change in unemployment before, during, or after the crisis.

Data sources on migrant workers are much patchier. Migrant workers who wander into local employment bureaus to browse the job ads might show up in the public employment services data on labor market supply and demand. But this does not provide comprehensive coverage of the migrant workforce. Academics and research institutes conduct surveys, such as the joint effort by Stanford and the Center for Chinese Agricultural Policy, and the results are sometimes reported in the press or can be found online. The NBS conducts an occasional survey of unemployment among migrant workers, taking advantage of the annual journey home for Chinese New Year to conduct a poll of migrant workers as they pass through train stations. News reports of factory closures or worker shortages are also a good source of anecdotal evidence. But no high-frequency official or private-sector survey provides a baseline for analysis.

Market Impact

Unemployment is a key indicator of the health of the economy, the outlook for domestic consumption, and the extent of inflationary pressure. In the United States, the unemployment data is probably the single most important data point for financial markets. But in China, the official unemployment data in its current format is too infrequent in publication and too partial in coverage to have an impact on equity, commodity, or currency markets.

PUBLIC EMPLOYMENT SERVICES LABOR MARKET SUPPLY-AND-DEMAND SITUATION

Market sensitivity: Medium

What is it? Quarterly report on the balance of supply and demand in urban labor markets, published in numbers of workers and ratio of job seekers to opportunities.

Chinese news release on the Internet: www.chinajob.gov.cn

English news release on the Internet: n/a

Release time: Around the end of the first month of the following quarter

Frequency: Quarterly

Source: MOHRSS

Revisions: No

Why Is It Important?

China's labor markets are a black spot for economic data. With a labor force of 790 million, the unemployment and wage data is based on a subset of 311 million urban workers. No regular or comprehensive source of data exists for more than half the labor force, including China's 275 million migrant and off-farm rural workers. Almost as bad, for the urban workers who are covered by the official data, the level of detail is woefully inadequate. Apart from a headline reading for unemployment and an average level and percentage change for wages, the official data offers few insights into the dynamics of China's labor market.

The MOHRSS data on the balance of supply and demand in urban labor markets is a light in the darkness. It doesn't shine into all the corners, but data on the ratio of job seekers to employment opportunities—shown in Figure 6.3—provides a way to track the shifting balance of supply and demand in China's labor markets. Data on the age, education, and motivation of China's job seekers puts some flesh on the bare bones of the unemployment data, and even the elusive migrant workers put in a cameo appearance.

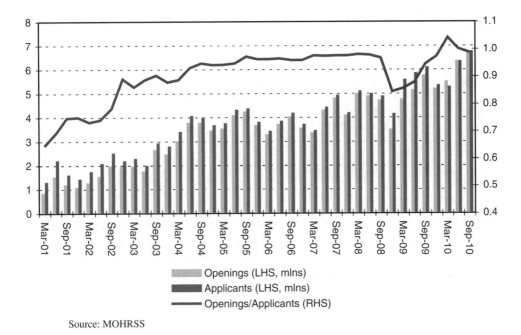

Source: MOHRSS

Figure 6.3 *Labor market conditions: ratio of job openings to job seekers*

How Is the Data Calculated?

The supply-and-demand survey started life in 2001, covering 59 cities nationwide with a total population of 107 million. Ten years later, the survey covers 100 cities with a population of 170 million, around 25% of the urban population. Data is collected by local employment bureaus, based on information provided by job seekers who register with the bureau and recruiters who advertise for employees. The bias toward urban workers is not as severe as in the wage and unemployment data. Migrant workers and peasants might not be able to register for unemployment benefit, but they can and do look for work at the employment bureau—and that means they show up in the data. An expanding sample set means comparisons over time need to be treated with caution. An increase in the number of job seekers or opportunities, or a change in the ratio, might reflect an increase in the number of cities covered by the survey, rather than a change in the labor market situation.

Interpreting the Data

Table 6.5 *Ratio of job opportunities to candidates (January to March 2010)*

	需求人数(人) (Job opportunities)	求职人数(人) (Job seekers)	岗位空缺与求职人数的比率 (Ratio of opportunities to seekers)	与上季度 相比变化 (Change from last quarter)	与去年同期 相比变化 (Change from same quarter last year)
本期有效数 (Numbers for this period)	5519321	5299216	1.04	+0.07	+0.18

Source: Adapted from MOHRSS

1. The highlight of the data release is the headline ratio of job opportunities to job seekers. A ratio of less than 1 means there are more people seeking work than there are opportunities. That means excess supply in the labor market, keeping a lid on rising wages. A ratio greater than 1 means there are more job opportunities than there are people looking for work. That means excess demand and upward pressure on wages. In Table 6.5, which covers the first quarter of 2010, the ratio shifted above 1 for the first time in the 10-year history of the series. Many analysts have latched on to this as evidence that China's surplus supply of labor is drying up, pushing wages and inflation higher.

Table 6.6 *Employment Opportunities and Job Seekers by Region (January to March 2010)*

区 域 (Region)	需求人数 (Employment opportunities)				求职人数 (Job seekers)			
	环比变化 (人数) (QoQ change (number of job opportunities))	环比变化 (百分比) (QoQ change (%))	同比变化 (人数) (YoY change (number of job opportunities))	同比变化 (百分比) (YoY change (%))	环比变化 (人数) (QoQ change (number of job seekers))	环比变化 (百分比) (QoQ change (%))	同比变化 (人数) (YoY change (Number of job seekers))	同比变化 (百分比) (YoY change (%))
东部 (East)	652858	27.1%	1073513	52.6%	417494	17.2%	528128	22.2%
其中：环渤海 (o/w Bohai Rim)	299280	38.6%	242302	29.1%	236543	28.7%	80949	8.3%
长三角 (Yangtze River Delta)	117878	13.3%	369193	57.9%	71199	7.6%	268522	36.4%
珠三角 (Pearl River Delta)	10853	21.9%	11755	12.1%	-6439	-16.3%	-34830	-25.8%
闽东南 (Fujian)	201342	30.2%	422791	94.8%	94331	16.1%	198127	41.0%
中部 (Center)	204594	17.1%	177659	14.8%	95693	7.3%	-94918	-6.5%
西部 (West)	86134	10.6%	138841	20.1%	25556	3.0%	-56341	-6.6%
合计 (Total)	943586	21.4%	1390013	35.4%	538743	11.7%	376869	8.0%

Source: Adapted from MOHRSS

1. MOHRSS also provides data on the change in the number of job seekers and job opportunities broken down by region. All the action is on the East Coast, and the data release provides a further breakdown of this area into the heavy industry of the Bohai rim, the Taiwanese factories of Fujian, the high-technology parks of the Yangtze River, and the sweatshops of the Pearl River Delta. Taken together, these regions account for the lion's share of China's exports. If the data shows labor supply is outpacing demand in the export-focused East Coast, that suggests wages are going to stay low, honing the competitive edge of Chinese products in global markets. If demand for labor starts to outstrip supply, the result will be rising wages, which could result in China losing out to lower-cost competitors such as Vietnam, or attempts by exporters to cut costs by moving production to cheaper inland provinces. In Table 6.6, the data shows the increase in demand for workers in the Yangtze and Pearl River Deltas in the first quarter of 2010 vastly outstripping the increase in supply. That shift from excess supply of workers to excess demand for workers helps explain the widespread reports of factory disputes and monster increases in wages that filled the press.

Table 6.7   *Job Seekers by Category (January to March 2010)*

求职人员类别 (Job seeker categories)	求职人数(人) (Job seekers)	所占比重(%) (% of total)	与上季度相比 求职变化 (百分点) (QoQ % change)	与去年同期相比 求职变化 (百分点) (YoY % change)
新成长失业青年 (Young adults entering labor market)	1268690	23.9	+1.1	+2.4
其中：应届高校毕业生 (o/w graduates from university this year)	565589	44.6	+4.8	+3.5
1► 就业转失业人员 (Previously employed now unemployed)	859173	16.2	-0.4	-
其他失业人员 (Other unemployed)	684470	12.9	-0.4	+1.3
在业人员 (Employed)	245880	4.6	-0.7	+0.4
下岗职工 (Redundant)	216611	4.1	+0.6	+0.8
退休人员 (Retired)	29526	0.6	-	+0.1
在学人员 (Students)	136294	2.6	-0.5	+0.1
2► 本市农村人员 (Local Peasants)	939007	17.7	+2.7	-0.7
外埠人员 (Workers from other towns)	919565	17.4	-2.4	-4.4
合计 (Total)	5299216	100.0	/	/

Source: Adapted from MOHRSS

1. The breakdown of job seekers by reasons for seeking a job is also revealing. If the reason for an increase in the number of job seekers is a surge in unemployment and redundancy, that is a troubling sign. An increase in employed workers looking for a change of occupation, on the other hand, is not something to worry about. In Table 6.7, the data shows that, in the first quarter of 2010, young workers entering the labor market,

especially those with a college education, were the main contributors to the increase in the number of job seekers.

2. Table 6.7 also casts a little light on the labor market situation of migrant workers. The categories of "local peasants" and "workers from other towns" are not exactly the same as migrant workers, but they are close enough. Looking at the change in job seekers in this category should provide insight into the labor market situation of this important but little understood group. Sure enough, the data for the period from 2008 to 2010 shows the number of peasants and out-of-town workers looking for a job surging with the collapse of the export sector in the first quarter of 2009, staying high through the second and third quarters, and starting to fall when the export sector picked back up at the end of the year.

Table 6.8   *Employment Opportunities and Job Seekers by Age (January to March 2010)*

年龄 (Age)	劳动力供求人数比较 (Labor Market Supply and Demand Balance)										
	需求人数 (人) (Job opportunities)	需求比重 (%) (% of opportunities)	与上季度相比需求变化 (百分点) (QoQ % change)	与去年同期相比需求变化 (百分点) (YoY % change)	求职人数 (人) (Job seekers)	求职比重 (%) (% of job seekers)	与上季度相比求职变化 (百分点) (QoQ % change)	与去年同期相比求职变化 (百分点) (YoY % change)	岗位空缺与求职人数的比率 (Ratio of job opportunities to job seekers)	与上季度相比供求变化 (QoQ change)	与去年同期相比供求变化 (YoY change)
16-24岁	1855114	33.6	+1.0	+3.2	2139904	40.4	-0.6	+2.4	1.01	+0.11	+0.19
25-34岁	1807235	32.7	+0.8	+0.9	1783251	33.7	+0.7	-0.3	1.16	+0.09	+0.23
35-44岁	860540	15.6	-1.4	-0.9	943025	17.8	-0.2	-2.5	1.06	+0.01	+0.23
45岁以上	238355	4.3	-1.1	-1.7	433036	8.2	+0.2	+0.5	0.69	-0.10	-0.11
无要求 (No requirement)	758077	13.7	+0.7	-1.6	/		/	/	/	/	/
合计 (Total)	5519321	100.0		/	5299216	100	/	/	/	/	/

Source: Adapted from MOHRSS

1. Youth unemployment is never good news, and idle juveniles have a track record of wreaking havoc in China. From the Red Guards who ran riot in the Cultural Revolution to the student protestors in Tiananmen Square, the devil of social disorder has found work for the idle hands of Chinese youth. One of the main fears when the financial crisis hit the mainland was that a generation of graduates would be cast into unemployment. The press was filled with stories of the outlandish lengths to which young graduates would go to find work. In November 2008, in Guangzhou, 15,000 students queued for 3 hours for a chance to submit their resume to recruiters for China Life Insurance. Thankfully, the worst fears did not materialize: The wheels of the economy kept turning and there were enough jobs to go around. But with history as its guide, the government remains understandably preoccupied with the problem of youth unemployment. As Table 6.8 shows, the

MOHRSS data includes a breakdown of job seekers by age. For the 16- to 24-year-old category, the table shows 2,139,904 job seekers in the first quarter of 2010, up 2.4% from a year earlier.

Market Impact

The data is published too infrequently and the coverage of labor markets is too partial to have an impact on day-to-day trading. But the balance of supply and demand in labor markets is a crucial factor in determining movements in wages, and movements in wages are a crucial factor in determining the strength of household demand, the competitiveness of China's exports, and the level of inflationary pressure. With China's labor markets entering a period of structural change, the MOHRSS data will receive close attention as a barometer of the transition from excess supply to excess demand.

C H A P T E R 7

Prices

CONSUMER PRICE INDEX

Market sensitivity: High
What is it? Index of changes in consumer prices in the Chinese economy
Chinese news release on the Internet: www.stats.gov.cn/
English news release on the Internet: www.stats.gov.cn/english/
Release time: 10 a.m. Beijing time, usually on the 11th day of the following month; March, June, September, and December data released later to coincide with the quarterly GDP data
Frequency: Monthly
Source: National Bureau of Statistics (NBS)
Revisions: No

Why Is It Important?

What was the underlying cause of the protests in Tiananmen Square that ended so brutally in summer 1989? History remembers the Tiananmen protestors as student idealists, crusaders for freedom and democracy. Idealism is an important part of the Tiananmen story, but it is not the entire story. Joining the students in China's capital and in similar protests around the country were workers who may have cared little about democratic ideals but who did care a lot about a more everyday issue: inflation. In 1989, consumer prices in China increased 18% from the year before. According to the official data, in the same year, wages for urban workers increased just 10.8%. Caught between a sharp increase in the price of food and other everyday items, and a much smaller increase in salary, Chinese households saw a major reduction in their real income. Salaries that had been enough to get by the year before were suddenly inadequate to make ends meet. The result was a sharp rise in social tensions, a ferment that threatened to tip student protest into a national uprising and that ended with the government's bloody response.

The Chinese Communist Party learned an important lesson from the confluence of rising social tensions and rising price pressures in summer 1989. Three times in the intervening period, inflation has run to high levels. From 1993 to 1996, inflation ran into double digits, and at the end of 1994, it touched 27%. In 2004, the Consumer Price Index

(CPI) pushed past 5% and forced the People's Bank of China (PBOC) to make the first upward adjustment in the interest rate in more than a decade. In 2008, a disease in the pig population provided the trigger for increases in the money supply to pass through into increases in prices, with the CPI pushing past 8%. That was enough for President Hu Jintao to start pounding the streets at local food markets in Beijing, sympathizing with vendors and customers about rising prices. But relative to the experience in Argentina, Brazil, and some of the countries of Eastern Europe, where hyperinflation has reduced the value savings to zero and brought governments to their knees, the Chinese experience of inflation post-1989 has been relatively benign.

What makes the success of the government in controlling consumer prices all the more remarkable is that the Chinese economy has a natural tendency toward inflation. China's exchange rate regime might be good news for exporters. But the consequence of an undervalued yuan, managed exchange rate, and massive current account surplus for the domestic economy is rapid growth in the money supply that is always threatening to tip over into inflationary pressure. So where is the inflation? Part of the answer is that the PBOC has done a good job of locking up increases in the money supply. Every week, China's Central Bank issues sterilization bonds, effectively paying the banks a small return to lock up a certain amount of liquidity and prevent too much cash from sloshing around in the real economy. If that's not enough, the Central Bank can raise the reserve requirement ratio, increasing the percentage of deposits that banks have to keep on reserve. This also has the impact of locking up liquidity and preventing increases in the money supply from impacting prices in the real economy. Part of the answer is that the inflation is there, if you know where to look for it. The price of land, the price of prop- erty, and the value of equities have ballooned in the last decade. When the government gets worried about irrational exuberance in property or equity markets, investment funds flow into more esoteric areas. Chinese art, antiques, and even garlic have all been the sub- ject of speculative frenzies in the last few years. But part of the answer is that China has not yet paid the inflationary price for its monetary expansion, and the outlook for infla- tion in the years ahead is not as benign as it was in the years gone by.

How Is the Data Calculated?

Compiling the CPI is a massive nationwide exercise, with survey teams hitting the streets in shops and markets to check prices for a representative sample of Chinese households' consumption basket. The CPI survey teams check price points for a representative sample of goods spread across 50,000 locations in 500 towns around the country. The frequency of checks depends on the type of goods under investigation. For some goods whose price is subject to frequent changes, checks take place on a weekly or even daily basis. For the goods whose price is most variable, checking prices is something of an art. Consider vegetables: Prices for greens sold in the wet market are higher in the morning, when the produce is fresh and customers are vying for the choicest selections, and lower in the evening, when vendors are eager to shut up shop and only a few moldy turnips remain to be sold. The survey teams have to make sure they are hitting the markets at the same time to ensure they are comparing like with like. On the 27th day of each month, the survey data is submitted from local statistical bureaus to the provincial level. On the 6th day of the following month, provincial data is submitted to the NBS head office in Beijing, which collates the data ahead of publication the following week.

The CPI tracks prices of eight types of goods: food; residence; transport and communication; recreation, education, and culture; tobacco and liquor; healthcare and personal items; clothing; and household facilities, articles, and services. Food and accommodation are the most important components, together making up almost 50% of the index. Weights of the components are set according to the breakdown of household expenditure, determined in a survey of 130,000 households. Items that make up a higher proportion of expenditure get a higher weight in the index. The NBS makes small changes to the weights each year in accordance with changes in spending patterns and recalculates the entire basket every five years. The latest change to the weights of the components took place at the beginning of 2011. The main change was to increase the weight given to the cost of accommodation and reduce the weight given to food.

Unlike most developed countries and some other developing countries, China does not publish the weights assigned to the different components of the CPI. In 2011, the publication of the first data set calculated using the new weights was accompanied by a bizarre statement that gave the *changes* to the weights, but not details of their absolute *levels*. The NBS data on the CPI is regarded with some skepticism by the Chinese public, with a widespread belief that the official numbers understate the real level of inflation. By treating information on weights of the components of the basket with a degree of secrecy more suited to guarding information on the location of nuclear weapon silos, the NBS does little to raise public confidence in the data. As Table 7.1 shows, even without official numbers, it is possible to calculate the weights with some degree of accuracy.

Table 7.1 *Weights of Components in CPI Basket (Estimates)*

Year	Food	Tobacco and Liquor	Clothing	Household Facilities, Articles	Healthcare	Transport and Communication	Recreation, Education, and Culture	Residence
2010	32.79%	3.68%	8.95%	6.54%	9.81%	10.94%	12.61%	14.69%
2011	30.58%	3.17%	8.46%	6.18%	9.45%	10.89%	12.36%	18.91%
Change	−2.21%	−0.51%	−0.49%	−0.36%	−0.36%	−0.05%	−0.25%	4.22%

Source: NBS, Capital Economics

The composition and calculation of the CPI are not without controversy. The main bone of contention is the accommodation item. In April 2010, the index of the cost of property in 70 major cities showed house prices up 12.8% for the year, a record high that was still widely regarded as understating the true rate of increases in house prices. As Figure 7.1 shows, in the same month, the CPI came in at just 2.8% year-on-year (YoY) and the accommodation component of the CPI came in at just 4.5%. How could there be such a glaring disparity between the change in house prices and the change in the cost of accommodation?

- The CPI basket gives a low weight to the cost of accommodation. On average, in Organization for Economic Cooperation and Development (OECD) countries, accommodation is about 25% of the CPI basket. In China, even after an increase in the weight in 2011, it is still around 19%. Within the accommodation component, in OECD countries, the cost of renting and buying a house together generally make up more than 60% of the total. In China, calculations by academics at the Chinese Academy of Social Science suggest that they account for just a third.

- Problems arise with the way the cost of buying a house is measured. The NBS uses the mortgage interest rate as the measure of the cost of buying a house. The mortgage interest rate is rather static, but the cost of property has risen rather fast, so this approach does not capture the real increase in the cost of buying a house.

- The largest part of the accommodation component is taken up by the cost of utilities. With the cost of water, electricity, and fuel controlled by the government and managed at artificially low levels, this also tends to bias the reading downward.

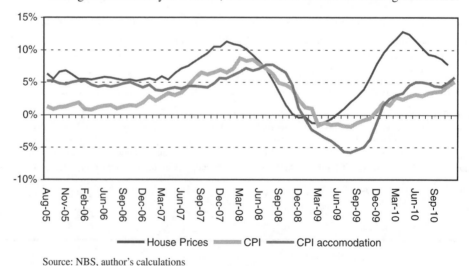

Source: NBS, author's calculations

Figure 7.1 *House prices versus CPI and CPI accommodation (YoY %)*

Behind the technicalities, a deeper issue is at stake. A house is not just something to be lived in (a consumption good); it is also an investment (a capital good). Should the CPI really be reflecting the change in the cost of capital goods? If the CPI surges in response to higher costs for luxury apartments in Shanghai and Beijing, would this reflect the experience of the peasant in Hunan who cares more about the cost of the next bowl of rice? The PBOC thinks the question is open for debate. In an editorial published in one of China's most free-thinking economics and finance magazines, *Caijing,* the head of the PBOC's monetary policy department Zhang Xiaohui argued that measures of inflation should do more to incorporate changes in the price of capital assets—including both property and equities. That change might not be an immediate prospect. In the meantime, looking at the CPI alongside the producer price index (PPI), the index of house prices, and the level of the Shanghai Composite Index provides a more complete picture of the state of inflationary pressure.

Interpreting the Data

Table 7.2 *Consumer Price Index by Category (January 2010)*

Item	The same month last year =100			The same period last year =100		
	Total	Urban	Rural	Total	Urban	Rural
1▶ Consumer Price Index	101.5	101.4	101.8	101.5	101.4	101.8
2▶ 1. Food o/w:	103.7	103.7	103.8	103.7	103.7	103.8
Grain	109.8	109.6	110.1	109.8	109.6	110.1
3▶ Meat, Poultry, and Their Products	96.5	96.6	96.2	96.5	96.6	96.2
[...]						
2. Tobacco, Liquor, and Articles	101.5	101.7	101.3	101.5	101.7	101.3
5▶ 3. Clothing	99.6	99.8	99.1	99.6	99.8	99.1
4. Household Facilities, Articles, and Services	98.9	98.7	99.4	98.9	98.7	99.4
5. Health Care and Personal Articles	102.3	102.2	102.6	102.3	102.2	102.6
6. Transportation and Communication	99.5	99.3	99.9	99.5	99.3	99.9
7. Recreation, Education, and Culture Articles	98.8	98.0	100.3	98.8	98.0	100.3
4▶ 8. Residence	102.5	102.7	102.1	102.5	102.7	102.1

Source: Adapted from NBS

1. The most important takeaway from the data is the headline reading for the CPI. This is the number that provides the best overall assessment of the extent of inflationary pressure in the Chinese economy. In Table 7.2, the data shows that consumer prices in January 2010 were up 1.5% YoY. What does that 1.5% number mean? Monetary policymakers in the U.S. often opine that inflation in the range of 1.5% to 2% is on target. The European Central Bank has a target of less than 2% change in price. In China, things are slightly different. The PBOC does not have a formal inflation target. But Premier Wen Jiabao's annual work report, delivered at the National People's Congress in March, often throws out a number for the year. Most often this is 4%, but in 2010, the premier signaled a stronger commitment to containing inflation with a target of 3%. Tolerance for a slightly higher level of inflation than would be acceptable in many

Western countries reflects a faster rate of growth, and the upward pressure from China's transition from artificially low government-controlled prices for gas, electricity, and water, to a market system with higher and more variable prices. The markets often interpret a monthly CPI reading above the government's target for the year as a sign that the PBOC is about to tighten monetary policy. A reading of 1.5% in January 2010 was well within the target and was also down from 1.9% in December 2009, a reassuring sign for the markets that inflation was not about to surge out of control.

The YoY change is important. But a year is a long time in the Chinese economy, and the markets also want to know the current direction of price changes. In 2009, the NBS began including the month on month change in the CPI in the text that accompanies its data release, although it has not yet found a place in the data table.

2. The largest component of the CPI basket is food. This is for the very straightforward reason that most households in China are poor, and poor people spend a high percentage of their income on food. As Figure 7.2 shows, food is also the most volatile component of the index. A disease in the pig population, a drought in the wheat fields of Henan, or a snowstorm that ruins Shandong's vegetable crop can pass through into changes in consumer prices. The question is whether the changes reflect a temporary disruption, gone with a change in the weather, or whether the change in food prices is a sign of wider inflationary pressure.

The Chinese government likes to focus on weather, disease, and other temporary factors as the explanation for changes in food prices. But there are also arguments in the other direction. Producing food is labor intensive, so rising labor costs are transmitted to higher food prices. In a developing country, rising incomes also tend to be reflected in changes in diet—with workers turning higher wages into higher spending on meat. The agricultural sector is also supply constrained. A field of wheat cannot be summoned out of the air—it has to be planted, tended, and harvested. If demand increases, it takes a while for supply to catch up. This is in contrast to the consumer goods sector, where overcapacity means supply can respond quickly to changes in demand. That means if there is inflationary pressure in the Chinese economy, it should show up in food prices first. Many China analysts maintain that too much money, as much as not enough pigs, is the cause of inflation in China.

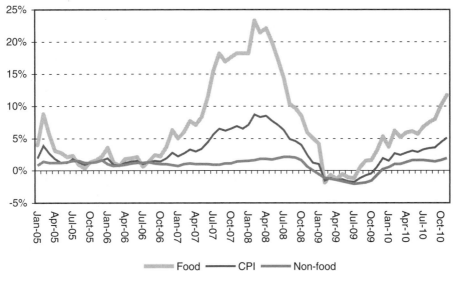

Source: NBS

Figure 7.2   *CPI, CPI food, CPI non-food (YoY %)*

3. Within the food component, the most important subcomponent is meat and poultry. Pork is China's favorite meat and changes in the prices of pork have a major impact on the CPI, so much so that some commentators have unkindly rechristened it the "China Pig Index." The dynamics of pork production in China mean that prices are quite volatile. Many of China's pigs are reared on backyard operations that are acutely sensitive to movements in price. Pig farmers respond to low prices by going slow on breeding. That means low prices today can result in a dearth of pork 6 months down the line. That dearth pushes prices up and encourages farmers to pipe Barry White tunes into the sty, with the result a glut of pigs and lower prices a few months later.

   Investors can get a heads-up on the change in the price of pork and other agricultural products, from daily and weekly prices published variously by the Ministry of Commerce, the National Development and Reform Commission, and the Ministry of Agriculture. The NBS also publishes average retail prices for 29 food items every 10 days. The Ministry of Commerce data has the best track record of forecasting movements in the CPI.

4. The next-largest component of the index is the cost of accommodation. Changes in the cost of accommodation in the CPI lag changes in the index of house prices in 70 cities by several months and are considerably less volatile. As discussed earlier, this is partly a problem with the way the accommodation component of the CPI is constructed. But it also reflects the structure of China's housing market, with a surplus of rental properties keeping rents down.

5. For some components of the CPI, improvements in manufacturing productivity, over-capacity, and government-controlled prices have resulted in continuous falls in prices. The cost of clothing has fallen every year for the last decade. The cost of healthcare, household facilities, and transport and communication has consistently undershot the CPI as a whole. This is a drag on the overall level of consumer prices. But as the cost of factor inputs increases and the government deregulates prices or increases taxes, these laggard components of the index will start to contribute more to overall price pressure.

Market Impact

Equities: Inflation pulls equities in conflicting directions. The higher and more volatile the increases in consumer prices, the more likely it is that the government will be forced to slam on the economic policy brakes, dampening both growth prospects and equity valuations. Rate hikes often come on Fridays and in weeks when rumors roil the markets, the Shanghai Composite Index can fall several percent in a single day, only to recoup some of the losses the following Monday if no action from the Central Bank has materialized. But higher inflation can also be a positive for equities. If higher prices push the real interest rates available to bank depositors into negative territory, that can trigger a rush into equities as a hedge against inflation.

Commodities: Inflation in China is a negative for global commodities prices. If consumer prices are running out of control, Beijing will be forced to slam on the monetary policy brakes. That pushes up the cost of investment and pushes down China's demand for commodities.

Currency: Changes in the exchange rate impact inflation through two channels. First, by raising the cost of exports, appreciation of the yuan reduces foreign demand for Chinese products, helping to cool off an overheated economy. Second, by reducing the cost of imports, appreciation of the yuan reduces the inflationary impact of crude oil, iron ore, and other imported commodities on the Chinese economy. Inflation is not the decisive factor in determining Beijing's approach to the exchange rate, but a higher reading for the CPI does make it more likely that the government will allow a more rapid appreciation of the yuan. In the period of yuan appreciation from 2005 to 2008, the pace of appreciation was most rapid in the first half of 2008, when inflation touched 8%.

INDICES OF URBAN RESIDENTS' CONFIDENCE ON INCOME AND PRICE LEVEL

Market sensitivity: Low

What is it? Survey of the views of households on the current price level, the outlook for inflation, and their choice between spending and saving; results are published in an index between 0 and 100, with 50 the dividing line between positive and negative sentiment

Chinese news release on the Internet: www.pbc.gov.cn/

English news release on the Internet: www.pbc.gov.cn/publish/english/963/index.html

Release time: The end of the quarter

Frequency: Quarterly

Source: PBOC

Revisions: No

Why Is It Important?

What do households think about prices? That's an important question. If households think prices are going to rise, they will demand higher wages. With more money in their pockets, they will bid up prices, making a reality of the inflation they expected to occur. As Figure 7.3 shows, in China, there is already a relationship between inflationary expectations and inflation. With the bargaining power in China's labor markets shifting in favor of the workers, the link will be reinforced. There are various ways of thinking about households' views on inflation. An increase in trading volume on the Shanghai Composite Index, more transactions in the residential property market, or a shift by households away from time deposits and toward demand deposits are all signs that inflationary expectations are elevated. But the simplest way to find out about households' inflation expectations is to ask them, and this is what the PBOC survey does.

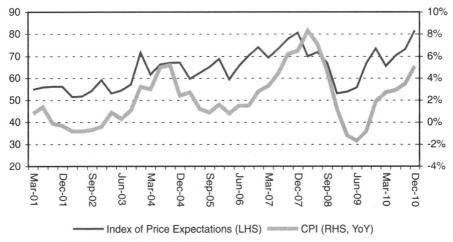

Source: PBOC, NBS, author's calculations

Figure 7.3   *CPI versus PBOC index of households' price expectations*

How Is the Data Calculated?

As the basis for the survey, the PBOC selects 50 representative cities from around the country. In each city, 8 banks are selected as the focus and 50 depositors are chosen from each bank. That adds up to 20,000 participants in the survey.

The survey collects participants' views on the current situation and future outlook for consumer prices, wages, house prices, and choice between spending and saving. For each question, participants can choose to give a positive, neutral, or negative answer. The results are aggregated into an index that gives a weight of 1 to the percentage of participants who gave a positive answer, 0.5 to neutral responses, and 0 to negative responses. So if 20% of respondents expect prices to rise, 40% think they will stay the same, and 40% think they will fall, the score for price expectation index would be this:

$$(20\% \times 1) + (40\% \times 0.5) + (40\% \times 0) = 40$$

The way the index is put together means that the result has to come out between 0 and 100, with 50 the dividing line that separates a positive from a negative reading. (This is the same as the way the PMIs are calculated.) Higher readings for an index are not necessarily good news. For the index of current consumer prices, a reading of 100 would mean 100% of participants are satisfied with the current price level (good news). But for the index of future price expectations, a reading of 100 would mean that 100% of participants expected consumer prices to rise in the next quarter (bad news). In the example just given, a score of 40 means that, on average, urban residents expect a slight fall in consumer prices.

Interpreting the Data

Table 7.3 *Indices of Urban Residents' Confidence in Income and Price Level*

		2010.01	2010.02	2010.03	2010.04
城镇储户收入与物价扩散指数表					
Indexes of urban residents' confidence on income and price level					
3▶	当期收入感受指数 Index of current income sentiment	55.0	49.5		
	未来收入信心指数 Index of future income confidence	56.2	53.6		
2▶	当期物价满意指数 Index of current price satisfaction	25.9	21.7		
1▶	未来物价预期指数 Index of future price expectation	65.6	70.3		

Source: Adapted from PBOC

1. The PBOC price expectation index has done a decent job of anticipating future movements in prices, rising ahead of the inflationary peaks in both 2004 and 2008. In Table 7.3, a reading of 70.3 in the second quarter of 2010 suggests that households expected a relatively sharp increase in prices in the next quarter. Sure enough, against the expectations of many professional economists, the CPI rose from 2.9% YoY in June 2010 to 5.1% in November.

2. The relationship between the current level of inflation and households' price satisfaction should be straightforward. If inflation is falling, households should be increasingly satisfied. If prices are rising, they should be increasingly dissatisfied. A reading of 21.7 for the index in the second quarter of 2010, down from 25.9 in the first quarter, suggests that households were not satisfied with the current price level and that the level of satisfaction was falling. This is consistent with a slight increase in the CPI over the same period.

But the straightforward relationship between the CPI and satisfaction with the price level does not always hold. As Figure 7.4 shows, over the last decade, inflation has risen and fallen, but households' satisfaction with the price level has been on an almost unbroken downward trend. The NBS points to an innocent explanation for the anomaly. People tend to pay more attention to prices that are going up than to prices that are staying the same. So even if just one of the hundred goods in the consumption basket is rising in price, it will be that one good that is the focus of attention. That tends to mean that households' perception of inflation is greater than actual inflation. But that is only part of the story. Chinese households' perception that prices are rising is based in large part on the fact that house prices are rising. With house prices not directly included in the CPI, this results in a mismatch between household satisfaction with prices and the level of inflation shown in the consumer price index.

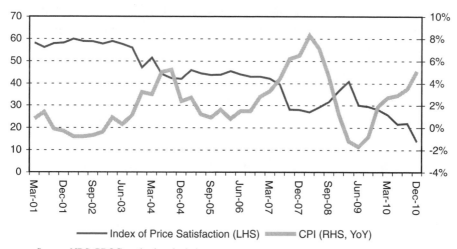

Source: NBS, PBOC, author's calculations

Figure 7.4 *CPI versus index of households' price satisfaction*

3. Understanding developments in China's labor markets is the key to understanding the outlook for growth and inflation. Unfortunately, there is no area in which the official data is weaker. By basing their wage data on wages for a privileged subset of workers in state owned enterprises, the NBS comes up with a growth rate that is implausibly high. By avoiding the bias in favor of state workers, the PBOC survey of household income satisfaction does a better job of capturing movements in wages. In contrast to the sedate undulations of the NBS data, the PBOC income survey tells a more believable story of volatile movements in wages. In particular, the survey data picks up the collapse in wage growth that occurred in 2009, with the index of current income sentiment falling from a high of 64 in the first quarter of 2008 to a low of 45 in the second quarter of 2009.

Included in the Chinese data release, but not in the tables, is an index of households' preference for spending, saving, or investing. One useful application of this index is as a cross-check against the NBS retail sales data. The retail sales data includes not just spending by households, but also spending by government and enterprises. The percentage of spending by households is not known. But it is a fair bet that if households in the PBOC survey are saying that they intend to save more and spend less, some of the acceleration in growth in retail sales shown in the NBS data is coming from spending by government and enterprises. In the second quarter of 2010, the data showed that just 18% of households intended to increase their level of consumption, compared to 45.7% that intended to save more. That suggests the continued strong growth in retail sales in the third quarter of 2010 was not all coming from an increase in spending by households.

Market Impact

The PBOC survey has several points of interest, especially on households' inflation expectations. But with the data available only quarterly, it does not normally inform day-to-day trading decisions.

PRODUCER PRICE INDEX

Market sensitivity: High

What is it? Index of change in producer prices

Chinese news release on the Internet: www.stats.gov.cn/

English news release on the Internet: www.stats.gov.cn/english/

Release time: 10 a.m. on the 11th day of the following month, except for March, June, September, and December data, which is released later to coincide with the publication of the quarterly GDP data

Frequency: Monthly

Source: NBS

Revisions: No

Why Is It Important?

Despite all the talk of a shift toward domestic consumption as a driver of growth, the Chinese economy remains an industrial economy. Profits are more important than wages, investment is more important than consumption, and enterprises are more important than households. Changes in the PPI do not have the same direct impact on the cost of living for Chinese households, or on monetary policy decisions made by the government, as the CPI. But with the industrial sector looming large, the PPI is an important gauge of inflationary pressure.

How Is the Data Calculated?

The NBS collects information on prices of around 11,000 products. The data is collected on the 8th and the 18th days of the month, in a survey that includes 50,000 enterprises in 430 cities. The average of the price on the two days is used for the calculation. To get from the price data to the index, products are weighted according to their share in the value of total output. The weights are updated every 5 years with the latest change coming in 2011, based on sales of industrial products from 2008 to 2010 and on a survey of 60,000 firms. The NBS does not publish data on the weighting, but it does say that weights are in line with the share of products in total industrial output.

How to Interpret the Data

Table 7.4   *Producer Price Index (May 2010)*

Indicators	May		Jan-May	
	Absolute Magnitude	Increased YoY (%)	Absolute Magnitude	Increased YoY (%)
1▶ **Producer Prices for Manufactured Goods**	...	**7.1**	...	**5.9**
Means of Production o/w:	...	8.8	...	7.4
Mining and Quarrying	...	31.1	...	32.3
2▶ Raw Materials	...	13.8	...	11.6
3▶ Processing	...	3.6	...	2.2
Means of Livelihood o/w:	...	1.8	...	1.2
Foodstuff	...	3.2	...	2.5
Clothing	...	1.9	...	1.7
Articles for Daily Use	...	1.7	...	0.9
4▶ Durable Consumer Goods	...	-0.3	...	-0.9

Source: Adapted from NBS

1. The focus of attention is on the headline change in the PPI. This is the number that gauges the extent of inflationary pressure in the industrial and manufacturing sector. The PPI is higher on average and more volatile than the CPI. In Table 7.4, a 7.1% YoY increase for the PPI in May 2010 compared with a reading of 3.1% for the CPI in the same month. A high reading for the PPI reflected a rebound in mining and raw material prices as China's real estate boom drove strong demand for iron ore, copper, and other inputs into the construction process. Evidence of mounting upstream inflationary pressure increased pressure on the government to tighten policy after the extraordinary stimulus of 2009, but it was not until the CPI rose above 4% several months later that the PBOC made its first move on interest rates.

   In theory, the PPI should also be valuable as a guide to the outlook for the CPI. In some way or another, all producer goods are inputs into the production of consumer goods. Higher prices at the factory door should translate into higher prices at the shops. In practice, as Figure 7.5 shows, the PPI as a whole does not have consistent leading properties. In 2007–2008, the major period of inflation in the Chinese economy in the last 10 years, the CPI led the way and the PPI followed. How could consumer prices be rising ahead of producer prices?

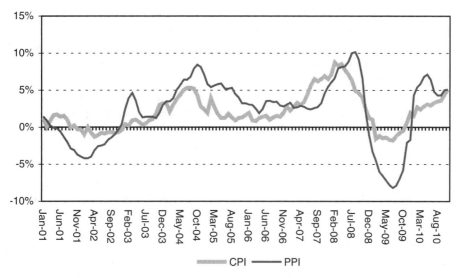

Source: NBS

Figure 7.5   *CPI and PPI (YoY %)*

- The PPI and the CPI measure different things. Food accounts for around a third of the CPI basket, and the focus is on the prices of unprocessed meat, fish, and vegetables, which is very volatile. The share of food in the PPI basket is considerably smaller, and the focus is on the price of processed food, where movements in price are less pronounced. Rent, communication, transport, and healthcare all loom large in the CPI. But there is no direct pass-through of the cost of producer goods to the cost of these services.

- Even for PPI components that do form part of consumers' shopping basket, overcapacity prevents Chinese manufacturers from passing on higher prices to consumers. The producer price for clothing has been rising almost continuously since 2004. Over the same period, the price consumers pay for clothing has continued to fall.

- Regulated prices also prevent producer price inflation from being passed on to consumers. The price for mining goods such as coal is volatile. But the price for electricity charged to consumers is set by the government. So even if the price of mining materials rises 31.1% YoY, as it did in May 2010, the impact is a profit squeeze for power producers, not an increase in the CPI.

2. Raw materials and mining and quarrying prices that make up a substantial part of the index are extremely volatile. With these categories including commodities like crude oil and iron ore, anything from a war in Iraq to a flood in Australia can have a marked effect on the index. With the price of many raw materials set by commodity markets, speculators can also drive prices in ways that have little relation to the fundamental dynamics of supply and demand. In summer 2008, when global oil prices pushed

toward USD150 a barrel and iron ore prices were at record highs, the PPI topped out at 10.1%. A year later, when the global financial crisis had turned the commodity bull run into a bear blowout, the PPI fell to –8.2%. Researchers at the International Monetary Fund estimate that movements in global commodity prices account for 20% of the movement in the PPI.

3. Lower and less volatile readings for the price of processed goods reflect overcapacity in China's manufacturing sector. With supply outstripping demand, market dynamics keep a lid on price rises. In Table 7.4, the data shows the price of processed goods up just 3.6% YoY in May 2010, undershooting the increase for the PPI as a whole.

4. The cost of consumer durables has fallen continually for the last decade. This reflects a surplus supply of factory labor that has kept wages for low skilled workers flat, improvements in productivity that have enabled manufacturers to do more with less, and overcapacity that has prevented producers from passing along increases in input costs to consumers. But the extent of falls in prices has been on a declining trend. Table 7.4 shows prices for consumer durables in May 2010 down just 0.3% YoY. That compares to a low of –7.3% in 2002. A switch from deflation to inflation in the price of consumer durables is only a matter of time. This will have implications for both the competitiveness of China's exporters and the extent of inflationary pressure in countries that import Chinese goods.

Market Impact

Equities: Equity markets are conflicted about the PPI. On one hand, high producer prices mean factories are charging more for their products, and that could mean higher profits supporting buoyant equity valuations. On the other hand, a high reading for the PPI is also a sign of overheating in the industrial sector, with the risk that Beijing will turn off the credit taps that keep business and investors flush with cash (bad news for equities).

Commodities: A high reading on the PPI is bad news for commodity producers, with the risk that the government might douse China's blast furnaces in cold water and dent demand for iron ore and other raw materials.

Currencies: With imported commodity costs one of the main drivers of producer price inflation in China, a high reading on the PPI can push policymakers to allow a faster pace of yuan appreciation.

Bond Market Yield Curve

Market sensitivity: Low
What is it? Yield on Ministry of Finance and PBOC debt
Chinese news release on the Internet: http://yield.chinabond.com.cn
English news release on the Internet: http://eyield.chinabond.com.cn
Release time: Chinabond publishes the benchmark yield curve for trading days at around 18:45
Frequency: Daily when the market is open
Source: China Central Depository and Clearing Co.
Revisions: No

Why Is It Important?

China's bond markets are a work in progress. The regulators, rating agencies, and industry associations all exist. The corporate, Ministry of Finance, and PBOC bonds are all available to trade. But the government has been dragging its feet on allowing the market to swing into operation, for reasons that are easy to understand. Controlling the pace of bank lending is the government's main lever to control the pace of growth in the economy. If enterprises can issue bonds to raise capital, they will not have to rely on loans from the banks, and the government's main policy lever will lose its effectiveness. For that reason, the powers-that-be keep tight control over the size of the bond market and the institutions that participate in it. The total outstanding value of bonds in the Chinese market at the end of 2009 was just CNY17.5 trillion, compared to total outstanding loans of CNY42.6 trillion. The Ministry of Finance, PBOC, and China Development Bank together account for 72% of all outstanding issuance. The commercial banks, which are majority owned by the government, hold 68% of all outstanding debt. With the government standing behind both sides of most transactions, trades sometimes take place at a price that has little to do with the dynamics of supply and demand.

To see how strange the operation of China's bond markets is, it's necessary to take a brief look at the world of interest rate policy. The PBOC sets both the deposit and the lending interest rate in the Chinese markets, with a wide margin in between to ensure the banks a fat profit. At the end of 2010, the commercial banks could borrow from depositors at 2.75% and lend at 5.81%. That guaranteed the banks at least 3.06% profit on every yuan they loaned out. In fact, with more than half of deposits held in demand accounts on which the banks pay virtually no interest the actual spread is considerably wider than that. Also at the end of 2010, the Ministry of Finance was offering a return of 2.15% on its 1-year paper, and the PBOC was offering 2.34%, little different from the Ministry of Finance yield after a difference in tax treatment is taken into account.

Why would the banks buy Ministry of Finance debt offering a return less than they were paying on 1-year deposits, when they could use the same capital to make a loan at a 3.06% profit? Part of the answer is that bonds issued by the Ministry of Finance and the

PBOC are risk free, so the banks are willing to accept a lower return. Ministry of Finance and PBOC bonds are also very liquid and can easily be converted back into cash if the need arises. But the real answer is that constraints on lending mean the banks cannot push as many loans out the door as they would like. When banks have hit their lending limits, any spare cash they have finds a less lucrative home on the fixed income markets. Yields reflect as much a lack of other options for the banks that are the main market participants as a calculated assessment of risk and reward.

With prices in the primary market set at an artificially low level, trading in secondary markets is thin. Trading volume in China's bond market in 2009 was CNY5.1 trillion (USD750 billion), compared to a CNY34.7 trillion (USD5.1 trillion) turnover on the Shanghai Composite Index. As a point of comparison, turnover in the market for U.S. Treasuries in 2009, an unusually weak year for trading volume, was around USD202.8 trillion.

Clearly, the Chinese bond market is not the U.S. bond market, and the shape of the yield curve does not have the same uncanny capacity to predict the future course of the economy. But the profit and loss of the banks that invest in China's bond markets is still affected by changes in inflation and movements in the benchmark interest rate set by the PBOC. The Chinese yield curve might not be the sensitive reflection of market views embodied by its U.S. cousin, but it does reflect the insights of thousands of professional investors, many of them working in institutions with strong links to the PBOC and moving around tens of billions of yuan every day. That makes it the canary in the coal mine of China's monetary policy, the most sensitive reflection of the market's view on the outlook for inflation and interest rates.

How Is the Data Calculated?

Trading in China's fixed-income markets is split between two separate platforms, the interbank market and the exchange market. But with almost all the action taking place on the interbank market, this is the one to watch. China Central Depository and Clearing Co. (Chinabond, for short) is the settlement house for all interbank market transactions. That means it has data on every transaction that takes place. At the end of every trading day, Chinabond reviews all the transactions that have taken place and takes a view on the representative yield for each point on the curve.

The main reason judgment rather than transactions plays a part in the construction of China's yield curve is that transactions are sometimes thin on the ground. Even in the market for PBOC paper, which is the most actively traded, the market turns over less than once a year. In 2009, the turnover of Ministry of Finance bonds was less than 6% of the outstanding value. That compares to a U.S. Treasury market that traded its own market capitalization 28 times in the year. For some maturities of Chinese Ministry of Finance debt, on some days, no transactions might take place. For these maturities, Chinabond has a formula for calculating the yield based on transactions that have taken place at shorter- and longer-term maturities.

Over time, a more mature market with a higher volume of transactions will strip away some of the role for judgment in construction of the curve. Until then, the fact that sections of China's yield curve are calculated based on a limited set of trades is one factor that reduces its value as an indicator of the outlook for the economy.

Interpreting the Data

Ministry of Finance Yield Curve

The yield on a bond represents the return that investors receive for holding it. Typically, the yield curve slopes upwards, as investors demand a modest return for holding short-term debt and a higher return for facing the greater uncertainties associated with holding longer-term debt. For Ministry of Finance debt, the risk of holding longer-term instru-ments is not the risk of default. Debt issued by the Ministry of Finance—and, for that matter, by the PBOC and the policy banks—is regarded as virtually risk free. At issue is the uncertainty about the outlook for the economy and the risk that a change in inflation will push up interest rates; the banks would then be left with a stream of income on low-yielding bonds while having to pay a higher rate to their depositors.

The slope of the yield curve, therefore, says a lot about investors' views on the out-look for the economy and interest rates. A steeply upward sloping yield curve suggests that investors believe that the economy is in danger of overheating and that there is a strong chance of an increase in benchmark interest rates. A flatter slope for the curve, or even a flat or downward-sloping curve, suggests that investors believe that there is slack in the economy and that benchmark interest rates are set to remain unchanged or even fall as the government attempts to stimulate growth.

At the beginning of August 2007, the economy was surging toward its seventh quar-ter of double-digit growth, and inflation was on the rise. As Figure 7.6 shows, the yield curve steepened, with the spread between the yield on 1-year and 10-year debt—a meas-ure of the steepness of the curve—widening to 1.31%. A steeper slope suggested that the markets were concerned about overheating and were pricing in another interest rate hike from the PBOC. Sure enough, on August 22, the Central Bank pulled the lever, raising the 1-year deposit rate from 3.33% to 3.6%.

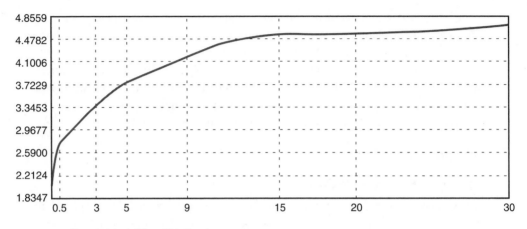

Figure 7.6 *Ministry of Finance Yield Curve, August 1, 2007*

In October 2008, the global economy was hovering on the brink of collapse, and the future of the Chinese economy was anyone's guess. As Figure 7.7 shows, the yield curve flattened, with the spread between the yield on 1-year and 10-year debt falling to around 0.25%. A flatter slope for the curve suggested that the markets were concerned about growth and were pricing in a fall in interest rates. Sure enough, at the end of October the PBOC cut the benchmark lending rate for a third time, taking the 1-year deposit rate to 3.87% from 4.14%. Two more cuts followed before the end of the year.

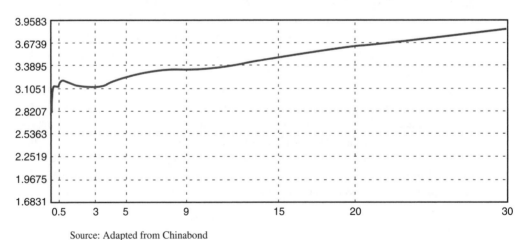

Figure 7.7 *Ministry of Finance Yield Curve, August 8, 2008*

Yield on 1-Year Central Bank Paper

The slope of the Ministry of Finance debt yield curve is not the only fortune teller in China's bond markets, and with trading in that market also thin on the ground, it is not necessarily the most reliable. The primary market yield on the PBOC's 1-year paper is regarded by bond market participants as an indicator of the Central Bank's intentions on interest rates. The thinking is straightforward. The deposit rate represents the cost of capital for China's banks. The yield on 1-year PBOC paper represents their return on capital. If the 1-year yield is higher than the 1-year deposit rate, the PBOC is giving the banks a risk-free return. That is an unnatural state of affairs. When the 1-year yield rises above the 1-year deposit rate, the few investors who follow China's fixed income markets interpret it as a clear sign that the PBOC is about to increase interest rates. As Figure 7.8 shows, in October 2004, August 2006, and March 2007, the increase in the yield on PBOC paper anticipated a move on interest rates. The fact that the 1-year yield did not move ahead of the increase in interest rates at the end of 2010 was interpreted by some analysts as a sign that the decision to raise rates came from the State Council, with the Central Bank not involved.

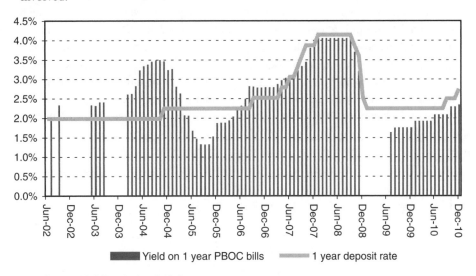

Source: PBOC, author's calculations

Figure 7.8   *One-year deposit rate versus yield on 1-year PBOC bills*

Short-Term Interest Rates

Some investors also focus on short-term interest rates as an indicator of the PBOC's intentions on monetary policy. Short-term interest rates—also known as money market rates or interbank rates—reflect the interest rates banks pay to borrow from each other, typically for short periods of time from a day to a few weeks. The idea is that movements in short-term interest rates, with the 7-day repo the biggest focus for attention, represent attempts by the Central Bank to guide rates to a different level. The 7-day repo rate is a sensitive reflection of liquidity conditions, but it is moved by many factors and it is difficult to distinguish the planned impact of PBOC operations from other influences. Initial Public Offerings (IPOs) that drain money from the financial system as investors rush to subscribe, inflows and outflows of hot money, and movements in fiscal deposits can all have a more marked impact on short-term interest rates than the Central Bank's carefully planned use of open market operations and the reserve requirement ratio.

The impact of IPOs on short-term interest rates is peculiar to the Chinese economy and can be especially marked. The price of shares at an IPO is typically set at a level that ensures a bounce on the first day of trading, guaranteeing a big profit to company insiders, strategic investors, and anyone lucky enough to get a piece of the action through subscription. The result is a massive drain on liquidity ahead of IPOs as investors marshal as much funds as possible in the hope of a subscription. The Petrochina IPO in October 2007 had CNY3.3 trillion in funds queuing up for subscription, the equivalent of 8% of deposits in the banking system. As Figure 7.9 shows, the resulting drain in liquidity saw the 7-day repo rate spiking above 10%. Those lucky enough to get a piece of the action were not disappointed. Petrochina's share price surged on the first day of trading.

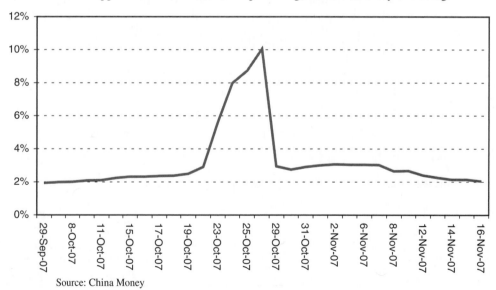

Source: China Money

Figure 7.9   *Seven-day repo rate spikes on Petrochina IPO*

Market Impact

One useful feature of China's bond markets is that investors are a rather sober, professional bunch and are not easily roiled by rumors. That is a stark contrast to China's equity markets, where legions of novice retail investors play a preponderant role. Anything from rumors in the Hong Kong press to speeches from academic members of the PBOC's Monetary Policy Committee can have the Shanghai Composite lurching up or down a few percent. It takes a bit more substance to move China's bond markets. If rumors of a move on interest rates have China's equity markets sharply up or down, it is worth glancing at how the bond markets are reacting. If yields are moving, that is a sign that not just impressionable equity investors, but also hard-boiled bond investors, are taking the rumor seriously.

CHAPTER 8

Financial Indicators

SOURCES AND USES OF FUNDS OF FINANCIAL INSTITUTIONS

Market sensitivity: High
What is it? Monthly record of changes in lending and deposits in China's banks, published in CNY100 millions
Chinese news release on the Internet: www.pbc.gov.cn/
English news release on the Internet: www.pbc.gov.cn/publish/english/963/index.html
Release time: Initial data release between the 10th and 15th of the following month; complete tables updated around the 19th of the following month
Frequency: Monthly
Source: People's Bank of China (PBOC)
Revisions: No

Why Is It Important?

Lenin is reported to have said that all socialist economies need one very large bank. His intellectual heirs in the People's Republic of China might have strayed a long way from the path of orthodoxy. But on this one point, they have held the line. The Chinese economy is a bank-based economy. Total loans outstanding in the financial system are greater than the combined value of all outstanding bonds and the market capitalization of the Shanghai and the Shenzhen exchanges. The biggest banks—Industrial and Commercial Bank of China, Bank of China, China Construction Bank, and Agricultural Bank of China—have all been listed. But the government retains a controlling interest. The heads of all the major banks are Communist Party members, appointed by the State Council, with careers that crisscross the commercial and government sectors.

A dominant role for the banks in intermediating between lenders and borrowers, and a controlling hand for the government in the behavior of the banking sector, gives Beijing a powerful tool that it can use to dictate the speed and direction of economic growth. At the end of 2008, with Wall Street's sneeze threatening to give the rest of the world pneumonia, attention initially focused on the promise of CNY4 trillion in additional fiscal spending as the inoculation that the Chinese economy needed. But it was CNY17.4

trillion in new loans—CNY9.5 trillion in 2009 and CNY7.9 trillion in 2010—that was the real miracle cure. Massive volumes of new lending funded an investment boom that kept growth above the government's 8% target, even as the rest of the world slid into recession.

How Is the Data Calculated?

A walk down Beijing's Finance Street makes clear the intimate relationship between the commercial banks and the PBOC. All of China's major commercial banks have their headquarters on the street, within easy walking distance of the PBOC. The Central Bank is in constant touch with the banks and receives frequent reports on changes in their lending and deposits. These reports are compiled every month to give a snapshot of the balance sheet of the financial sector.

But that frequent communication does not mean the data is free from problems. One difficulty in interpreting the new loan data is that banks' attempts to game the annual lending quota set by the government have resulted in rapid growth in off-balance sheet lending. This effectively adds to total credit but is not recorded in the PBOC loan data. In 2010, the PBOC has belatedly acknowledged that off-balance sheet lending came in at close to CNY1.5 trillion, a significant addition to the CNY7.9 trillion official total.

In a new development in 2011, the PBOC began publication of a quarterly figure for "social finance" (社会融资, shehui rongzi). This includes loans issued by trust companies and capital raised through initial public offerings (IPOs) and the sale of bonds. In part, this is a recognition by the PBOC of the need to capture the creation of off-balance sheet credit by the banks. It is also a recognition that, while bank loans remain the dominant vehicle for finance, equity and bond markets are assuming a larger role, and keeping track of developments in these areas provides a more complete picture of credit conditions.

Interpreting the Data

Table 8.1 *Summary of Sources and Uses of Funds of Financial Institutions by Sectors (February 2010)*

项目 Item	2010.01	2010.02	2010.03
来源方项目 **Funds Sources**			
一、各项存款 Total Deposits o/w:	612877.3	622436.8	
1.住户存款 Deposits of Households o/w:	267079.3	282726.8	
(1)活期及临时性存款 Demand & Temporary Deposits	100502.2	107019	
(2)定期及保证性存款 Time & Marginal Deposits	166577.2	175707.9	
2.非金融企业存款 Deposits of Non-financial Enterprises o/w:	259215.2	255098.8	
(1)活期及临时性存款 Demand & Temporary Deposits	160263.8	153543.4	
(2)定期及保证性存款 Time & Marginal Deposits	98951.35	101555.4	
[...]			
资金来源总计Total Funds Sources	**697197**	**705516.1**	
运用方项目 **Funds Uses**			
一、各项贷款 Total Loans o/w:	413679.6	420678.4	
(一) 境内贷款 Domestic Loans o/w:	413413.1	420478.5	
1.住户贷款 Loans to Households	88231.94	90226.18	
[...]			
2.非金融企业及其他部门贷款 Loans to Non-financial Enterprises and Other Sectors o/w:	325181.2	330252.3	
(1)短期贷款及票据融资 Short-term Loans and Bill Financing o/w:	141031.7	141252.8	
短期贷款 Short-term Loans	118978.7	120946.6	
票据融资 Bill Financing	22053.03	20306.17	
(2)中长期贷款 Medium & Long-term Loans	176949.9	182029.8	
[...]			
四、外汇占款 Position for Forex Purchase	196094.1	197889.1	
资金运用总计 Total Funds Uses	**697197**	**705516.1**	

Source: Adapted from the PBOC

1. The markets are obsessed with China's new loan data—and for good reason. New loans are the main source of credit in the Chinese economy and a key determinate of the pace of growth and level of inflation. Controlling the pace of loan growth is one of the main instruments the government uses to keep control of the economy. Banks are told how much they can lend over the course of the year, and regulators tighten or loosen the quota depending on the outlook. A fair chunk of new loans also make their way illegally onto the equity and property markets—with a direct impact on the value of investments.

As Figure 8.1 shows, lending follows a strong seasonal pattern, and the banks normally start the year with a bang. In 2009, new loans in January pushed up to CNY1.6 trillion, 16% of the total for the year. In 2010, new loans in the first two weeks of January were so high that the PBOC was forced to fire a warning shot across the bows of the banking sector by raising the reserve requirement ratio (RRR). A lending officer at one of the big banks explained the reason for the January surge like this: "You know who your best customers are, and you know what your loan quota for the year is. You go to your best customer and say, 'How much do you want?' They ask for all of it, and you give them most of it. The rest of the year is your other customers scrambling to scrape up whatever is left over."

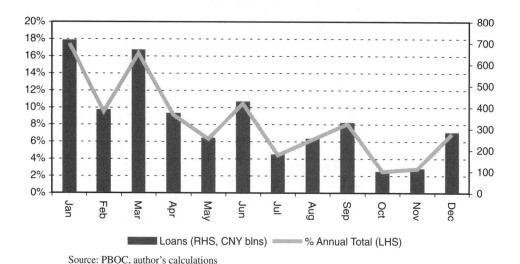

Source: PBOC, author's calculations

Figure 8.1 *Average monthly new loans, 2004–2009 (CNY billions)*

After the January feeding frenzy, lending typically stays high in the first half of the year, often with peaks in March and June as loan officers rush to improve their performance ahead of quarterly financial reports. By the second half of the year, the most creditworthy customers have all the funds they need, loans officers have met their targets for the year, and the banks are pushing up against the limits of their lending quotas. Lending starts to fall away in the third quarter, and by the fourth quarter, new loans are thin on the ground. This annual lending cycle is not particularly healthy for the economy. There is no good reason, other than the operating environment of the banks, for a credit feast at the beginning of the year and a lending famine at the end. But this is the reality that needs to be kept in mind when interpreting the monthly lending data. Massive new loans in January, March, or June do not mean that growth is about to surge forward; likewise, a sharp fall in new loans in October, November, and December does not mean the world is about to end.

2. The data also includes a breakdown of credit between short-term loans, medium and long-term loans, and bill financing. Medium- and long-term loans to businesses fund investments in industry, infrastructure, and real estate. Short-term loans and bill financing are used to cover short-term operating costs. The level of bill financing is changeable, with massive quantities of new bills issued one month and falling due a

few months later. The lending data is published on a net basis, so when these short-term notes fall due, they are subtracted from the total for new loans. As Figure 8.2 shows, netting out short-term bills that are falling due can have a marked impact on the total volume of new loans. In summer 2009, the PBOC data showed total new loans collapsing from CNY1.53 trillion in June to CNY355 billion in July. But a glance at the breakdown between different maturities reveals that medium- and long-term loans held relatively steady; a large volume of short-term loans and bills falling due explained the fall in the total.

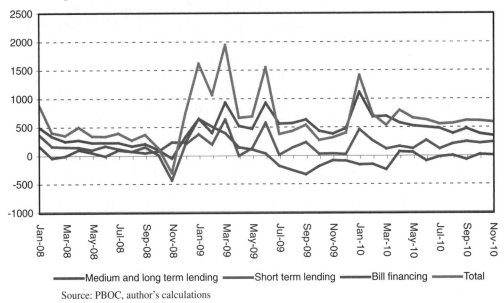

Source: PBOC, author's calculations

Figure 8.2 *Composition of new lending (CNY billions)*

3. Dollars and other foreign currency received by China's exporters in payment for their goods can either be used to pay for imports, or converted into yuan and put to use in the domestic economy. That means banks' forex purchases should be basically equal to the current account surplus. Because it is published monthly, the bank data on forex purchases provides a more timely insight into China's balance with the rest of the world than the quarterly current account and foreign exchange reserve data.

Not included in Table 8.1, but included in the PBOC's data release, is a total for foreign currency loans. This is an important data point for two reasons:

• Foreign currency loans are not included in the headline figure for new lending; only by adding them can we get a complete picture of how much credit has expanded. Foreign currency loans can sometimes add or subtract substantially from the total. In June 2009, China's banks made USD37 billion (CNY251 billion) in foreign currency loans, taking total new loans from the already monstrous CNY1.5 trillion evident in the yuan loan data to a gargantuan CNY1.7 trillion.

- Appetite for foreign currency loans is closely tied to expectations of yuan appreciation. If borrowers expect the yuan to appreciate, it makes sense to borrow a fistful of dollars, convert them into yuan, wait for the yuan to appreciate, convert a portion back into a few dollars more, repay the loan, and pocket the difference. High levels of foreign currency loans indicate that borrowers expect a period of strong yuan appreciation to come.

4. The immediate focus of market attention is always on growth in new loans. But the massive growth in deposits in the Chinese banking system is also a source of interest and controversy. A cultural tendency toward thrift, inadequate welfare state, and the need to save vast sums to get a foot on the housing ladder have pushed China's household savings rate up to phenomenal levels. In 2009, the average urban household saved almost 30% of its income. That compares to a savings rate in the United States that, until the crisis forced a reversal, was in negative territory.

China's household savers have played a key part in the mainland's development story. By channeling the capital amassed by savers to priority projects, Beijing has been able to play a game of rapid catch-up in the construction of a modern industrial base and public infrastructure. But aside from the benefits of rapid growth, household savers have received little reward for their thriftiness. For the last decade, real interest rates—meaning the interest rate paid to depositors minus the change in consumer prices—have, on average, been in negative territory. That means that China's households are paying a tax on their own savings, to subsidize the supply of cut-price capital to the industrial sector.

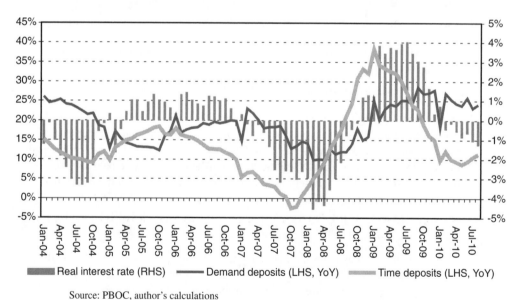

Source: PBOC, author's calculations

Figure 8.3　*Growth in household demand and time deposits versus real interest rate*

5. Changes in real interest rates, or the anticipation of changes in real interest rates, affect households' choice between time and demand deposits. If households think that real interest rates are going to shift into negative territory, they pull funds out of time deposits and push them into demand deposits, where they can be accessed before inflation lays waste to their value. If they think that real interest rates are moving into positive territory, they are happy to earn a few extra yuan by holding their funds in time deposits.

That means the relative growth rates of time and demand deposits are a gauge of household's inflationary expectations, and a useful way into thinking about the outlook for the CPI. The growth rate of households' time deposits fell throughout 2006, anticipating the rise in inflation that pushed real interest rates into negative territory at the beginning of 2007. In 2009, even with consumer prices falling, households saw the inflationary risk in the massive surge in bank lending and growth in time deposits started to decelerate. In October 2010, with real interest rates in negative territory for the previous 9 months and inflation picking up, households voted with their feet and withdrew CNY700 billion from the banking sector, a record amount. That threat of an exodus of funds from the banking sector was one of the factors that pushed the government into an earlier-than-expected move on interest rates, as it sought to reassure households that the value of their deposits was safe.

Market Impact

Equities: New loans impact equity markets through three channels. First, higher lending, contributes to higher investment and higher consumption, buoying company profits and equity valuations. Second, new loans add directly to banks' profitability, and banks are the most important single component of the Shanghai Composite and Hang Seng Indexes. Third, some loans are used illegally to fund speculation on the markets. In February 2007, the State Council dispatched a team to Shanghai to investigate illegal use of loans for speculation. The Shanghai Composite Index fell 8.8% the next day. That fall triggered a 3.5% slide in the S&P, one of the first times the Chinese tail wagged the U.S. dog. In 2009, the word on the street was that CNY1 trillion of the CNY7 trillion loaned out in the first half of the year had found its way onto the equity markets. News that the China Banking Regulatory Commission (CBRC) was sending a team to investigate resulted in a temporary reversal of the market's bull run.

Commodities: The relationship between new loans and investment means that commodities markets also watch the data closely. Strong new loans mean more investment in infrastructure projects, productive capacity, and the real estate sector. All of that means more demand for crude oil, iron ore, and copper.

Currency: The new loans data provides little clue to the government's intentions on the exchange rate. But a high number for foreign currency loans is a sign that the market expects rapid appreciation ahead. For commodity currencies such as the Australian dollar and proxies for China's growth in the Korean won and the Singapore dollar, a high number for new lending can be bullish.

Money Supply

Market sensitivity: High
What is it? Monthly indicator of the quantity of money in the Chinese economy, published in CNY100 millions
Chinese news release on the Internet: www.pbc.gov.cn/publish/main/index.html
English news release on the Internet: www.pbc.gov.cn/publish/english/963/index.html
Release time: Between the 10th and 15th of the following month
Frequency: Monthly
Source: PBOC
Revisions: No

Why Is It Important?

China's money supply is like the Yangtze River, always threatening to flood its banks. The Yangtze has seasonal rains that turn spring's muddy trickle into summer's torrent. The equivalent for China's money supply is the steady drip of the current account surplus. Continuous inflows from the current account surplus make managing growth of China's money supply a tricky business. The engineers charged with preventing the current account trickle from turning into an inflationary torrent are the PBOC. In general, the Central Bankers have done a pretty good job. Aggressive use of open market operations and the RRR have sterilized the impact of inflows, taking cash out of circulation before it can turn into higher loans from the banks. Growth in the money supply has been reigned in to an average 18% for the last decade. But the PBOC has not always been so strict. The money supply river has sometimes been allowed to break its banks, with the result a short-term boost to growth and a bull run on the equity markets, but a long-term cost to be paid in higher inflation.

How Is the Data Calculated?

The Central Bank collects data on the money supply from deposit organizations—mainly the banks. The data is aggregated into three different categories:

- **M0**—The bills and coins actually in circulation.
- **M1**—M0 + demand deposits.
- **M2**—M1 + time, savings, and other deposits.

Counting the amount of money in the Chinese economy seems fairly straightforward and not the sort of exercise that is prone to problems. In fact, China's money supply data has not kept up with developments in the economy, and this introduces two distortions into the data. First, both households' time and demand deposits are classified as part of M2. This harks back to an earlier time when household deposits were not particularly liquid. In the age of ATMs and online banking, household demand deposits are extremely liquid and their exclusion from M1 is something of an aberration.

Second, the data fails to capture the impact of new developments in financial products which take funds out of the traditional bank deposit system. Interest rates for depositors in the banking system are capped by the government at an artificially low level. To get around this problem, banks have created wealth management products which offer savers a higher rate in return. These funds are not classified as deposits, and so are not included in M2, but as they are effectively deposits by another name, their exclusion from the calculation reduces the value of M2 as a measure of the money supply.

Interpreting the Data

Table 8.2 *Money Supply (April 2010)*

单位: 亿元人民币
Unit: 100 Million Yuan

项目 Item	2010.01	2010.02	2010.03	2010.04	2010.05	[...]
2▶ 货币和准货币 (M2) Money and Quasi-money	625609.29	636072.26	649947.46	656561.22		
1▶ 货币 (M1) Money	229588.98	224286.95	229397.93	233909.76		
流通中货币 (M0) Currency in Circulation	40758.58	42865.79	39080.58	39657.54		

Source: Adapted from the PBOC

1. Growth in the money supply on its own does not create inflation. If the economy is running at below capacity, an increase in the money supply will not pass through into higher prices. But when growth is on track and the economy is operating at capacity, increases in the money supply create the conditions for prices to rise. With growth in the Chinese economy typically proceeding at a torrid pace, changes in the money supply have a close relationship with changes in inflation. In 1994, growth in M1 peaked at close to 32% YoY. With the money supply out of control, the CPI ran above 27%, the highest level in the reform era. A peak in growth of M1 at 22.1% YoY in September 2007, supported growth in GDP at 13.0% for the year but, as Figure 8.4 shows, was followed by a rise in the CPI to a heady 8.7% in February 2008. In 2009, the government responded to the global financial crisis by opening the liquidity floodgates. Growth in M1 surged above 30% YoY, supporting growth in GDP at a steady 9.1%. But in 2010, with growth back on track and the economy operating at close to capacity, that increase in the money supply started to pass through into higher prices. The CPI rose to 5.1% YoY in November, and the PBOC warned darkly that the real inflationary price had yet to be paid. With the exception of the previous example, when the peak in inflation came a long time after peak growth in money supply, the lesson of the last decade is that peaks in the CPI follow 6 months to a year after peaks in growth of M1.

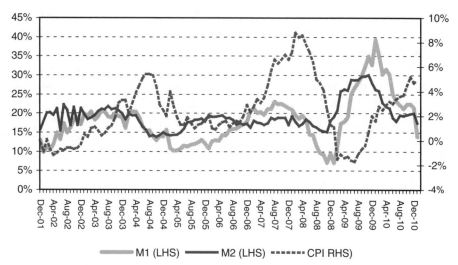

Figure 8.4 *M1 and M2 growth versus CPI (YoY %)*

Source: PBOC, National Bureau of Statistics, author's calculations

2. M2 is the broadest measure of money supply, and the government uses it as an intermediate target for monetary policy. At the annual government work conference, which
takes place in March, the premier often announces a target for M2 growth for the year.
But this is typically only a loose pointer toward the government's thinking and is
sometimes exceeded by a wide margin. In 2009, Premier Wen Jiabao set a target of
17% YoY growth in M2. In fact, money supply grew by 27.7% for the year.

Beyond the published data, investors and policymakers keep an eye on two important
indicators as a guide to the outlook for inflation:

• The ratio of M2 and GDP is an indicator of the overall state of monetary conditions. An increase in the ratio means there is more money chasing less output,
  resulting in a risk of higher inflation. A decrease in the ratio means less money is
  chasing more output, which should help control inflation but maybe at the expense
  of lower growth. Zhang Jianhua, the head of the PBOC's research department, has
  said that the Central Bank looks at this ratio as an indicator of overall monetary
  conditions.

• The difference between growth in M1 and M2 is a measure of the extent of inflationary expectations. As Figure 8.4 shows, times when growth in M1 has accelerated past growth in M2, including the end of 2006 and the end of 2009, have
  coincided with the beginning of rising consumer prices. One complicating factor
  here is that both households' time and demand deposit accounts are classified as
  part of M2, so shifts in the relative pace of growth reflect changes in behavior by
  enterprises, not by households. For a read on households' preferences for liquidity
  and return in managing their finances, the PBOC's data on the banking system provides a breakdown between time and demand deposits.

Market Impact

Equities: Investors who want a rule of thumb to gauge turning points in the equity markets could do a lot worse than looking at growth in money supply. The highs and lows of the Shanghai Composite Index map closely with the peaks and troughs in growth of M1.

Commodities: If China is opening the money supply flood gates, that means more investment spending and stronger demand for raw materials. If the Central Bank is in tightening mode, that means less investment spending and a smaller appetite for commodities a few months down the road.

Currency: The relationship between the money supply and the exchange rate is a major headache for China. Keep the yuan stable at an undervalued exchange rate, and a continued current account surplus will feed the money supply and add to inflationary pressure. Allow appreciation, and speculators will bring hot money into the country to benefit from the rising yuan—and the result will be the same. Either way, the direction of travel is from the decision on the exchange rate to the impact on the money supply, not the other way around.

NONPERFORMING LOANS

Market sensitivity: Medium
What is it? Quarterly indicator of the quantity of nonperforming loans (NPLs) in the banking sector, published in CNY100 millions and as a percentage of total loans
Chinese news release on the Internet: www.cbrc.gov.cn/chinese/home/jsp/index.jsp
English news release on the Internet: www.cbrc.gov.cn/english/home/jsp/index.jsp
Release time: About 7 weeks after the end of the quarter for Chinese version
Frequency: Quarterly for the Chinese release, annually for the English release
Source: CBRC
Revisions: No

Why Is It Important?

Government control of the banking sector has its advantages. Directing lending to strategic sectors and finance available on favorable terms has enabled China to rapidly catch up in the development of its public infrastructure and industrial base. The ability to turn on the lending taps has also helped get the government out of more than one tight spot. A surge in new loans to CNY9.5 trillion in 2009, more than double the CNY4.2 trillion in loans issued in 2008, pulled the Chinese economy back from the brink. But political interference in the commercial operation of the banking sector also has a cost. Loans that are made to achieve policy objectives or, even worse, to further the pet project of some local party chief, are more likely to go bad than loans that are made to make a profit.

The Chinese banking system has already dealt with one NPL horror show. At the end of the 1990s, decades of policy-directed lending had stuffed the banks full of loans that had little chance of repayment. Root and branch reform of the state owned enterprises meant that many of the borrowers were actually facing bankruptcy, so bad loans could not continue to be rolled over. The Asian Financial Crisis added to China's economic woes and underlined the risks that accompany weakness in the banking system. At the end of the decade, the official statistics put NPLs as a percentage of total loans at 30%. Unofficial estimates put that number much higher, some as high as 50%.

The government solved the problem by ingenious means. The bad loans were not written off. They were separated out and sold at face value to asset-management companies, one for each of the big banks. The asset-management companies took more than CNY1 trillion of NPLs off the banks' books, paying for the purchases with the proceeds of bonds that they sold to the banks themselves. That incestuous arrangement still left the banks exposed to credit risk from the asset-management companies, who would be relying on turning the banks' own old NPLs into performing loans to repay interest and capital on the bonds. If that all sounds like so much reshuffling of deck chairs on the *Titanic*, consider that the banks and asset-management companies are all majority owned by the Ministry of Finance. So if all that smoke and mirrors created the illusion that the banks were better off, no one could be under any illusion about the balance sheet of the government, which was left completely unchanged.

In the years that followed, the banks' balance sheets continued to improve and the NPL ratio continued to fall. In an economy growing at more than 10% a year, it is pretty difficult to make bad loans. Going into the financial crisis, China's banks could boast an NPL ratio of just 2.42%; at the midpoint of 2010, that number had fallen to 1.30%. Does that mean that China's banks have mended their ways and solved the problem of bad loans? Probably not. The CNY9.5 trillion in loans made in 2009 and the CNY7.9 trillion more issued in 2010 were directed as much by policy as by financial imperatives. Throw slower growth into the mix, and like the villain in a horror movie that you thought was dead, China's NPLs might be set for a comeback, hacking a bloody path through the banks' books. If it's going to be *NPLs II,* you can catch the previews and see the main feature in the CBRC's quarterly data release.

How Is the Data Calculated?

The banks are under their own recognizance to monitor and report on the level of NPLs. Loans are classified into one of five categories:

- **Normal loans**—Loans where the borrower has been performing its obligations and there are no signs the borrower will default on principal or interest.

- **Special notice loans**—Loans where the borrower is currently able to make principal and interest payments, but is experiencing factors that may be prejudicial to repayment.

- **Substandard loans**—Loans where the borrower is clearly experiencing factors jeopardizing its ability to meet payment obligations, and it is clear that the borrowers' income from its ordinary course of business does not allow it to make principal and interest payments in full. These loans may result in a loss even after enforcement of collateral.

- **Doubtful loans**—Loans where the borrower is unable to meet its payment obligations. These loans will result in material loss even after the enforcement of collateral.

- **Loss**—Loans where no, or only a minimal amount of, principal and interest are collectible, even after exhausting all collection efforts and all available legal means.

Every quarter, banks review their own loan portfolios and report on the status of their loans to the CBRC. The criteria used for classifying loans are in line with international practice, and the regulations require the banks to have robust systems in place for monitoring and evaluation, with senior leadership in the frame if anything goes wrong. The CBRC also monitors the quality of loans of commercial banks through both on-site inspections and off-site monitoring activities. But interpretation plays an important part in the classification of loans, and that leaves scope for under-reporting.

Banks might under-report their NPLs for two reasons. First, the same political pressure that pushes banks to lend to local leaders' vanity projects is likely to prevent them from foreclosing on the loan. Even if loans to local state-owned enterprises or government investment entities have little chance of being repaid, the pressure on the banks will be to keep rolling them over into perpetuity. Second, if the banks do acknowledge NPLs, they have to set aside a certain percentage of capital—currently, 150% of the value of the NPL—to cover the loss. The fewer NPLs they report, the less capital they have to set aside, and the more scope they have to make new loans.

Interpreting the Data

Table 8.3 *Commercial Banks Nonperforming Loans Situation (January to June 2010, CNY100mlns)*

Year 2010	Q1		Q2	
	Outstanding balance	Share in total loans	Outstanding balance	Share in total loans
1▶ **Non-Performing Loans by Five-Category Classifications**	4701.2	1.40%	4549.1	1.30%
2▶ Substandard	1786.6	0.53%	1673.3	0.48%
Doubtful	2288.8	0.68%	2226.7	0.64%
Loss	625.8	0.19%	649.1	0.19%
By Institutions				
Major Commercial Banks	4009.6	1.41%	3839.8	1.30%
State Owned Commercial Banks	3400.0	1.59%	3247.7	1.46%
3▶ Joint Stock Commercial Banks	609.6	0.86%	592.1	0.80%
City Commercial Banks	365.9	1.19%	360.7	1.11%
Rural Commercial Banks	265.8	2.47%	288.2	2.34%
Foreign Banks	59.8	0.74%	60.4	0.72%

Source: Adapted from CBRC

1. The headline grabber in the data release is total NPLs, and NPLs as a ratio of total banking system loans. Table 8.3 shows NPLs as a percentage of total loans falling to 1.30% in the second quarter of 2010, a record low. All appears quiet. But with the CNY17.4 trillion in new loans issued in 2009 and 2010 directed as much by political as financial logic, NPLs might be set for a comeback. CNY2.9 trillion of those loans were made to a bubbly real estate sector. CNY7.7 trillion more were dropped into the murky world of local government investment projects. Another few hundred billion were handed over to industries in which overcapacity and restructuring threaten to trigger bankruptcies. How many of those loans will turn bad is anyone's guess. With total loans outstanding in the banking system at the end of 2010 around CNY37 trillion, if every loan made to local government investment entities and the real estate sector in 2009 and 2010 went bad, that would result in an NPL ratio of around 29%. That is a nightmare scenario and is unlikely to occur. But many analysts believe the rapid expansion in the loan book in 2009 and 2010 cannot have occurred without compromising credit standards. A rebound in the NPL ratio above the current low level would not be a surprise.

Properly understood, NPLs are not just a problem for the banks; they are also a problem for the government. If NPLs reach a level that threatens the solvency of the banks, the government would be forced to step in and assume responsibility. The level of public debt acknowledged by Beijing is very low, about 17% of GDP at the end of 2010. But when analysts attempt to estimate the real level of public debt, they add in an estimate of the level of NPLs that might end up on the government's books. CNY454.9 billion in NPLs in the second quarter of 2010 equaled around 1.3% of GDP. But if loans issued to the real estate sector and local government investment entities start to go bad, that number could rise much higher—adding to the government's debt burden.

2. The CBRC divides NPLs into four categories—with progressively higher levels of severity. Special notice loans are the first rung on the ladder. In horror movies, it's the absence of a mobile phone signal that is the first sign the hapless teens are about to be picked off by the faceless killer. If NPLs are going to make a comeback, a rise in special notice loans should be the first sign of trouble ahead.

3. The CBRC also breaks down NPLs by the different broad categories of banks. The most important category is the state-owned commercial banks. These are the giants that dominate the Chinese banking sector, accounting for around two-thirds of total outstanding loans. Industrial and Commercial Bank of China, Agricultural Bank of China, Bank of China, China Construction Bank, and Bank of Communications are included in this category.

   The joint stock commercial and city commercial banks, including major players such as China Merchants and China Minsheng, make up the second tier of the Chinese banking sector, accounting for about a third of total outstanding loans. At the bottom of the pile are the rural commercial banks. With the major state-owned, joint stock, and city banks taking all the best customers, the rural banks are left making loans to high-risk small businesses and shady local government operations in low-growth rural areas. Throw weaker risk-management capacity and stronger political control over lending in village backwaters into the mix, and NPLs at the rural banks are the highest of the bunch.

   One oddity of the NPL data is that the China Development Bank, the Import Export Bank of China, and the Postal Bank (all of which remain 100% owned by the state) are not included in the calculation. It is reasonable to assume that NPLs at these policy banks are higher than at their more commercially orientated peers. As recently as 2007, before its balance sheet was prettied up for the IPO, the NPL ratio at the Agricultural Bank of China was a whopping 23%. If the NPLs of the remaining policy banks were included in the published total, the NPL level and ratio would be higher.

Market Impact

The NPL data is not really a market mover. It is published infrequently and with an extended delay, and it measures a problem that does not have a direct impact on the growth outlook. That said, a high level of NPLs is a negative not just for the banking sector that is a big part of the Hang Seng and the Shanghai Composite Index, but also for the government that might ultimately have to foot the bill for a bailout. If NPLs do lumber out of the grave for a sequel to the late-1990s original, the markets will pay close attention.

CHINA FOREIGN EXCHANGE TRADING SYSTEM CENTRAL PARITIES

Market sensitivity: High
What is it? Daily announcement of the trading band for the yuan against the dollar and other major currencies
Chinese news release on the Internet: www.chinamoney.com.cn/
English news release on the Internet: n/a
Release time: 9:15 a.m.
Frequency: Daily
Source: China Foreign Exchange Trading Center (CFETC)
Revisions: No

Why Is It Important?

The most visible expression of China's control of the exchange rate is the central parities published by the CFETC every morning. These parities set the value of the yuan against the dollar, the euro, the yen, and other major currencies at which the Central Bank will buy foreign currency that day. The changes in the parities can be big, as when exchange rate reform began with a bang on July 21, 2005, or resumed with a whimper on June 19, 2010. But they are usually small, as the government continues on a path of gradual reform. Big or small, movements in the central parities are eagerly awaited by the markets as a daily indicator of the government's intentions on the exchange rate.

How Is the Data Calculated?

The PBOC has delegated responsibility for setting the daily central parities to the CFETC. Every day, before the mainland's FX markets open, the CFETC calls a group of market participants and asks for quotes on the dollar–yuan exchange rate. A list of 26 market makers includes big Chinese banks such as Industrial and Commercial Bank of China and Agricultural Bank of China, as well as smaller banks such as Guangdong Development Bank, and some foreign players such as HSBC. The CFETC removes the highest and lowest quotes and then takes an average of those that remain. The parities for the yuan against the euro, Japanese yen, British pound, and Hong Kong dollar are a function of the yuan–dollar parity and the dollar's exchange rate against these other currencies. If the yuan is set at 6.6303 to the dollar, and the dollar is currently trading at 1.3706 to the euro, then the yuan must also be set at 9.0875 to the euro ($6.6303 \times 1.3706 = 9.0875$). The parity for the yuan against the Malaysian Ringgit, which is a recent addition to the daily parities, is also the average of quotes taken from market makers, although, in this case, only three Chinese banks are asked for their opinion.

In theory, the average of quotes from market makers should reflect the balance of supply and demand in the FX markets. In practice, China's Central Bank is a major player in FX markets, intervening to the tune of tens of billions of dollars a month to keep the yuan on an even keel. China's closed capital account also prevents the markets from taking a genuine position on the value of the yuan. With these constraints, there can be no genuine market view on the value of the currency. But even within the context of an interventionist Central Bank and a closed capital account, the central parities do not always reflect the market view. Market makers will reveal in private that they sometimes see little relationship between the price in the market and the parity set by the CFETC. FX strategists believe that on some days the PBOC itself, or even higher levels of government, are calling the shots. That is no surprise. The central parities are an instrument of government control as much as they are an expression of supply and demand in the market.

Interpreting the Data

Table 8.4   *Yuan Daily Parities (November 15, 2010)*

	Currency	Central Parity
1 ▶	USD/CNY	6.6303
	HKD/CNY	0.85536
	100JPY/CNY	8.0362
2 ▶	EUR/CNY	9.0875
	GBP/CNY	10.6950
	CNY/MYR	0.47048

Source: Adapted from CFETC

1. The main focus for the markets is the dollar–yuan parity. In Table 8.4, the data shows that on November 15, 2010, the yuan was set at 6.6303 to the dollar. The Central Bank tolerates trading in a band 0.5% above or below the central parity. So on that day, the yuan could fall to 6.6635 or rise to 6.5971 without fear of Central Bank intervention. Any suggestion of movement outside that band would have the PBOC wading in with its wallet to bring the exchange rate back within the target range.

   Movements in the dollar–yuan parity are typically rather small. But on two occasions, the government has used larger movements to signal significant shifts in the policy position. On July 21, 2005, the PBOC got the exchange rate reform ball rolling with a one-off 2% appreciation, taking the yuan from 8.27 against the dollar (the level it had held for the last several years) to 8.11. On June 22, 2010, after the financial crisis had kicked reform into the long grass for almost 2 years, the Central Bank signaled a resumption with a 0.4% appreciation, taking the yuan from 6.82 to the dollar to 6.79. A 0.4% move in June 2010 was less spectacular than the 2% jump in July 2005. But following 2 years of near stasis in the dollar–yuan exchange rate, it was enough to get the ball back into play.

   The rest of the time, the market is left puzzling over the significance of rather smaller movements. Just what is going on in the minds of China's policymakers when they set the exchange rate is a mystery. The Ministry of Commerce, the chief cheerleader for China's export lobby, is vociferous in its support for stability in the exchange rate. The PBOC, chief cheerleader for reform, occasionally plucks up the courage to make the intellectual case for a floating yuan. But the real decision makers in the State Council are as inscrutable as their stereotypes. Official announcements repeat that reform will be gradual and determined by the national interest. But that provides little information about the principles that inform the pace of appreciation. Adding to the mystery, the Central Bank also claims that the value of the yuan is set with reference to a basket of currencies. That was certainly not true in the period from 2005 to 2008, when the yuan was clearly tracking the dollar. In the latest period of reform, the jury is still out on whether the exchange rate is referencing a basket or continuing to focus on the greenback.

China's leaders might keep mum. But developments in the period since July 2005, suggest a certain rhyme and reason to China's exchange rate policy:

- The main reason for managing the exchange rate is to support the competitiveness of the export sector. A cheap yuan means cheap Chinese products, enabling the exporters of the Pearl and Yangtze River Deltas to win a larger share of global markets and supporting high levels of employment in the textile sweatshops and mobile phone factories. In the period from 2005 to 2008, with export growth running comfortably above 20% a year, the government felt relaxed enough to allow the pace of yuan appreciation to accelerate. The annualized rate of appreciation hit a peak of higher than 20% in January 2008. But when the global crisis hit and the collapse in export demand threatened to throw tens of thousands of firms into bankruptcy and millions of workers into unemployment, appreciation came grinding to a halt. From summer 2008, for almost 2 years, the yuan held steady against the dollar. Not until consumers in the rest of the world had returned to the shops in summer 2010, export growth was back above 20%, and fears of mass unemployment were disappearing into the rear view mirror did appreciation of the yuan resume.

- The exchange rate is also a tool that can be used to control inflation. A higher value for the yuan should choke off demand, slowing growth and taking some of the heat out of the economy. At the same time, a higher value for the yuan means China's industrial sector are paying a lower price for imported commodities such as crude oil and iron ore, keeping a lid on upstream inflationary pressure. For both these reasons, periods of high inflation can push the Chinese government to allow the yuan to appreciate at a faster rate. The period of most rapid yuan appreciation at the beginning of 2008 was also a peak for inflation, with the CPI hitting 8.7% in February 2008.

- The Chinese government would swear until blue in the face that the exchange rate is set in accordance with national priorities. But actions speak louder than words, and China's actions make clear that international pressure does have some impact. During Hank Paulson's reign as U.S. Treasury Secretary, the pace of appreciation had a habit of picking up ahead of the biannual meeting of the U.S.–China Strategic Economic Dialogue. At the end of 2008, with the export sector teetering on the brink, Beijing flirted with the possibility of depreciation, but the risk to China's reputation as a responsible player in the global economy held it back. In the first half of 2010, with the global recovery on track and pressure on China mounting to resume appreciation, the PBOC announced the end of the yuan's peg to the dollar the week before a crucial G20 meeting. Later in the year, when the U.S. Congress was set to vote on legislation aimed at toughening the administration's stance on the yuan, Beijing allowed the pace of appreciation to creep up a few notches. The extent of appreciation might be determined by domestic considerations, but the lesson of the last 5 years is that the timing has a lot to do with international pressure.

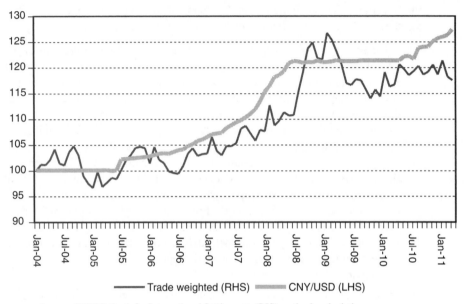

Source: CFETC, Bank for International Settlements (BIS), author's calculations

Figure 8.5 *Nominal yuan–dollar versus real trade-weighted exchange rates (Index: Jan 2004=100)*

2. The focus of the markets is on the dollar–yuan exchange rate. But a focus on a single exchange rate is, in many ways, misleading. Less than 15% of China's total trade is with the United States. Adding up all of China's trade with dollar block countries takes the number closer to 50%. But still more than half of China's trade takes place with countries that deal in euros, yen, won, rupees, real, and other currencies. The best guide to the overall competitiveness of China's exports is not the dollar–yuan exchange rate, but rather the trade-weighted exchange rate.

The government does not publish the trade-weighted exchange rate. But the Bank for International Settlements publishes real and nominal trade-weighted exchange rates, updated every month, that can be downloaded from its website. As Figure 8.5 shows, the trade-weighted exchange rate often tells a different story than the dollar–yuan exchange rate:

- In the period from 2005 to 2008, the yuan appreciated 21% in nominal terms against the dollar. But on a real trade-weighted basis, the Chinese currency gained only 16%, a less serious hit to the competitiveness of exports than suggested by the change in the dollar–yuan rate.

- At the end of 2008, the Chinese government repegged the yuan to the dollar as a way to support the competitiveness of exports. Ironically, the impact was exactly the reverse. With a flight to quality pushing the dollar through the roof, the yuan went with it. Between August 2008 and February 2009, the yuan was flat against the dollar, but on a real trade-weighted basis, it picked up 10%.

- In the period from June 2010 to the end of the year, Beijing won a few friends in Washington, DC by allowing the yuan to appreciate 3.1% against the dollar. But on a trade-weighted basis, the yuan actually fell 2.2%. Six months after the start of reform, China's exports were more, not less, competitive than they had been before the PBOC announced the end of the yuan's dollar peg.

The PBOC has always claimed to manage the value of the yuan against a basket of currencies, and the announcement of a return to flexibility on June 19, 2010, was accompanied by a lengthy paper extolling the benefits of a basket regime. PBOC Deputy Gov. Hu Xiaolian has also gone on record saying that it makes more sense to track the trade-weighted exchange rate than the dollar–yuan exchange rate. For now, the focus for policymakers and markets remains the dollar–yuan exchange rate. But the benefits of tracking and monitoring a basket of currencies mean the trade-weighted exchange rate can only rise in prominence.

Market Impact

Equities: More rapid appreciation of the yuan might be bad for the export sector, but it is often good news for the equity markets, for three reasons:

- Appreciation of the yuan means that the value of yuan assets (such as shares of companies listed on the Shanghai exchange or the yuan profits of Chinese companies listed in Hong Kong) rises.

- Companies such as Petrochina and Baosteel that have a major weight on the mainland's markets are importers of commodities and, therefore, benefit from yuan appreciation. The exporters who lose out are often smaller private-sector firms whose shares are not publicly traded.

- Appreciation, or the expectation of appreciation, increases the appeal of China for speculators, and some of the inflows of hot money find a home on the equity markets.

Commodities: The exchange rate is a focus of attention for commodities markets, for two reasons. First, movements in the yuan change the price that Chinese companies pay for their imported commodities. A faster rate of appreciation means Chinese firms can buy up supplies of crude oil and iron ore at a lower yuan price, supporting strong demand. Second, for many commodities, China is the marginal producer. That means Chinese production costs put a ceiling on global prices. If the yuan appreciates against the dollar, that can raise the market's estimate of the ceiling on global aluminum and other metal prices.

Currencies: Movements in the central parity have an obvious impact on the market's estimate of the likely pace of yuan appreciation. The dollar–yuan exchange rate is also a major factor affecting other regional currencies. If the yuan appreciates against the dollar, that creates room for the Taiwanese dollar, the Singapore dollar, and the Korean won to make up ground without damaging the competitiveness of domestic exporters. Where the yuan goes, other Asian currencies often follow.

HONG KONG BANKING SYSTEM YUAN DEPOSITS

Market sensitivity: Low
What is it? Monthly data on the stock of yuan deposits in the Hong Kong banking system, published in CNY millions
Chinese news release on the Internet: www.info.gov.hk/hkma/
English news release on the Internet: www.info.gov.hk/hkma/gb_chi/index.htm
Release time: Around 6 weeks after the end of the month
Frequency: Monthly
Source: Hong Kong Monetary Authority (HKMA)
Revisions: No

Why Is It Important?

The Hong Kong dollar's peg to the U.S. dollar has turned the former colony into a barometer of island opinion on the outlook for yuan appreciation. The peg to the U.S. dollar means that Hong Kong's currency tracks the greenback's movement against the yuan. If the yuan appreciates 5% against the U.S. dollar, it also appreciates 5% against the Hong Kong dollar. Hong Kong residents are entitled to convert Hong Kong dollars into yuan up to the value of CNY20,000 per day. If the investment-savvy Cantonese expect the yuan to rise against the greenback, it makes sense for them to exchange as many Hong Kong dollars into yuan as possible. If they expect the yuan to depreciate against the U.S. dollar, it makes sense for them to convert those yuan back into Hong Kong dollars. In the period from 2005 to 2010, the level of yuan deposits in the Hong Kong banking system did as good a job as the professional economists in forecasting the outlook for appreciation. In 2010, a move to turn Hong Kong into an offshore center for yuan finance, with the rapid expansion of yuan trade settlement, has led to a surge in growth in yuan deposits that is only partially related to island opinion on the outlook for the exchange rate.

How Is the Data Calculated?

As part of its bank supervision, the HKMA conducts a monthly survey of all the banks under its jurisdiction, including collecting data on the total quantity of yuan deposits and the breakdown between time and demand deposits.

Interpreting the Data

Table 8.5 *Yuan Deposits in the Hong Kong Banking System*

Renminbi deposits 人民幣存款				RMB million yuan 百萬元人民幣
As at end of 期末數字	Demand and Savings 活期及儲蓄存款	Time 定期存款	Total 總計	No. of authorized institutions engaged in RMB business 經營人民幣業務 的認可機構數目
2010 Feb 2月	42,499	23,593	66,092	71
Mar 3月	44,609	26,145	70,755	73
Apr 4月	50,237	30,657	80,894	72
May 5月	51,266	34,345	85,611	76
June 6月	52,427	37,275	89,702	77
July 7月	55,724	47,960	103,684	77
Aug 8月	62,864	67,548	130,412	84

Source: Adapted from HKMA

The main takeaway from the data is the change in the total value of yuan deposits in the Hong Kong banking system. An increase suggests that Hong Kong residents, peering over the short stretch of ocean that separates them from the mainland, have concluded that the yuan is set to rise against the dollar. A leveling off suggests that the outlook for appreciation is more muted. As Figure 8.6 shows, Hong Kong residents have been better than most at reading the runes.

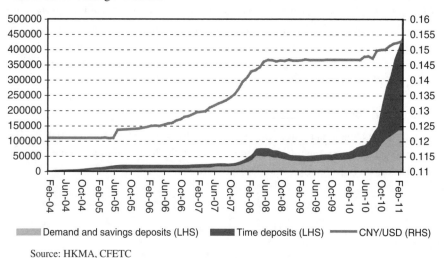

Source: HKMA, CFETC

Figure 8.6 *Yuan deposits in Hong Kong (CNY millions) versus yuan–dollar exchange rate*

- In 2004 and the first half of 2005, with expectations of the end of the yuan's peg to the dollar elevated, yuan deposits rose from CNY895 million in February 2004 to CNY20,898 million in June 2005.

- In spring 2008, with concerns about the impact of the burgeoning global crisis on China's exporters, growth in yuan deposits topped out in April, two months before appreciation came grinding to a halt.

- In the beginning of 2010, with the worst of the crisis over, Hong Kong residents anticipated the resumption of yuan appreciation. Yuan deposits started to rise at the beginning of 2010, and growth accelerated in April, two months ahead of the PBOC's announcement of the next stage of reform.

In 2010, the move by China's Central Bank to turn Hong Kong into a pool of off-shore yuan liquidity changed the nature of the game. The level of yuan deposits in the Hong Kong banking system soared from CNY89,702 million in June 2010 to CNY370,635 million in January 2011. As in the period from 2004 to the first half of 2010, the expectation of yuan appreciation contributed to the appeal of holding the mainland's currency. But the supercharged increase in deposits was related as much to the experiment in yuan internationalization—with a surge in yuan bond issuance and trade settlement—as to the outlook for the yuan dollar exchange rate. It remains to be seen if a more stable environment after the early stages of the experiment restores the value of yuan deposits as an indicator of opinion on the exchange rate, or if a continued rapid growth says more about the development of Hong Kong as an offshore financial center for the yuan than it does about the outlook for appreciation.

Market Impact

The main value of the deposit data is as a barometer of expectations on the yuan–dollar exchange rate. With China's capital account closed, the options for using that information to take a position on the prospects for appreciation are somewhat limited. But movements in the exchange rate do have broader implications for other categories of assets, with expectations of appreciation generally bullish for mainland equities, commodities, and other Asian currencies.

PEOPLE'S BANK OF CHINA REPORTS

Market sensitivity: Medium
What is it? Reports from the Central Bank on monetary policy and macroeconomic conditions, and the statement of the Monetary Policy Committee (MPC)
Chinese news release on the Internet: www.pbc.gov.cn/
English news release on the Internet: n/a
Release time: The macroeconomic report is typically published in the first month of the following quarter and the monetary policy report in the second month. The statement of the MPC is published after the meeting of the committee, which normally takes place at the end of the quarter.
Frequency: Quarterly
Source: PBOC
Revisions: No

Why Is It Important?

The minutes of the Federal Open Markets Committee (FOMC) are like a window into the mind of the decision makers on U.S. monetary policy. Arguments are made, evidence is put forward, and decisions are explained. They might not always be the right decisions, but at least the process is clear, and that transparency takes a lot of the surprises out of policy making. PBOC reports are like the black-tinted windows of the Audi A6s in which senior officials are chauffeured around Beijing. Shapes and outlines are discernable within, but there's no clear view of the current thinking of China's monetary policy decision makers. When decisions do come, they often take the markets by surprise.

Why so mysterious? In the United States, the FOMC can be clear about the direction of policy because it is making policy. As an independent central bank, the Fed has the authority to shift the interest rate or use other tools to achieve its objectives on inflation and growth. In China, the PBOC and the MPC are confined to an advisory role. The premier, in consultation with the State Council, makes the final decision about the direction of monetary policy and the use of key instruments such as the interest rate and exchange rates. The PBOC cannot give a clear read on the direction of policy because it does not decide the direction of policy—in some cases, does not even know what it is.

A recent example illustrates the difficult position in which the PBOC finds itself. Speaking to an audience in Washington, D.C., on October 11, 2010, Gov. Zhou Xiaochuan said that use of the RRR and open market operations would be sufficient to keep inflation under the government's target for the year. The markets, reasonably enough, interpreted these words as a sign that, despite higher-than-expected inflation, a hike in interest rates would remain on hold for a while longer. Just 8 days later, on October 19, the PBOC announced a hike in interest rates. With that decision coming straight from the highest level of the government, the Central Bank may well have been as surprised as anybody else.

The PBOC's Monetary Policy Report and Macroeconomic Report, and the Statement of the MPC, do not provide the same level of insight into the thinking of policymakers in China as the FOMC minutes or the Fed's Beige Book do into that of policymakers in the United States. But even dimly discerned outlines are of some value, and China analysts parse the reports in some detail.

Interpreting the Monetary Policy Report

The PBOC Monetary Policy Report is a quarterly review of the state of the financial markets, the implementation of monetary policy, and the Central Bank's views about the economic outlook.

Loose, Stable, or Tight?

The report is typically around 50 pages long, but readers can safely skip over much of the first 48. The markets are looking for the characterization of the overarching policy stance, and this appears in the last few pages, in a section titled "Important Policies in the Period Ahead" (下一阶段主要政策思路):

- In the first quarter of 2008, the financial crisis was still a glint in a subprime mortgage broker's eye, and controlling inflation was the top priority. The PBOC promised to "persist with a tight monetary policy." (坚持实施从紧的货币政策)

- By summer 2008, inflationary pressure had faded and uncertainties about the global outlook had increased. The PBOC promised a "stable" monetary policy (保持货币政策的连续性和稳定性), with "fine tuning in response to a changing domestic and international economic outlook." (根据国内外形势变化适时微调)

- By the third-quarter report, Lehman Brothers was bankrupt, the global economy was hovering on the brink, and the Central Bank was promising an "appropriately loose" (适度宽松) monetary policy.

- A year later, in the final quarter of 2009, "appropriately loose" had become a mantra for the Central Bank. But with the worst of the crisis over, the appearance of "balancing the objectives of growth, reform, and controlling inflationary expectations" (保持经济平稳较快发展、调整经济结构和管理好通胀预期的关系) showed that the policymakers were considering a broader set of priorities.

- In the third quarter of 2010, with the economy back on an even keel and inflation rearing its ugly head again, the PBOC offered up that it wanted to "gradually return monetary conditions to a normal state" (引导货币条件逐步回归常态水平), to signal that tightening was on the way.

Often policy actions change first and words run to catch up. By the time the third quarter 2008 report got around to announcing a shift to an "appropriately loose" monetary policy, the Central Bank had already cut interest rates. At the end of 2010, a hike in interest rates came before the announcement of a return of monetary conditions to a "normal state." The PBOC is also often parroting a formulation first articulated by the premier or the state council. But the headline characterization of policy is still an important signal of the direction of the government's thinking, and it has analysts turning hastily to the final pages of the report to see whether the Central Bank is planning to keep it loose, stable, or tight.

Exchange Rate Boilerplate

The report also offers a glimpse into the Central Bank's plans for the exchange rate. Language here often has a boilerplate quality, with the report's authors cutting and pasting from a stock of well-worn phrases:

- "Follow the principles of autonomy, controllability, and gradualism" (按照主动性、可控性和渐进性原则)
- "Take further steps to perfect the yuan exchange rate mechanism, with market supply and demand as the basis, and make adjustments with reference to a basket of currencies" (进一步完善人民币汇率形成机制，重在坚持以市场供求为基础，参考一篮子货币进行调节)
- "Maintain stability of the yuan exchange rate at a balanced equilibrium level" (保持人民币汇率在合理均衡水平上的基本稳定)

The phrases might be well worn, but sometimes variations on a theme can attract the attention of the markets. In the report on the third quarter of 2009, the PBOC rang alarm bells by omitting the commitment to maintaining the "stability" of the exchange rate. That was enough to excite headlines in the financial press, to the effect that the end of the yuan's peg to the dollar was in sight. As it happened, the end of the peg did not come until 7 months later in June 2010, illustrating the dangers of reading too much significance into the PBOC's exact choice of words.

Excess Reserves, Yuan Trade Settlement, Interest Rates, and Lending Breakdown

The report also contains a few interesting details on the state of the economy that are not available elsewhere:

- "Excess reserves" refers to the amount of cash commercial banks hold with the Central Bank in excess of required reserves. When the PBOC shifts the RRR, the level of excess reserves dictates whether the shoe starts to pinch immediately. If excess reserves are low, an upward shift in the RRR generates an immediate scramble for cash that pushes money market rates higher and dents the banks' capacity to make new loans. If excess reserves are high, the banks already have enough cash with the PBOC to cover the new requirement without too much trouble. In January 2010, the PBOC raised the RRR by 0.5 percentage points, and the markets interpreted that as a sign that the tightening process had begun. But the Monetary Policy Report for the final quarter of 2009 showed that the bank already held reserves 3 percentage points in excess of the required level, suggesting that a small increase in the RRR could be easily absorbed. The hike was a sign that the policy stance was changing, but its real impact on the banks' ability to lend was limited. That fact was borne out by continued hand-over-fist credit creation, which saw the banks issue CNY1.3 trillion in new loans in January.

- The PBOC sets benchmark interest rates in China, but the commercial banks have freedom to set lending rates slightly below or as far above the benchmark rate as they can find customers willing to pay. Information on the percentage of loans issued above or below the benchmark rate, which is included in the Monetary Policy Report, provides an important read on credit conditions. Between January 2010 and September 2010, the benchmark interest rates set by the PBOC did not change, but the Monetary Policy Report shows that actual lending rates rose considerably. In January, the banks were pushing 35% of loans out the door below the benchmark rate and 33% above the benchmark rate. By September, the situation had reversed. Just 25% of loans were issued at a discount, and 44% of customers were being forced to pay a premium for access to credit.

- Not all Chinese banks are created equal. The big four banks—Industrial and Commercial Bank of China, Agricultural Bank of China, China Construction Bank, and Bank of China—control the bulk of the deposits and issue the majority of loans. The second-tier banks—such as Shanghai Pudong Development Bank and Bank of Guangzhou—have a smaller deposit base and account for a lower share of total lending. The big banks tend to take the best customers. The smaller banks are left lending to local projects. The Monetary Policy Report provides a breakdown of lending among different categories of banks.

- China's financial system remains a bank-based one, and loans are the main show in town—but they are no longer the only show in town. China's enterprises can also raise capital by issuing shares or fixed-income products. The Monetary Policy Report provides a summary of total funds raised through all these channels. That provides a more complete picture of credit conditions and offers insight into the changing mix of financing options for China's enterprises. In 2010, for example, the Monetary Policy Report for the fourth quarter showed new loans sharply down from the previous year. But higher equity issuance meant financing circumstances for Chinese enterprises were not as straightened as the loan data suggests. In 2011, the PBOC began publishing a separate quarterly report on social finance (社会融资, shehui rongzi) which also includes figures for lending by trust companies, and capital raised through IPOs and the sale of bonds.

- Trade transactions settled in yuan show the progress of the Central Bank in pushing the yuan as an international currency. In the middle of 2009, the PBOC launched and then extended a program to allow China's trade transactions to be settled in yuan. Progress in the first year and a half was rapid, but from an extremely low base. In the first half of 2009, none of China's trade transactions were settled in yuan. By September 2010, the Monetary Policy Report showed more than CNY50 billion, or 2.8% of total trade for the month, was settled using the Chinese currency.

Interpreting the Macroeconomic Report

The Macroeconomic Report sets out the Central Bank's view on the current situation and the future outlook for the economy.

Quarter-on-Quarter Seasonally Adjusted Annualized Growth

Until 2011, the Macroeconomic Report was the only place you could find an official esti-mate of China's quarter-on-quarter seasonally adjusted annualized GDP growth (QoQ SAAR). Most countries around the world, including the United States, use the QoQ SAAR as the benchmark for assessing the state of the economy. Until 2011, China was unique among the large economies in publishing only a YoY growth figure, with the National Bureau of Statistics (NBS) pleading difficulties in seasonal adjustment caused by a week-long moving holiday for Chinese New Year. But the Central Bank had obvi-ously invested in a superior quality abacus. From 2009 to 2010, Macroeconomic Reports included an estimate of China's QoQ SAAR. This estimate often pointed to a direction or pace of growth that was substantially different from the official YoY data published by the NBS. In the second quarter of 2009, the PBOC estimated the QoQ SAAR growth rate at 14.9%, way higher than the 7.9% YoY growth rate the NBS published. One interpreta-tion of the PBOC figure is that the Central Bank was hinting that the stimulus had already achieved its objective and that it was time to slam on the breaks, before the massive increase in lending started to tip over into overheating and inflationary pressure. With the NBS now publishing its own figure for the QoQ growth rate, it seems likely that the PBOC will fall in line behind the official data, rather than publishing its own independent estimate.

Output Gap

The report includes the PBOC's calculation of the output gap. The output gap is a measure of the difference between potential output (how much the economy could produce, firing on all cylinders) and actual output (how much it is actually producing). It is closely related to the extent of inflationary pressure. If actual output is close to or even exceeding potential output, that must mean demand is pushing up against the limits of supply and that higher prices are sure to follow. If actual output is below potential output, this means there is slack in the economy. Output could increase without tipping over into overheating and price pressure. Even in developed economies, calculating the output gap is fraught with difficulty. In China, with a rapidly changing economy and less than perfect statistical system, those problems are compounded. The PBOC is tight-lipped on how it is making its calculation. But with no data available elsewhere, the PBOC estimate is the only show in town.

Interpreting the Monetary Policy Committee Statement

China's MPC meets once a quarter to discuss the economic situation and advise the State Council on the right course for monetary policy. Membership is dominated by the PBOC, with the governor in the chair, two vice governors participating, and the head of the State Administration of Foreign Exchange (which is part of the PBOC) in attendance. Outside the PBOC, virtually every part of the central government's economic and financial apparatus has a seat at the table. The State Council, National Development and Reform Commission, Ministry of Finance, National Bureau of Statistics, Banking Regulatory Commission, Securities Regulatory Commission, and Insurance Regulatory Commission are all represented. The commercial banks are represented by the China Banking Association. Finally, the MPC generally has at least one academic member (it currently has three).

Investors familiar with the rich detail of the FOMC statements and minutes, or the European Central Bank (ECB) Governing Council's statement and press conference, might feel a little disappointed by the statement from China's MPC. A few brief paragraphs cover, at a very high level of generality, the economic situation and outlook, along with the priorities for policy. Reports from at least one former member of the MPC suggest to us that discussions at the meeting are actually rather interesting, and that a detailed and pointed set of recommendations is transmitted to the State Council. But the published statement has no hint of this and mainly consists of boilerplate language that China-watchers have seen many times before.

The MPC as a committee might be tight-lipped, but the academic members are quite gregarious. Former members Yu Yongding and Fan Gang, and current members Li Daokui, Xia Bin, and Zhou Qiren have a flair for public speaking and a willingness to chit-chat with members of the financial press unlike their official colleagues. It is a rare week when China's financial press does not carry at least one or two remarks from the academic members of the MPC on interest rates, the exchange rate, or the hot topic of the day. These remarks get more attention than comments from run-of-the-mill academics because, as MPC members, Li, Zhou, and Xia are privy to internal discussions and, it is assumed, mandated to speak on behalf of the PBOC. With a constant stream of chatter, the difficulty is sorting the informed insight wheat from the throwaway quote chaff.

Market Impact

The PBOC reports are an important statement of the views of an important organization and often contain data points or language that enable a more informed understanding of what is going on in the Chinese economy and the discussion in policy circles. But they are normally more grist to the analyst's mill than adrenalin for the trading desk's itchy fingers.

Index

Numbers

A

B

C

D

F

O

S

T

FINANCIAL TIMES

In an increasingly competitive world, it is quality
of thinking that gives an edge—an idea that opens new
doors, a technique that solves a problem, or an insight
that simply helps make sense of it all.

We work with leading authors in the various arenas
of business and finance to bring cutting-edge thinking
and best-learning practices to a global market.

It is our goal to create world-class print publications
and electronic products that give readers
knowledge and understanding that can then be
applied, whether studying or at work.

To find out more about our business
products, you can visit us at www.ftpress.com.